Gifts of Promise

Theodore Clymer

Leo Ruth

Consultants

Ken Johnson
Deborah Dashow Ruth
Roger W. Shuy
E. Paul Torrance

GINN AND COMPANY

Acknowledgments

Grateful acknowledgment is made to the following publishers, authors, and agents for permission to use and adapt copyrighted materials:

Atheneum Publishers for the adaptation of "Deer Hunt" by Vera and Bill Cleaver. Copyright © 1973 by Vera and Bill Cleaver. From *The Whys and Wherefores of Littabelle Lee.* Used by permission of Atheneum Publishers. Also for the abridgment of "Make My Bed in the River" by Jean McCord. Copyright © 1968 by Jean McCord. From *Deep Where the Octopi Lie.* Used by permission of Atheneum Publishers.

Brigham Young University Press for "Grandmother's Eagles." Louis, Ray Baldwin *Child of the Hogan,* Provo, Utah: Brigham Young University Press, 1975.

Doubleday & Company, Inc., for "After Twenty Years" from THE FOUR MILLION by O. Henry. Reprinted by permission of Doubleday & Company, Inc. Also for "The Three Heroines of Shirley Chisholm" adapted and abridged excerpts from SHIRLEY CHISHOLM by Susan Brownmiller. Copyright © 1970 by Doubleday & Company, Inc. Reprinted by permission of the Publisher. Also for "A Gentleman Scientist" adapted and abridged excerpts from THE HIDDEN CONTRIBUTORS by Aaron E. Klein. Copyright © 1971 by Aaron E. Klein. Reprinted by permission of Doubleday & Company, Inc. Also for "The Dream of the Golden Mountains" adapted from PASSAGE TO THE GOLDEN GATE by Daniel Chu and Samuel Chu. Copyright © 1967 by Doubleday & Company, Inc. Reprinted by permission of the Publisher.

E. P. Dutton & Co., Inc., for "I Hole Up in a Snowstorm" from *My Side of the Mountain* by Jean George. Copyright © 1959 by Jean George. Reprinted by permission of the publishers, E. P. Dutton. Also for "August Heat" abridged from *The Beast With Five Fingers* by William Fryer Harvey. Copyright 1947 by E. P. Dutton & Co., and reprinted with their permission.

Field Enterprises Educational Corporation for "The Nez Percé Indians" by Allen P. Slickpoo, Sr., and "Joseph, Chief" by Cecil Corbett both from *The World Book Encyclopedia.* © 1977 Field Enterprises Educational Corporation. Used by permission.

Harcourt Brace Jovanovich, Inc., for the poem beginning "Freedom is a hard-bought thing--" on page 385 from "Song of the Settlers" by Jessamyn West. Copyright 1947, 1975 by Jessamyn West. Reprinted from her volume *A Mirror for the Sky* by permission of Harcourt Brace Jovanovich, Inc. First published in *The New Yorker.* Also for the poem beginning "The doors are twisted on broken hinges" on page 388 from "Four Preludes on Playthings of the Wind" in *Smoke and Steel* by Carl Sandburg, copyright, 1920, by Harcourt Brace Jovanovich, Inc.; renewed, 1948, by Carl Sandburg. Reprinted by permission of the publisher.

Harper & Row, Publishers, Inc., for "Climbing Kloochman" slightly adapted and abridged from *Of Men and Mountains* by William O. Douglas. Copyright 1950 by William O. Douglas. Reprinted by permission of Harper & Row, Publishers, Inc., and The Lantz Office, Incorporated. Also for "On Equal Terms" slightly adapted and abridged from *If You Could See What I Hear* by Tom Sullivan and Derek Gill. Copyright © 1975 by Thomas J. Sullivan and Derek L. T. Gill. Reprinted by permission of Harper & Row, Publishers, Inc.

Holt, Rinehart and Winston for the poem "Dust of Snow" from *The Poetry of Robert Frost* edited by Edward Connery Lathem. Copyright 1923, © 1969 by Holt, Rinehart and Winston. Copyright 1951 by Robert Frost. Reprinted by permission of Holt, Rinehart and Winston, Publishers. Also for "Tapestry: The Islands and the Man" adapted from *I Walked with Heroes* by General Carlos P. Romulo. Copyright © 1961 by Philip Andrew Wells, trustee under the Carlos

3

5

Contents

8

Moments of Recognition

What can we learn
In these
Moments of recognition?

His first reaction was panic. Inside the heavy diving suit under sixty feet of ocean he was panting—and using up precious oxygen.

TRAPPED

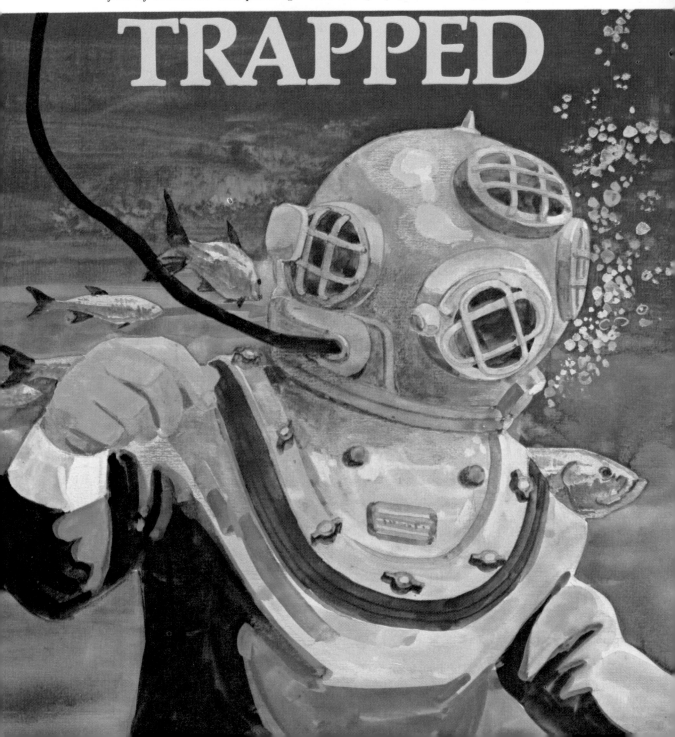

Have you ever asked yourself the questions, How brave am I? How much raw courage have I? How would I conduct myself in a life-and-death emergency?

Most of us are never given the chance to find answers to these questions. The opportunity was mine when some years ago I went with a friend to Alaska as a deep sea diver to inspect the underwater sections of the fish traps in Prince William Sound.

"You can do part of the diving," Virgil explained. "That way the cannery will pay your expenses."

"But I don't know a thing about diving."

"I'll teach you." Virgil was a professional with twenty years' experience diving in northern waters. It had all begun when he arrived in Alaska virtually penniless. However, it wasn't long before he was paid one hundred dollars for ten minutes' work. The job called for going below in a diving suit and cutting a killer whale out of a salmon trap with wire nippers. Thereafter, when something went wrong in the chill depths off the Alaskan shore, Virgil was the man they called. It might be a whale tangled in a trap, or a sunken warehouse full of canned salmon, or a dropped ten-ton anchor worth fifteen cents a pound, or a seventy-ton Caterpillar crane toppled over into forty feet of water.

"We'll get there a couple of weeks early," Virgil explained to me now, "then go out in the boat and make some practice dives before the real work starts."

I agreed. I wanted to see the north.

The day before we left I had breakfast with an editor friend at the Benson Hotel in Portland.

"So you're really going to dive?" he asked me.

"I am, if I have enough courage," I answered.

My friend looked at me a moment, then said, "During the Second World War I was in OSS and I flew a lot of men behind enemy lines. Everyone knew that his chance of coming back alive was slim. But a lot of them came back because they refused to panic in an emergency. You'll be all right, I'm sure."

To one who'd never been beneath the sea, just the sight of the suit was a little frightening. The metal helmet and breastplate weighed seventy-five pounds, the lead shoes forty pounds, the lead belt around my middle ninety pounds. Slightly more than two hundred pounds of dead weight to take me to the bottom and hold me there.

"We don't use a lifeline," Virgil explained. "It's just extra gear to drag around at a hundred feet or more. To come up, let the air pressure build in the suit and you'll float to the surface." There was a mike in the helmet and one on deck so the diver and tender could talk back and forth. Air was supplied by a one-cylinder gas motor that ran the compressor.

My first two practice dives went off perfectly. Both dives were shallow, thirty and forty feet. In between dives Virgil hammered diving knowledge and warnings into me. "Remember, if you get into trouble you've got to get yourself out. I can't come down. As far as we know this is the only diving suit in Alaska. Don't take chances. Keep me informed what's happening below."

After the third dive he said, "You went in like an old pro. You're doing fine."

The fourth dive took place opposite the native village of Tatitlik. A couple of hundred yards away on shore the schoolteacher and his wife were hacking chunks of ice off a small iceberg that had drifted in. It was 11:00 P.M. The sun was still high.

"It's about sixty feet here," Virgil said, "a nice sandy bottom. We've got enough gas left for an hour's dive. Tomorrow we'll get more. You want to go down?"

My appetite was whetted by three successful dives. Of course I did.

"Remember," he warned as he locked on the helmet, "you've got the last of the gas. When I say 'Come up,' you'd better come!"

The bottom was just as he'd said. I could see about twenty-five feet. The shape of the boat had disappeared. I was alone in a watery world. A strong tide was running and the long coarse grass was lying 13

almost flat, as if blown by a hard wind. I leaned forward about forty-five degrees, dug my lead toes into the sand, and began walking. A school of sea trout swirled around me, then dashed away. A big halibut flapped into view and disappeared back into the liquid distance. The long, tough grass kept tangling around my feet. Once I fell.

I went out about a hundred feet, turned right and explored a short distance, found nothing and came back. "See anything interesting?" Virgil's voice crackled in over the mike.

"Just sand and grass," I said. "But somebody forgot to pull the plug. There's water all over the floor." It was old and corny, but I was enjoying myself and feeling comfortable under sixty feet of ocean.

I wandered around for some time getting used to the suit and the feel of pressure. Finally I started back, following my air line toward where the boat should be. Virgil would soon be telling me to come up.

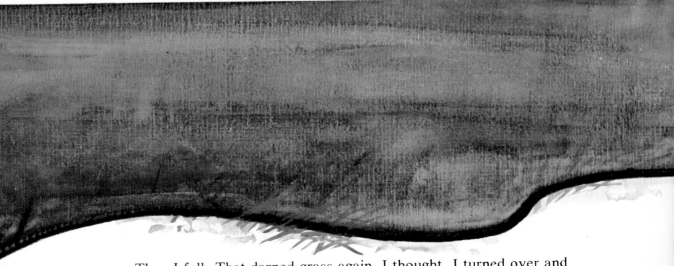

Then I fell. That darned grass again, I thought. I turned over and sat up. Shock rolled through me. I'd walked into a great coil of partially silt-buried, rusty inch-thick cable. Like all old, hard-used cable it was twisted into compact kinks and knots. Somehow I'd shoved one of my big lead shoes through one of those kinky loops and it had sprung tight on my foot. I bent forward, got hold of each side of the loop, and tried to pry it open. I couldn't even budge the cable. That coil weighed hundreds of pounds and I could see more snaking out across the bottom. I was held fast, as if caught in a bear trap.

That moment all Virgil's cautions took on terrible meaning. This was our only diving suit. I had to get out on my own. No one could come down to help me. The last gas was in the compressor. When the motor stopped I'd be out of air.

Suddenly panic was right in the helmet with me. I tore at my cable with my bare hands, trying to pry that closed loop open. The cable was covered with jaggers, needle-sharp ends of broken strands. They slashed both my palms, and a thread of blood began drifting toward the surface. Oh, no! I thought. Sharks!

I've no idea how long the panic lasted. Twenty seconds, thirty, a minute. Sweat poured down my face into my eyes, nostrils, mouth. I was panting, using up precious oxygen.

Then for a reason I've never been able to explain I heard my editor friend's voice say, "You'll be all right, I'm sure." His voice was as clear as it had been that morning in the Benson Hotel dining room in 15

Portland. I seemed to go through fear, like passing through an open door. I became perfectly calm.

I quit struggling and began to think. How much gas was left? Enough for ten minutes, fifteen? It's hard to judge time under water. But all the time in the world wouldn't help me. I, alone, had to get my foot out of the vise created by the twisted cable. I desperately needed another pair of hands. I thought of Virgil's forearms, almost as big around as my neck. He'd once been a professional wrestler. If I just had his arms down here.

"You found something?" Virgil's voice came in over the mike in my helmet. We had a rule that the tender always checked when the air bubbles streaming to the surface from the helmet kept coming up in one spot; it meant the diver had stopped for some reason.

I explained what had happened and Virgil's voice came back completely calm, "What do you want me to do?"

Then I knew. "Send down a line."

A minute later a half-inch rope snaked down, with a wrench tied to the end to sink it to me. I tied the rope to one side of the loop. "When I say 'Pull,' " I said, "give it all you've got." I dug my free heel into the sandy bottom, got hold of the opposite side with both hands and said, "Pull, Virg. Pull."

The line became taut as Virgil's 220 pounds strained on it. I did the same on my side. At first there was nothing. Then fine scales of rust broke away. Reluctantly the loop parted. I yanked my foot out, let go, and the loop snapped closed again.

I let air build in the suit and shot to the surface. Virgil twisted the helmet off, and I looked at the beautiful sky and the sun and the sea. Neither of us said a word. He was beginning to unbuckle the suit a minute later when the compressor motor sputtered and died.

Resting on the bunk later I realized I had found a partial answer to my third question. In an emergency at least I would act. To the other two questions I still have no satisfactory answer.

16   WALT MOREY

"You've got brains," Granny told me. "And when you've got brains, it's a ticket to anyplace you want to go—a ticket to the whole world."

LEGACY

Granny had adored me. Every time my father lost his job or left the house I was sent to live with her, and I couldn't wait to get there. I'd sit on the train coach overnight with my cardboard suitcase on the seat beside me and I could barely sleep for being so happy. She had a little farm in Deepwater, Missouri that had hardly any kind of a house

on it at all, just a little ramshackle place in the backlands,
but I thought it was wonderful.
It made me smile just to think
about it now. All the house had
was one tiny bedroom that, even
though it was three feet above
the kitchen, had no stairs to it.
Whenever Granny and I went to
bed we had to shinny ourselves
up. She must have been close to
seventy the last time I was there,
but she was able to scramble up
almost as fast as I.

Living with her had been
like living with another little girl
who was just older and smarter
than I was. There wasn't anything she couldn't do, except
maybe handle a plow. At home
my father had never let me help
him because he said that I
couldn't do anything right, but
Granny had let me help with
everything—milking the cow,
tending the chickens, cooking
and baking. She even let me help
plant the vegetable garden, another thing my father wouldn't
let me do. I couldn't keep the
rows straight, he used to tell me.
But Granny said she didn't give
a hoot about straight rows. The
potatoes I planted in her garden
grew all over, sometimes crossing into the spinach, which
curved around behind the
18   tomatoes. It was less of a garden

than a living salad, but when it all came out of the ground Granny couldn't get over how smart I was to have performed such a miracle, or so she told me.

I'd lived with her for a whole year that last time, and I'd never forget how terrible I'd felt when my mother finally wrote me to come home because my father was working again. Granny couldn't read, so I'd even thought of not telling her what was in the letter, but I couldn't lie to her. She felt as bad as I did, but there wasn't anything we could do.

That last night we'd spent together we tried to pretend that it was just like any other night. We went to bed right after supper the way we always did and I read to her from the Bible for a while. I knew the Book of Psalms was her favorite, so I was reading from that. Granny had decided she couldn't abide beds after my grandfather died, so we were lying on thick patch-work quilts on the floor. It was warm enough so that we didn't need a blanket, and she was curled up beside me, her knees pulled up and poking at the cotton nightie, her hair done in a long braid down to her waist. Her eyes were closed, and after a while I thought she was asleep, 19 so I put the Bible away.

Before I leaned over to turn down the oil lamp I looked at her face, seeing the deep lines in it. She wasn't asleep, though. Her eyes popped open and she smiled at me. She was a tiny little thing, thin in the shoulders and heavy in the waist. Even though I was only eleven I was bigger than she was.

"You fooled me," I said.

It was a game we played sometimes. If she fell asleep while I was reading I could go without washing my hands and face the next morning. But if she caught me I had to wash my neck and my ears.

"No, I jus' dozed off. I really did."

She took my hand and squeezed it. I could feel the calluses on hers. "I'm gonna miss you, Annie."

I'd tried hard not to whine or cry up to then, but I couldn't keep it up. I managed to blurt out, "Granny, I don't want to go home ever again. I just don't want to. Please let me stay." Then I started to bawl so hard I didn't think I'd ever be able to stop. Granny got up and held onto me the whole time. She didn't say a word until she knew I was done.

20

"Annie. . . ."

"Uh-huh."

"You know I don't want you to go home. . . ."

"Yes?"

"An' you know I never told you a lie."

"I know."

"Then you know if I tell you you're a lucky girl, that's the truth."

"How can I be lucky?"

"'Cause a lot of people when they're unhappy, they can't do anything about it. But you can, 'cause you're smart. You've got brains. An' when a person's got brains they got a ticket to any place they want to go—a ticket to the whole world."

"What kind of a ticket?"

She tapped her head. "Right up here. Didn't you tell me that if you worked hard an' really studied you could be teachin' school by the time you're sixteen?"

"That's what my teacher said."

"Then that's what you got to think about, about bein' a teacher an' gettin' outta those dirty minin' places."

"I'll never be able to do it, Granny, never." I was ready to start crying all over again, but Granny told me to stop right away. "An' listen to me, 'cause I'm not gonna say this twice."

She told me to sit up. "You're gonna do big things some day, Annie—real big things. But you can't do big things if you're gonna go round feelin' sorry for yourself." She stopped for a second and she looked a little sad. "Your pa's my son, child. He's not an easy man, but he's not a bad man either. Whatever you think about 'im you just remember he always stood on his own two feet an' he taught you the same. An' he always paid his own way. That's what the Hobbses is like—all of 'em. Maybe he and your ma haven't been too understandin' of you, but they fed you an' gave 21 you a roof. That's more than many's got. . . ."

"But they don't really want me, Granny."

"Yes they do. They jus' don't know how to show it. But never mind that. If you got just one person in the whole world who loves you an' believes in you, why that's wonderful, don't ya see. An' you got one—me. I love you, an' I believe in you. So anytime you get to thinkin' you're not gonna make it, or that you can't do somethin' for your own self's sake, you do it for my sake. Will you?"

"Yes."

"Promise?"

"I promise."

"That's what I want to hear. You'll see, Annie. Some day you're gonna go off to a new land just like a pioneer—just like your grampa an' me did. 'Cause you're that kind—a big person. An' that's the kind that goes to a new land."

"But there's no new lands, Granny. They're all gone."

"Shoot, child, there'll always be new lands."

"Where?"

"California maybe, I don't know. Or Alaska. . . . Now there's a new land, Alaska."

I asked her what she knew about it, but she'd begun to get sleepy and so had I. A few minutes later we were asleep.

When it was close to train time a neighboring woman had ridden into the yard with a buckboard. Granny had gone as far as the main road with us, then we hugged each other good-bye. She'd felt like a strong little bird.

As the buckboard drove off and I turned around to see her waving to me I had to fight to hold in the tears. "Don't worry," the driver said, "you'll be back some day."

I hadn't answered her, not knowing how to explain that I wasn't crying because I was going away, but because my grandmother had looked so small and alone as she stood in the middle of the road gently waving good-bye.

I'd never seen her again after that. She'd died during the first year I'd been teaching. I hadn't found out about it until three weeks after it happened. She had died in her sleep, my mother wrote me, and she had left me a legacy.

She sure had, but it wasn't the legacy my mother had written me about. It was one she'd given me a long time ago when I needed it most. And for that I'd never forget her.

ROBERT SPECHT

What's It All About?

1. Both Walt and Annie receive good advice in these two selections—Walt from his editor friend in Portland, Annie from her Granny. What is this advice? How does it help each person?
2. How do both Walt and Annie demonstrate that clear, reasoned thinking is important?

---

1. What warnings does Virgil give Walt as he learns to dive?
2. When Walt is trapped, his first reaction is panic. How does this increase his danger?
3. What does Walt learn from his experience?
4. Why does Annie enjoy staying with her grandmother so much?
5. How does Granny help Annie understand her parents?
6. Annie's mother informs Annie of her grandmother's legacy—probably a little money and some possessions—after Granny dies. But what is the legacy that Annie values the most?

PUTTING IDEAS TO WORK

If you were asked by a younger brother, sister, cousin, or friend for one piece of good advice, what would you say? Write a paragraph that offers someone younger than yourself the one best piece of advice that you can think of.

DUST OF SNOW

The way a crow
Shook down on me
The dust of snow
From a hemlock tree

Has given my heart
A change of mood
And saved some part
Of a day I had rued.

24   ROBERT FROST

Sam Gribley was scared by the coming of the snowstorm. Did he have enough food? Would his tree home protect him from the cold? Would he survive?

I Hole Up in a Snowstorm

I am on my mountain in a tree home that people have passed without ever knowing that I am here. The house is a hemlock tree six feet in diameter, and must be as old as the mountain itself. I came upon it last summer and dug and burned it out until I made a snug cave in the tree that I now call home.

"My bed is on the right as you enter, and is made of ash slats and covered with deerskin. On the left is a small fireplace about knee high. It is of clay and stones. It has a chimney that leads the smoke out through a knothole. I chipped out three other knotholes to let fresh air in. The air coming in is bitter cold. It must be below zero outside, and   25 yet I can sit here inside my tree and write with bare hands. The fire is small, too. It doesn't take much fire to warm this tree room.

"It is the fourth of December, I think. It may be the fifth. I am not sure because I have not recently counted the notches in the aspen pole that is my calendar. I have been just too busy gathering nuts and berries, smoking venison, fish, and small game to keep up with the exact date.

"The lamp I am writing by is deer fat poured into a turtle-shell with a strip of my old city trousers for a wick.

"It snowed all day yesterday and today. I have not been outside since the storm began, and I am bored for the first time since I left home eight months ago to live on the land.

"I am well and healthy. The food is good. Sometimes I eat turtle soup, and I know how to make acorn pancakes. I keep my supplies in the wall of the tree in wooden pockets that I chopped myself.

"Every time I have looked at those pockets during the last two days, I have felt just like a squirrel, which reminds me: I didn't see a squirrel one whole day before that storm began. I guess they are holed up and eating their stored nuts, too.

"I wonder if The Baron, that's the wild weasel who lives behind the big boulder to the north of my tree, is also denned up. Well, anyway, I think the storm is dying down because the tree is not crying so much. When the wind really blows, the whole tree moans right down to the roots, which is where I am.

"Tomorrow I hope The Baron and I can tunnel out into the sunlight. I wonder if I should dig the snow. But that would mean I would have to put it somewhere, and the only place to put it is in my nice snug tree. Maybe I can pack it with my hands as I go. I've always dug into the snow from the top, never up from under.

"The Baron must dig up from under the snow. I wonder where he puts what he digs? Well, I guess I'll know in the morning."

When I wrote that last winter, I was scared and thought maybe I'd never get out of my tree. I had been scared for two days—ever since the first blizzard hit the Catskill Mountains. When I came up to the sunlight, which I did by simply poking my head into the soft snow and standing up, I laughed at my dark fears.

Everything was white, clean, shining, and beautiful. The sky was blue, blue, blue. The hemlock grove was laced with snow, the meadow was smooth and white, and the gorge was sparkling with ice. It was so beautiful and peaceful that I laughed out loud. I guess I laughed because my first snowstorm was over and it had not been so terrible after all.

Then I shouted, "I did it!" My voice never got very far. It was hushed by the tons of snow.

I looked for signs from The Baron Weasel. His footsteps were all over the boulder, also slides where he had played. He must have been up for hours, enjoying the new snow.

Inspired by his fun, I poked my head into my tree and whistled. Frightful, my trained falcon, flew to my fist, and we jumped and slid down the mountain, making big holes and trenches as we went. It was good to be whistling and carefree again, because I was sure scared by the coming of that storm.

I had been working since May, learning how to make a fire with flint and steel, finding what plants I could eat, how to trap animals and catch fish—all this so that when the curtain of blizzard struck the Catskills, I could crawl inside my tree and be comfortably warm and have plenty to eat.

During the summer and fall I had thought about the coming of winter. However, on that third day of December when the sky blackened, the temperature dropped, and the first flakes swirled around me, I must admit that I wanted to run back to New York. Even the first night that I spent out in the woods, when I couldn't get the fire started, was not as frightening as the snowstorm that gathered behind the gorge and mushroomed up over my mountain.

I was smoking three trout. It was nine o'clock in the morning. I was busy keeping the flames low so they would not leap up and burn the fish. As I worked, it occurred to me that it was awfully dark for that 27 hour of the morning. Frightful was leashed to her tree stub. She seemed restless and pulled at her tethers. Then I realized that the forest was dead quiet. Even the woodpeckers that had been tapping around me all morning were silent. The squirrels were nowhere to be seen. The juncos and chickadees and nuthatches were gone. I looked to see what The Baron Weasel was doing. He was not around. I looked up.

From my tree you can see the gorge beyond the meadow. White water pours between the black wet boulders and cascades into the valley below. The water that day was as dark as the rocks. Only the sound told me it was still falling. Above the darkness stood another darkness. The clouds of winter, black and fearsome. They looked as wild as the winds that were bringing them. I grew sick with fright. I knew I had enough food. I knew everything was going to be perfectly all right. But knowing that didn't help. I was scared. I stamped out the fire, and pocketed the fish.

I tried to whistle for Frightful, but couldn't purse my shaking lips tight enough to get out anything but *pfffff*. So I grabbed her by the hide straps that are attached to her legs and we dove through the deerskin door into my room in the tree.

I put Frightful on the bedpost, and curled up in a ball on the bed. I thought about New York and the noise and the lights and how a snowstorm always seemed very friendly there. I thought about our apartment, too. At that moment it seemed bright and lighted and warm. I had to keep saying to myself: There were eleven of us in it! Dad, Mother, four sisters, four brothers, and me. And not one of us liked it, except perhaps little Nina, who was too young to know. Dad didn't like it even a little bit. He had been a sailor once, but when I was born, he gave up the sea and worked on the docks in New York. Dad didn't like the land. He liked the sea, wet and big and endless.

Sometimes he would tell me about Great-grandfather Gribley, who owned land in the Catskill Mountains and felled the trees and built a home and plowed the land—only to discover that he wanted to be a sailor. The farm failed, and Great-grandfather Gribley went to sea.

As I lay with my face buried in the sweet greasy smell of my deerskin, I could hear Dad's voice saying, "That land is still in the family's name. Somewhere in the Catskills is an old beech with the name *Gribley* carved on it. It marks the northern boundary of Gribley's folly—the land is no place for a Gribley."

"The land is no place for a Gribley," I said. "The land is no place for a Gribley, and here I am three hundred feet from the beech with *Gribley* carved on it."

I fell asleep at that point, and when I awoke I was hungry. I cracked some walnuts, got down the acorn flour I had pounded, with a bit of ash to remove the bite, reached out the door for a little snow, and stirred up some acorn pancakes. I cooked them on a top of a tin can, and as I ate them, smothered with blueberry jam, I knew that the land was just the place for a Gribley.

JEAN GEORGE   29

*Shipwrecked. Alone on an island.
Nothing but a cave for a home.
I despair of any rescue.*

From The Journal of Robinson Crusoe

September 30, 1659

I, poor miserable Robinson Crusoe, being shipwrecked, during a dreadful storm, came on shore on this dismal unfortunate island, which I called the Island of Despair. All the rest of the ship's company was drowned, and myself almost dead.

All the rest of that day I spent in afflicting myself at the dismal circumstances I was brought to. I had neither food, house, clothes, weapon, nor place to fly to. In despair of any relief, I saw nothing but death before me. Either I should be devoured by wild beasts, murdered by savages, or starved to death for want of food. At the approach of night I slept in a tree, for fear of wild creatures, but slept soundly, though it rained all night.

Crusoe's main problem was staying alive. His journal for the next six and a half months tells of the building of his cave home. Crusoe removed supplies from the wrecked ship before a storm destroyed the vessel completely. Setting up a tent under an overhanging rock, he gathered his things in a semi-circle around it. Gradually he dug a cave beneath the rock, enlarging it to hold all his belongings, hand-made furniture and tools. Posts and beams held up the ceiling of the cave. A thick wall, camouflaged with earth on the outside, surrounded the entire camp. The wall could stand up to any disaster. But a cave is not always the best place to be.

April 17, 1660

The very next day after this wall was finished, I had almost had all my labour overthrown at once, and myself killed. The case was thus:— As I was busy in the entrance into my cave, I was terribly frighted with a most dreadful surprising thing indeed. On a sudden I found the earth come crumbling down from the roof of my cave. Over my head two of the posts I had set up in the cave cracked in a frightful manner. I was heartily scared, but thought nothing of what was really the cause, only thinking that the top of my cave was falling in, as some of it had done before. For fear I should be buried in it, I ran forward to my ladder and got over my wall. I was no sooner stept down upon the firm ground, but I plainly saw it was a terrible earthquake. The ground I stood on shook three times with three such shocks as would have overturned the strongest building that could be supposed to have stood on the earth. A great piece of the top of a rock, which stood about half a mile from me next to the sea, fell down with such a terrible noise as I never heard in all my life. I perceived also the very sea was put into violent motion by it; and I believe the shocks were stronger under the water than on the island.

I was so amazed with the thing itself, having never felt the like, that I was like one dead or stupefied. The motion of the earth made my stomach sick, like one that was tossed at sea; but the noise of the falling of the rock awaked me and filled me with horror. I thought of nothing 31 then but the hill falling upon my tent and all my household goods, and burying all at once.

After the third shock was over, and I felt no more for some time, I began to take courage. Yet I had not heart enough to get over my wall again, for fear of being buried alive, but sat still upon the ground, not knowing what to do.

While I sat thus, I found the air overcast, and grow cloudy, as if it would rain. Soon after that, the wind rose by little and little, so that in less than half an hour it blew a most dreadful hurricane. The sea was all on a sudden covered over with foam and froth. The shore was covered with the breach of the water. The trees were torn up by the roots. A terrible storm it was. This held about three hours and then began to abate. In two hours more it was stark calm and began to rain very hard.

All this while I sat upon the ground, very much terrified and dejected. On a sudden it came into my thoughts, that the earthquake was spent and over, and I might venture into my cave again. With this thought my spirits began to revive, and, the rain also helping to persuade me, I went in and sat down in my tent. But the rain was so violent, that my tent was ready to be beaten down with it. I was forced to go into my cave, though very much afraid and uneasy, for fear it should fall on my head.

The violent rain forced me to a new work, namely, to cut a hole through my new fortificaton like a sink, to let water go out, which would else have drowned my cave. After I had been in my cave some time, and found still no more shocks of the earthquake follow, I began to be more composed.

The fear of being swallowed up alive made me that I never slept in quiet. Still, when I looked about, and saw how every thing was put in order, how pleasantly concealed I was, and how safe from danger, it made me hate the thought of leaving.

DANIEL DEFOE

The Real Robinson Crusoe

RAUL DUQUE, REUTERS

Santiago. A film has been made on a Chilean island about the life of one of the least-lucky Scots of all time—Alexander Selkirk, whose four year exile alone on the island inspired Daniel Defoe to write "Robinson Crusoe."

Selkirk, despite being the inspiration for the novel, is still relatively unknown. But to set matters right, English producer Mike Gibbon has made a film of Selkirk shot on location on the

same island off Valparaiso where the sailor was marooned in 1704.

But centuries ago it was deserted and the first known human being to set up residence there was Selkirk.

•   •   •

Selkirk, a crewman of the 96-ton English ship Cinque Ports, was left behind on Mas Afuera after a quarrel with a Captain Strandling. His plan was to hitch a ride back home on the first English ship he saw.

That's where his bad luck comes in—it took four years.

Selkirk, then 28, set foot on the island with only his Bible, a knife, a rifle, an axe, a pound of gunpowder, some tobacco and a box of clothes.

According to Selkirk's account, his first 18 months on the islands was the worst period of his life. He suffered bouts of depression and spent most of his time perched on a high hill looking for rescue.

But he gradually overcame his loneliness and lived off the game and fish.

•   •   •

33

His loneliness finally ended on January 31, 1709, when on climbing his watchpost he saw the English ships Duke and Duchess which five months previously had sailed from Bristol.

He went along on one of the ships as a boatswain and took part in the plundering of Spanish galleons before returning with the crew to England on October 14, 1711.

Selkirk went to Sussex to settle down and get married.

He was widowed and married again but the call of the sea proved too much for him and a few years later he volunteered for duty in the Royal Navy.

He died at the age of 47 while serving aboard a British warship.

What's It All About?

1. What do you think would be the greatest difficulty to overcome for anyone who is marooned or left alone?
2. How did each of the three characters in these accounts—Gribley, Crusoe, and Selkirk—come to be separated from the rest of civilization?

---

1. What kinds of shelters do Gribley and Crusoe make for themselves?
2. What frightens both Sam Gribley and Robinson Crusoe? What is each one most worried about?
3. What preparations does Sam Gribley make for spending the winter in his tree home in the Catskills?
4. What do you think made Sam Gribley want to get away from the city and try living off the land?

PUTTING IDEAS TO WORK

Imagine yourself living alone far from civilization. Describe the place where you are and the shelter you build yourself.

Most states require that automobiles have certain equipment before they can be used on streets and highways.

A Safe Driver Is Only as Good as a Safe Car

Study the diagram below. What reasons can you give for each requirement? What is the major reason for all the requirements?

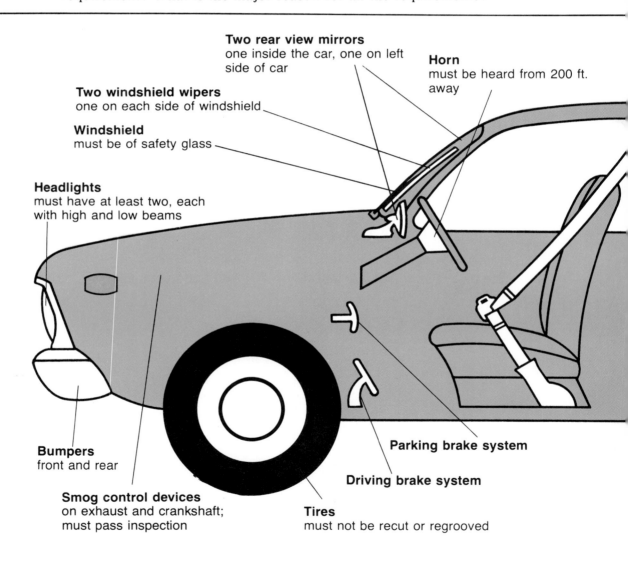

Two rear view mirrors
one inside the car, one on left side of car

Horn
must be heard from 200 ft. away

Two windshield wipers
one on each side of windshield

Windshield
must be of safety glass

Headlights
must have at least two, each with high and low beams

Bumpers
front and rear

Smog control devices
on exhaust and crankshaft; must pass inspection

Parking brake system

Driving brake system

Tires
must not be recut or regrooved

1. Do you find this information is easier to understand because it is presented with a diagram? Why? Why not?
2. Do you see ways that the information could be presented in a better way? How?

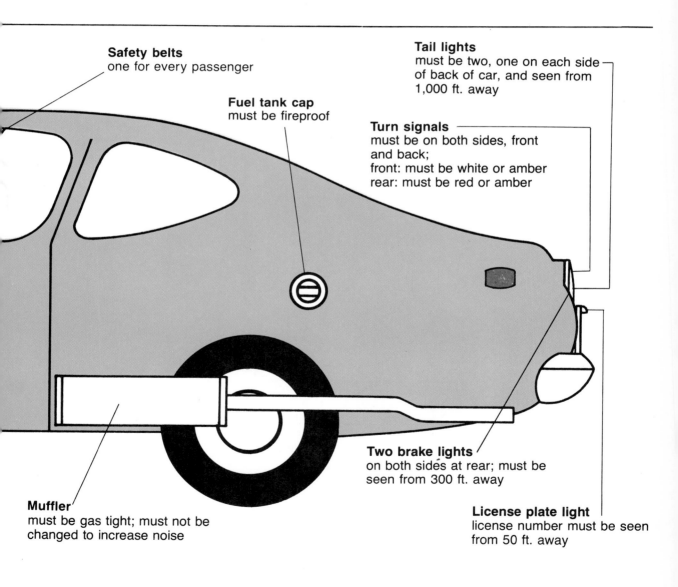

Safety belts
one for every passenger

Tail lights
must be two, one on each side
of back of car, and seen from
1,000 ft. away

Fuel tank cap
must be fireproof

Turn signals
must be on both sides, front
and back;
front: must be white or amber
rear: must be red or amber

Two brake lights
on both sides at rear; must be
seen from 300 ft. away

Muffler
must be gas tight; must not be
changed to increase noise

License plate light
license number must be seen
from 50 ft. away

The more familiar you are with road and highway signs and what they mean, the easier it will be for you when you learn to drive.

Alert Passengers = Good Drivers

Now, while you are still a passenger, is a good time to become familiar with the signals a good driver must follow in order to be a safe driver. There are several different kinds of road signs. If you and your family were traveling in a place that was new to you, reading the road signs correctly would help your journey go smoothly.

Study the groups of signs below and on the next page, notice the differences in shapes and colors of each group of signs. Discuss each sign's meaning with your class.

Diamond Shaped, Yellow Signs give *Warnings*

DIVIDED HIGHWAY   ROAD NARROWS   SLOW

TWO WAY TRAFFIC   PED XING   BIKE XING   HORSE XING   DEER XING   SLIPPERY WHEN WET

Diamond and Rectangular Shaped, Orange Signs give *Construction Warnings*

ROAD WORK 1 MILE   ROAD MACHINERY AHEAD   MEN WORKING   ROAD CONSTRUCTION 5 MILES   SLOW

NO LEFT TURN   **NO RIGHT TURN**

PEDESTRIANS BICYCLES MOTOR-DRIVEN CYCLES PROHIBITED

SPEED LIMIT 55

$500 FINE FOR LITTERING

EMERGENCY PARKING ONLY   **DO NOT PASS**   **NO U TURN**

Square or Rectangular Shaped, White Signs give *Information*

This sign is usually on the back of slow-moving vehicles.

This sign means what it says; "stop" before going on.

This sign means slow down, look for other cars, and let them go first.

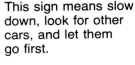

Three Signs with special shapes and colors

1. What differences do colors make in traffic signs? What differences do shapes make?
2. How many different signs did you know before discussing them with your class?
3. Name two signs that have to do with people. Name two other signs that have to do with animals.
4. Which sign might be found near a hospital?
5. What is the fine for littering?
6. What does a yield sign mean?
7. Draw the sign often seen on slow-moving vehicles. What kind of vehicle might carry it?
8. What other signs have you seen that aren't given here?

How Well Did You Learn Your Road Signs?

Test yourself to see how well you can read the road signs. On a separate sheet of paper, write the letter that is before the correct explanation for each traffic sign.

Road Sign Examination

1
(a) right turn ahead
(b) left turn ahead
(c) cross road

6
(a) slippery road
(b) campground ahead
(c) merge left

2
(a) no passing
(b) pavement ends
(c) signal light ahead

7
(a) narrow traffic
(b) two-way traffic
(c) hill ahead

3
(a) local traffic only
(b) stop
(c) other driver goes first

8
(a) no right turn
(b) no left turn
(c) narrow road

4
(a) curving road
(b) no u-turn
(c) steep hill ahead

9
(a) dangerous hill
(b) crossing roads ahead
(c) gravel road ahead

5
(a) slow vehicle
(b) two right turns ahead
(c) stop

10
(a) curves in road
(b) cross winds
(c) chains needed

The faster a car is driven, the longer it takes to come to a stop.

Stopping Takes Longer Than You Think

Information explaining stopping time is presented below in two different ways. Study both charts.

M.P.H.*	Distance Traveled in "Thinking Time"	Distance Traveled in Braking Time	Total Distance Traveled**
25	30 ft.	35 ft.	65 ft.
35	40 ft.	65 ft.	105 ft.
45	50 ft.	110 ft.	160 ft.
55	60 ft.	165 ft.	225 ft.
65	70 ft.	230 ft.	300 ft.

*Miles Per Hour   **Under ideal road conditions

MPH

| 25 | 30 ft. | 35 ft. | 65 ft. |

Thinking Distance

| 35 | 40 ft. | 65 ft. | 105 ft. |

Braking Distance

| 45 | 50 ft. | 110 ft. | 160 ft. |

| 55 | 60 ft. | 165 ft. | 225 ft. |

| 65 | 70 ft. | 230 ft. | 300 ft. |

With perfect 4-wheel brakes and ideal conditions

1. Which method of explaining braking distance seems better to you? Why?
2. Charts of this kind usually have titles. Make up titles for each one.
3. Now create a new presentation with this same basic information. Can you present the information more clearly?

If this was just a coincidence, it was the strangest coincidence Withencroft had ever known.

August Heat

PHENISTONE ROAD, CLAPHAM

August 20th, 190-. I have had what I believe to be the most remarkable day in my life; and while the events are still fresh in my mind, I wish to put them down on paper as clearly as possible.

Let me say at the outset that my name is James Clarence Withencroft.

I am forty years old, in perfect health, never having known a day's illness.

By profession I am an artist, not a very successful one, but I earn enough money by my black-and-white work to satisfy my necessary wants.

My only near relative, a sister, died five years ago, so that I am independent.

I breakfasted this morning at nine, and after glancing through the morning paper, I lighted my pipe and proceeded to let my mind wander in the hope that I might chance upon some subject for my pencil.

The room, though door and windows were open, was oppressively hot, and I had just made up my mind that the coolest and most comfortable place in the neighborhood would be the deep end of the public swimming bath, when the idea came.

I began to draw. So intent was I on my work that I left my lunch untouched, only stopping work when the clock of St. Jude's struck four.

The final result, for a hurried sketch, was, I felt sure, the best thing I had done.

It showed a criminal in the dock immediately after the judge had pronounced sentence. The man was fat—enormously fat. The flesh hung in rolls about his chin; it creased his huge, stumpy neck. He was clean shaven (perhaps I should say a few days before he must have been clean shaven) and almost bald. He stood in the dock, his short, clumsy fingers clasping the rail, looking straight in front of him. The feeling that his expression conveyed was not so much one of horror as of utter, absolute collapse.

There seemed nothing in the man strong enough to sustain that mountain of flesh.

I rolled up the sketch, and without quite knowing why, placed it in my pocket. Then with the rare sense of happiness which the knowledge of a good thing well done gives, I left the house.

I believe that I set out with the idea of calling upon Trenton, for I remember walking along Lytton Street and turning to the right along Gilchrist Road at the bottom of the hill where the men were at work on the new tram lines.

From there onward I have only the vaguest recollections of where I went. The one thing of which I was fully conscious was the awful heat, that came up from the dusty asphalt pavement as an almost palpable wave. I longed for the thunder promised by the great banks of copper- 45

colored cloud that hung low over the western sky.

I must have walked five or six miles, when a small boy roused me from my reveries by asking the time.

It was twenty minutes to seven.

When he left me, I began to take stock of my bearings. I found myself standing before a gate that led into a yard bordered by a strip of thirsty earth, where there were flowers, purple stock, and scarlet geranium. Above the entrance was a board with the inscription—

CHAS. ATKINSON

MONUMENTAL MASON

WORKER IN ENGLISH

AND

ITALIAN MARBLES

From the yard itself came a cheery whistle, the noise of hammer blows, and the cold sound of steel meeting stone.

A sudden impulse made me enter.

46   A man was sitting with his back toward me, at work on a slab of

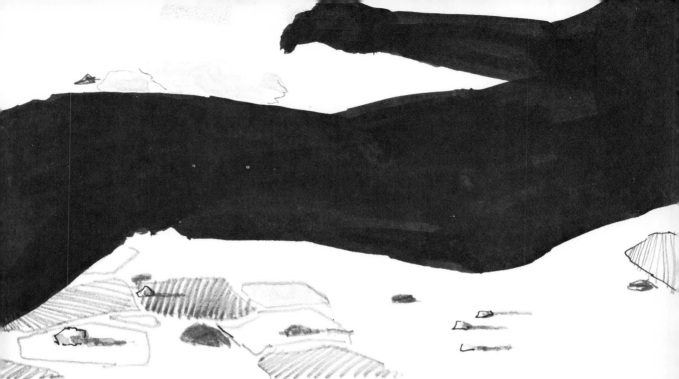

curiously veined marble. He turned round as he heard my steps and I stopped short.

It was the man I had been drawing, whose portrait lay in my pocket.

He sat there, huge and elephantine, the sweat pouring from his scalp, which he wiped with a red silk handkerchief. But though the face was the same, the expression was absolutely different.

He greeted me smiling, as if we were old friends, and shook my hand.

I apologized for my intrusion.

"Everything is hot and glary outside," I said. "This seems an oasis in the wilderness."

"I don't know about the oasis," he replied, "but it certainly is hot. Take a seat, sir!"

He pointed to the end of the gravestone on which he was at work, and I sat down.

"That's a beautiful piece of stone you've got hold of," I said.

He shook his head. "In a way it is," he answered; "the surface 47 here is as fine as anything you could wish, but there's a big flaw at the back, though I don't expect you'd ever notice it. I could never make really a good job of a bit of marble like that. It would be all right in the summer like this; it wouldn't mind the blasted heat. But wait till the winter comes. There's nothing quite like frost to find out the weak points in stone.''

"Then what's it for?'' I asked.

The man burst out laughing.

"You'd hardly believe me if I was to tell you it's for an exhibition, but it's the truth. Artists have exhibitions; so do grocers and butchers; we have them too. All the latest little things in headstones, you know.''

He went on to talk of marbles, which sort best withstood wind and rain, cold and heat, and which were easiest to work; then of his garden and a new sort of carnation he had bought. At the end of every other minute he would drop his tools, wipe his shining head, and curse the heat.

I said little, for I felt uneasy. There was something unnatural, uncanny, in meeting this man.

I tried at first to persuade myself that I had seen him before, that his face, unknown to me, had found a place in some out-of-the-way corner of my memory; but I knew that I was practicing little more than a plausible piece of self-deception.

Mr. Atkinson finished his work, spat on the ground, and got up with a sigh of relief.

"There! What do you think of that?" he said, with an air of evident pride.

The inscription which I read for the first time was this—

SACRED TO THE MEMORY OF
JAMES CLARENCE WITHENCROFT.
BORN JAN. 18TH, 1860.
HE PASSED AWAY VERY SUDDENLY
ON AUGUST 20TH, 190—

*"In the midst of life
we are in death."*

For some time I sat in silence. Then a cold shudder ran down my spine. I asked him where he had seen the name.

"Oh, I didn't see it anywhere," replied Mr. Atkinson. "I wanted some name, and I put down the first that came into my head. Why do you want to know?"

"It's a strange coincidence, but it happens to be mine."

He gave a long, low whistle.

"And the dates?"

"I can only answer for one of them, and that's correct."

"It's a rum go!" he said.

But he knew less than I did. I told him of my morning's work. I took the sketch from my pocket and showed it to him. As he looked, the expression of his face altered until it became more like that of the man I had drawn.

"And it was only the day before yesterday," he said, "that I told Maria there were no such things as ghosts!"

Neither of us had seen a ghost, but I knew what he meant.

"You probably heard my name," I said.

"And you must have seen me somewhere and have forgotten it! Were you at Clacton-on-Sea last July?"

I had never been to Clacton in my life. We were silent for some time. We were both looking at the same thing, the two dates on the gravestone, and one was right.

"Come inside and have some supper," said Mr. Atkinson.

His wife is a cheerful little woman, with the flaky red cheeks of the country-bred. Her husband introduced me as a friend of his who was an artist. The result was unfortunate, for after the sardines and watercress had been removed, she brought me out a Doré Bible, and I had to sit and express my admiration for nearly half an hour.

THE NCROFT 1860 SUDDENLY 190-

I went outside and found Atkinson sitting on the gravestone smoking.

We resumed the conversation at the point we had left off.

"You must excuse my asking," I said, "but do you know of anything you've done for which you could be put on trial?"

He shook his head.

"I'm not a bankrupt, the business is prosperous enough. Three years ago I gave turkeys to some of the guardians at Christmas, but that's all I can think of. And they were small ones too," he added as an afterthought.

He got up, fetched a can from the porch, and began to water the flowers. "Twice a day regular in the hot weather," he said, "and then the heat sometimes gets the better of the delicate ones. And ferns, they could never stand it. Where do you live?"

I told him my address. It would take an hour's quick walk to get back home.

"It's like this," he said. "We'll look at the matter straight. If you go back home tonight, you take your chance of accidents. A cart may run over you, and there's always banana skins and orange peel, to say nothing of fallen ladders."

51

He spoke of the improbable with an intense seriousness that would have been laughable six hours before. But I did not laugh.

"The best thing we can do," he continued, "is for you to stay here till twelve o'clock. We'll go upstairs and smoke; it may be cooler inside."

To my surprise I agreed.

We are sitting in a long, low room beneath the eaves. Atkinson has sent his wife to bed. He himself is busy sharpening some tools at a little oilstone, smoking one of my cigars.

The air seems charged with thunder. I am writing this at a shaky table before the open window. The leg is cracked, and Atkinson, who seems a handy man with his tools, is going to mend it as soon as he has finished putting an edge on his chisel.

It is after eleven now. I shall be gone in less than an hour.

But the heat is stifling.

It is enough to send a man mad.

WILLIAM FRYER HARVEY

Mini·Mysteries

NOTE to an UNKNOWN WOMAN

Although Sara Hull was a librarian by profession, her special interest was solving mysteries even faster than the police. After all, she did have the same initials as Sherlock Holmes.

53

"Miss Hull, have you seen the paper?" The tall boys in blue jeans thrust a copy of *The Gazette* across the library desk. "Arch Vanderhorn's been kidnapped! We knew you'd want to know right away, since you were such a good friend of his."

Sara Hull took the paper and read the headline: VANDERHORN HEIR ABDUCTED. There was a photograph of Arch's gentle, sensitive face, and another of the peculiar note found in his room and the envelope in which it had been contained. The letter had been painstakingly pieced together with words and letters, some capitals, some small, cut from newspapers and magazines. But the address on the envelope and the signature were in Arch Vanderhorn's familiar handwriting: *For Roselle McKhosh*, the address read.

As Sara held the paper up to the light for a closer look, blown-up prints of the same photographs were pushed under her nose. Bill Tawson's voice said, "Here. These ought to be easier to read."

Sara looked up at her friend, the detective inspector, and smiled in spite of her concern for Arch. She had sometimes thought she was the only friend the lonely boy had made since he had graduated from the expensive prep school his always-traveling parents had chosen. His only interest had seemed to be word games—anagrams, puzzles of all kinds, and she had enjoyed recommending books about them to him.

"Is this really how it happened, Bill?" she asked, scanning the newspaper account.

"Yes, the bedroom was ripped apart as if the boy had fought like a tiger," Bill said. "Of course, the parents were in Europe—they're flying back—and the servants sleep in another part of the house, so nobody heard anything. Must have been carefully planned—that note took a while to put together. But the mystery is—not why they forced the kid to address it—but who is Roselle McKhosh? The butler's been there twenty-five years, and says they've never had a servant named that. I think the kid was trying to tell us something, but what?"

54   Again Sara examined the picture of the pasted letters:

no polIce or they May FINish mE. JUST
WAit uNTil thEy Dial you. They will sOon,
So pleAse none of Your FAncy tRickEry.
WhEre they'LL take me, i don't know, but if
you LOVE me, wait. ARCH.

The librarian laughed aloud. Bill Tawson and the two teenagers looked at her in amazement as she said, "You brought it to the right place. This note is addressed to me."

"To you?" the three chorused.

"Yes, to me." Sara looked at her watch. "If this was found last night, I'm sure it's all right to tell you. Arch must be wherever he's going by now. He hasn't been kidnapped. He staged this whole thing himself. He knows his parents will find him, but this way he thought he might have a little time away from that cold, lonely house to think things out and enjoy some freedom. But he wanted to tell me good-bye, so he did it with the things he likes best: an anagram, and a very simple puzzle. Come on, Bill Tawson—do you think you're the only person who realizes that SH stands for both Sara Hull and Sherlock Holmes?"

JULIA REMINE PIGGIN

What did Sara mean?

The name Roselle McKhosh is an anagram. Unscramble the letters and you'll have—Sherlock Holmes. And if you read only the capital letters in Arch's note, it says: I'm fine. Just wanted to say farewell. Love, Arch.

55

Mini·Mysteries
The Followed Friend

"Shut the door, please, Sara. I'm afraid someone will hear."

Obligingly, Sara Hull shut the door of her office in the public library. Shirley Yerby moved her chair to the least conspicuous corner, her mouth working nervously.

"Someone is following me," she explained in a hoarse, frightened whisper. "Oh, Sara, call Bill Tawson, please."

"I will, but tell me what to tell him," Sara pulled her telephone closer, but did not lift the receiver.

"Well, you know I have to go to business luncheons—it's part of my job at the store. The kind where they feed you, but at the same time give a pitch for the product they want you to stock—you know the kind. Well, today there was a big one, full scale, at the Hotel Dollinger. I won't go into the details—"

"Yes, you will," said Sara. "Tell me exactly what happened, from the time you went in."

"Oh, all right. I went to the hotel, took the elevator to the Gladiola Room where the luncheon was being held. They had tables set up outside the room—you know, secretaries check to make sure you're invited, give you a plastic name tag to pin on, and a big portfolio full of advertising for the product. This was a new kind of laundry hamper, put 57 out by Silkwick—I went into the Gladiola Room with the folder under my arm, had a drink, then sat down at the table for lunch. I sat between two old friends—Mary Loll from Americo Advertising and Tim Sage from *House-to-House* magazine. We had some kind of Italian dish—lasagna, I think—then the Silkwick people got up and told us how wonderful the hamper was, and after that we all said 'see ya' and left. I felt sort of sleepy from the big lunch, and decided to go home instead of back to work—it was nearly four. Well, I got on the bus, and that's when it happened. This big red-haired man got on. He came over to me, looked me right in the face, and said, 'Hello, Miss Yerby.' Then he went and sat in the back. I was scared to death. Sara, I swear, he wasn't at that luncheon. I didn't meet him there; never saw him before in my life. Well, I didn't get off at my stop—I went one beyond. And sure enough, he got off when I did. He went the other way—I suppose he doubled back, but—well, that's not all. I walked around the block, then made a rush for my house. I got inside the hall and a man—another one I'd never seen—was coming out. He smiled and he spoke to me too: 'Miss Yerby, how are you?' Sara, please call Bill. They're after me for something. I don't know what, but how did these men know my name if they haven't been put on my trail? Please, Sara.''

Sara stood up, and held out her hand to her friend.

"I'll call Bill, but first I want you to come over here," she said. She guided Shirley to the far corner of the room, and pointed to the wall. "Look," she said. "Take a good look. See it? Do you still want me to call the Detective Bureau?''

JULIA REMINE PIGGIN

What did Sara point to?

A mirror. Shirley had forgotten to take off the name tag that had been given to her before the luncheon—the men had simply read her name and called her by it for fun.

What's It All About?

1. What do you think happens to Withencroft after he completes his writing? Why do you think so?
2. What are the key pieces of information in each of the two mini-mysteries that help Sara Hull solve the mysteries?

---

1. Why do you think Withencroft includes all the details about himself at the beginning of his letter?
2. Why is Withencroft startled when he first sees Atkinson's face?
3. Explain two possible different meanings for this statement in Withencroft's letter: "I shall be gone in less than an hour."
4. How would you explain the incredible coincidence that brings Withencroft, at the end of his long walk, to Atkinson's place?
5. Why did Arch Vanderhorn leave a coded message?
6. Why does Sara Hull ask her friend to look in the mirror?

PUTTING IDEAS TO WORK

Try making an anagram, a scrambled version of your own name. Then write a message like Arch Vanderhorn's in which a second message is hidden in the first.

Jeremy wanted his father's approval more than anything in the world, but he wished he didn't have to shoot a wild duck to get it.

First Hunt

His father said, "All set, boy?" and Jeremy nodded quickly, picking up his gun with awkward mittened hands. His father pushed open the door and they went out into the freezing dawn together, leaving behind them the snug security of the shack, the warmth of the kerosene stove, the companionable smell of bacon and coffee.

Not that Jeremy had eaten much breakfast. It had stuck in his throat, and his father, noticing this, had said, "Just a touch of duck fever, son; don't let it bother you." And he added, almost wistfully, "Wish I were fourteen again, getting ready to shoot my first duck. You're luckier than you realize, Jerry boy."

They stood for a moment in front of the shack, their breaths white in the icy air. Ahead of them was only flatness; not a house, not a tree, nothing but the vast expanse of marsh and water and sky. Ordinarily Jeremy would have been pleased by the bleak arrangements of black and gray and silver that met his eye. Ordinarily he would have asked his father to wait while he fussed around with his camera, trying to record these impressions on film. But not this morning. This was the morning, solemn and sacred, when he was to be initiated at last into the mystic rites of duck shooting.

This was the morning. And he hated it, had hated the whole idea ever since his father had bought him a gun, had taught him to shoot clay pigeons, had promised him a trip to this island in the bay where the point shooting was the finest in the state.

He hated it, but he was determined to go through with it. He loved his father, wanted more than anything in the world his approval and admiration. If only he could conduct himself properly this morning, he

knew that he would get it.

Plodding now across the marshland, he remembered what his father had said to his mother after the first shotgun lesson: "You know, Martha, Jerry's got the makings of a fine wing shot. He's got coordination and timing. And—the kind of nerve it takes, too."

They came to the blind, a narrow, camouflaged pit facing the bay. In it was a bench, a shelf for shotgun shells, nothing else. Jeremy sat down tensely, waited while his father waded out with an armful of decoys. Light was pouring into the sky now. Far down the bay a string of ducks went by, etched against the sunrise. Watching them, Jeremy felt his stomach contract.

To ease the sense of dread that was oppressing him, he picked up his camera and took a picture of his father silhouetted blackly against the quicksilver water. Then it occurred to him that this might not be the thing to do. He put the camera hastily on the shelf in front of him and picked up his gun again.

His father came back and dropped down beside him, boots dripping, hands blue with cold. "Better load up. Sometimes they're on top of you before you know it." He watched Jeremy break his gun, insert the shells, close it again. "I'll let you shoot first," he said, "and back you up if necessary." He loaded his own gun, closed it with a metallic snap. "You know," he said happily, "I've been waiting a long time for this day. Just the two of us, out here on the marshes. We. . . ."

He broke off, leaning forward, eyes narrowed. "There's a small flight now, headed this way. Four, no, five. They'll come in from left to right, against the wind, if they give us a shot at all. Keep your head down; I'll give you the word."

Jeremy kept his head down. Behind them the sun had cleared the horizon now, flooding the marshes with tawny light. He could see everything with an almost unbearable clarity: his father's face, tense and eager, the faint white rime of frost on the gun barrels. His heart was thudding wildly. *No*, he prayed, *don't let them come. Make them stay away, please!*

But they kept coming. "Four," his father said in a whisper. "One mallard. Keep still."

Jeremy kept still. High above them, thin and sweet, he heard the pulsing whistle of wings as the flight went over, swung wide, began to circle. "Get set," Jeremy's father breathed. "They're coming."

In they came, gliding down the sunlit aisles of space, heads raised alertly, wings set in a proud curve. The mallard was leading; light flashed from the iridescent feathers around his neck and glinted on his ruddy breast. Down dropped his bright orange feet, reaching for the steel-colored water. Closer, closer. . . .

"Now!" cried Jeremy's father in an explosive roar. He was on his feet, gun ready. "Take him! Take the leader!"

Jeremy felt his body obey. He stood up, leaned into the gun the way his father had taught him. He felt the stock cold against his cheek, saw the twin muzzles rise. Under his finger the trigger curved, smooth and final and deadly.

In the same instant, the ducks saw the gunners and flared wildly. Up went the mallard as if jerked by an invisible string. For a fraction of a second he hung there, poised against wind and sun, balanced between life and death. *Now*, said something sharply in Jeremy's brain, *now!* And he waited for the slam of the explosion.

But it didn't come. Up went the mallard, higher still, until suddenly he tipped a wing, caught the full force of the wind, and whirled away, out of range, out of danger, out of sight.

There was no sound, then, except the faint rustle of the grasses. Jeremy stood there, gripping his gun.

"Well," his father said at last "what happened?"

The boy did not answer. His lips were trembling.

His father said, in the same controlled voice, "Why didn't you shoot?"

Jeremy thumbed back the safety catch. He stood the gun carefully in the corner of the blind. "Because they were so alive," he said, and burst into tears.

He sat on the rough bench, face buried in his hands, and wept. All hope he had had of pleasing his father was gone. He had had his chance, and he had failed.

Beside him his father crouched suddenly. "Here comes a single. Looks like a pintail. Let's try again."

Jeremy did not lower his hands. "It's no use, Dad. I can't."

"Hurry," his father said roughly. "You'll miss him altogether. Here!"

Cold metal touched Jeremy. He looked up, unbelieving. His father had taken the camera out of its case, was offering it to him. "Quick, here he comes. He won't hang around all day!"

In swept the single, a big pintail drake driving low across the water, skidding right into the decoys. Jeremy's father clapped his hands together, a sound like a pistol shot. The splendid bird soared up; the pressure of his wings sent him twelve feet. One instant he was there, not thirty yards away, feet retracted, head raised, wings flailing, white breast gleaming. The next he was gone, whistling like a feathered bullet downward.

Jeremy lowered the camera. "I got him!" His face was radiant.

"Did you?" His father's hand touched his shoulder briefly. "That's good. There'll be others along soon; you can get all sorts of shots." He hesitated, looking at his son, and Jeremy saw that there was no disappointment in his eyes, only pride and sympathy.

64   ARTHUR GORDON

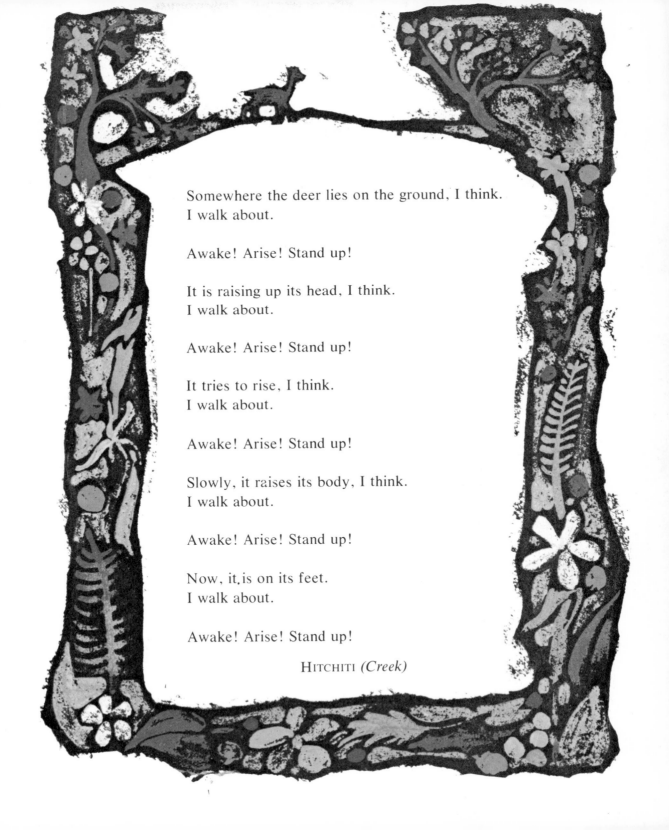

Somewhere the deer lies on the ground, I think.
I walk about.

Awake! Arise! Stand up!

It is raising up its head, I think.
I walk about.

Awake! Arise! Stand up!

It tries to rise, I think.
I walk about.

Awake! Arise! Stand up!

Slowly, it raises its body, I think.
I walk about.

Awake! Arise! Stand up!

Now, it is on its feet.
I walk about.

Awake! Arise! Stand up!

HITCHITI (*Creek*)

"In other times," said Littabelle Lee, "I had killed for food, and the experience had not been bad. Yet this time . . . "

DEER HUNT

Pup rubbed his cold-red ears. "I saw a deer just now. If I had a gun, I would've killed it, but all I've got is this here knife."

I got down and stood beside Pup. "Where did you see a deer?"

Pup pointed. "Through there. Back in the trees. You ever killed one?"

"No."

"Me either. I bet it'd be fun."

"Pup," I said, "it is wrong to kill anything for fun. For food, that is different."

"Let's go get that deer," said Pup, and took Little Boy's reins from my hand and tied them to an evergreen. He did that as if we were related, and we started off down the slope in front of us as if we had suddenly become that way. Clannish and staunch together. We did not

66

speak. Pup put his hand on my arm and patted it. The shadows of the trees lay black on the snow sheen, and the breath from our mouths was faintly blue. We went down the slope, the snow crunching beneath our feet, sinking sometimes in places where it had not hardened, and we saw the tracks of the deer. We went on several more paces before we saw the animal standing alone in a deer trail. It was a buck with antlers and a white, powder-puff tail. Pup's hand, closing around my arm, commanded me. We stopped, and the animal lifted his head; we observed each other. I could not gauge the distance between us. He was without fear. He stood motionless, watching.

Pup whispered to me, "Don't move quick. Bring your gun up slow."

There was the distance between us, and there were the blue-shadowed snow dunes. I could not have seen the animal's clear, beautiful eyes, yet I saw them. And I thought I saw in them what all of nature should be to human beings—a glimpse of God.

In other times I had killed for food and the experience had not been bad. I had not been squeamish about it, yet this time 67

I could not, could not. Something inside me unfolded, rushing, illuminating. Stunned by this feeling I could not understand, I could not move. I felt ugly and naked.

Pup whispered urgently, "Bring your gun up slow."

I brought the gun up slow. It was heavy, heavier than in reality it was. I lowered it.

Pup's eyes were ablaze. He whispered urgently. "What's wrong?"

"Nothing."

"You sick?"

"No."

"Why you cryin'?"

"I'm not."

"Aren't you gonna kill him? Don't you want him?"

"No."

"But he's right there! It'd only take one shot! One!"

"No. I would rather die."

"Gimme the gun then, I'll do it."

"No. Get away from me. You want a slap? I'll give you one. Back off."

Mad, Pup backed off. The clouds were going across the frosty sky, and we two humans and the wild, beautiful animal continued to stand there, watching each other. I thought—He has used all of his powers to stay alive. You have no right, no right.

Away down the deer trail there was a movement of some kind and the deer, alerted, turned and bounded off, his hooves sending up little floes of snow.

Pup and I went back up the slope to the spot where we had left Little Boy. Pup was very much irked and put out with me. He said, "You had him dead to rights. You could have had him with one shot, just one."

How could I tell him what I felt? It was not just the deer to be explained. It was the flashing, tumbling shift I had felt inside myself while standing with my gun raised and pointed at the animal. He had brought me to some kind of a crossroad in my existence. It was an arrival, adding in some way, pointing in some way, to the meaning of my life. The deer was an ingredient of our land, and so he was an ingredient of myself. But I could not tell Pup these things. So I said, "Pup, I could not kill that deer. He trusted me too much. He has been out here in the woods a long time and he loves being here as much as we do. Don't you see?"

"You talk crazy," said Pup and kicked at the snow. After a moment he said, "He was sure pretty. Want me to give you a boot-up?"

VERA *and* BILL CLEAVER

69

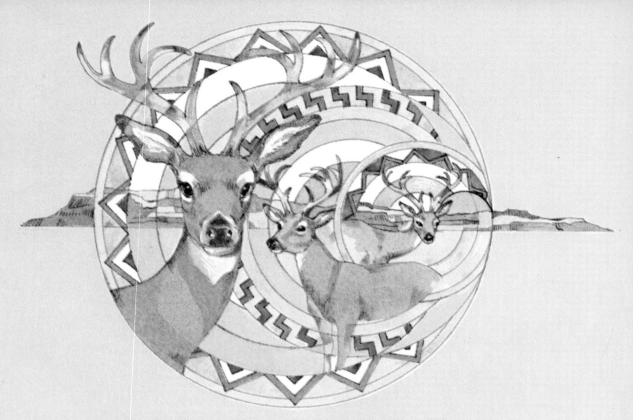

Comes the deer to my singing,
Comes the deer to my song,
Comes the deer to my singing.

From the Mountain Black,
From the summit,
Down the trail, coming, coming now,
Comes the deer to my singing.

Starting with his left fore-foot,
Stamping, turns the frightened deer,
Comes the deer to my singing.

Comes the deer to my singing,
Comes the deer to my song,
Comes the deer to my singing.

70   NAVAJO

What's It All About?

1. Jeremy feels he must "conduct himself properly" to earn his father's approval. At the beginning of the story, what does Jeremy think "proper conduct" is? What does he find out at the end about proper conduct?
2. Why is Littabelle Lee reluctant to shoot this deer?
3. Both Jeremy and Littabelle Lee discover that they are unable to shoot a living creature. Compare their experiences. How does each one feel about the prey?

1. What are the first indications that Jeremy hates the idea of going hunting with his father?
2. What did you think the father would do when Jeremy said he couldn't shoot the duck? What does he actually do? Why?
3. In what way do Littabelle Lee and Pup disagree about killing the deer?
4. Compare the reactions of Jeremy's father and Pup when Jeremy and Littabelle Lee refuse to shoot.

PUTTING IDEAS TO WORK

Do you agree or disagree with the statements: "Killing wild animals for food is all right; killing them for sport is wrong." Choose a point of view and write your arguments for it.

A lot of people gave up on David Pearson, but he never gave up on himself.

I Learned to Win by Losing

Judgments on who is the best stock car driver may differ, but it is clear that David Pearson was one of the top four or five.

Pearson was a shy and modest man, a withdrawn, soft-spoken sort. He never became a public spokesman for his sport because he lacked the polish and confidence. "I just don't have the education to speak at banquets and such, and it depresses me because I love racing," he confessed.

73

He got the nickname "Li'l David" not because he was small but because he defeated many stock car giants, just as the biblical David defeated Goliath. In 1961 he was in his second year on the tour, when he suddenly hit the headlines with three surprising super-speedway wins. He upset all the favorites, and a big future seemed to be ahead of him. But he was not ready to follow up such success, and for the next few years he was considered a disappointment, struggling along a rough road back to the top.

"A lot of people gave up on me," he said, looking back, "but I never gave up on myself. I wanted it too much. I had ability, but I needed experience. I got lucky early, but I had a lot to learn."

His handsome face showed traces of his Cherokee Indian ancestry, but Pearson was a typical southern small-town boy. He was born in 1934 and raised in the tiny mill town of Whitney, near Spartanburg, in South Carolina. His father and mother worked hard in the cotton mills to earn a living for their family, and David developed powerful arms and shoulders lifting heavy spools of cotton to help out. He quit school at 16.

"From the time I was ten and saw my first race, from the time I was a little shaver, racing was all I ever wanted," he once said. "Me and my buddies used to sneak over the old board fences at the Spartanburg Fairgrounds and watch the stock cars flying on that dirt track, and I always knew that was for me."

His older brother owned a body repair shop, and David volunteered to sweep the place just so he could be near the beat-up racers that were brought in. On the country roads around Whitney, he would race anyone who'd challenge him or take up his challenge.

In 1952, when David was 18, he married Helen. Four months after their first child was born, Pearson bought an old racing car for $40 and told his wife he was going racing. David fixed up his car and entered it in a race at Woodruff Speedway in September 1953, finishing second and winning $13.

Pearson had the enthusiasm, but in the beginning he didn't have the know-how. "I didn't know anything about how to set up a car for races," he recalled. "Some of my buddies were helping me and they knew about what I knew. We thought the car had to lean to the left like all good race cars, so we all jumped up and down on the left running board of my old jalopy and actually knocked it over to one side. We used iron from an old bed for roll bars. That's what we knew."

By 1959 Pearson had joined NASCAR's sportsman circuit, and that year he won 30 of 42 races and the South Carolina state championship.

He determined to move up to the big time, but he didn't have the money. "I was working in a service station days and racing nights," he recalled, "but I was doing so well on the dirt tracks some of my friends wanted to see how I could do on the super-speedways. The owner of the service station, a local cop and my father started a drive to raise money to send me on the circuit. My policeman friend even went on

the radio station in town to appeal to the public for funds to buy me a car. So I got a car."

It wasn't enough of a car. He didn't win any races during 1960, but he came close several times and did well enough in 22 starts to be named "Rookie of the Year" on the Grand National tour.

That showing earned David his big chance—a factory ride with the Pontiac team operated by Ray Fox. David grabbed it and shocked the circuit in his sophomore season by winning three super-speedway classics— the World 600 at Charlotte, the Dixie 400 at Atlanta and the Fire-cracker 250 at Daytona.

His wife remembered that first triumph at Charlotte vividly.

"I watched the race from the infield," she recalled, "and I wasn't scared until a driver had a real bad crack-up. Later, he lost his leg. I shuddered at David having to continue the race after such a horrible accident, but he was leading and he did go on to win."

She laughed wistfully. "That first race, David earned $28,000 and a new convertible. His cut was $12,000, including the car, the first new one we'd ever owned. When he told me he wanted to put the money into a house, I was thrilled. We decided our home would be in the same mill village surroundings that we both knew and loved. I was really proud of David when he told me he didn't care for a big house with a lot of fancy trimming. Maybe he knew it wouldn't always be as easy as it was that year."

Pearson earned almost $50,000 in purses that year. "I don't know how I did it," he said years later. "I wasn't that good, only I didn't know it. I'm a charger, I had a good car, it held up and I won. I soon found out I had a lot to learn, however. I had to learn how to win in a car that wasn't way out the best."

During the next six years he didn't win a single super-speedway event. In fact, in 1962 and 1963 he did not win a race of any sort. After 1962, Ray Fox let him go and Pearson drove Dodges for Cotton Owens, a championship driver who had retired. He drove them so hard they kept breaking on him.

"He was still wild," Owens recalled. "At Richmond in 1964 I told him I could still beat him even though I was washed up, because I had more experience even if he had more talent. I had two equal cars and I gave him his choice. He took one, I took the other one and I won. After that, he was more likely to listen to my advice."

Pearson won eight races in 1964. The next year he won only two, but he finished in the top ten in more than half his starts. He was improving, and in 1966 he won 15 races, the driving championship and almost $50,000. He began to enjoy life again.

"It's a funny game," he said. "Stock car racing is two ends of the world. You win and you're at the very top. You're surrounded by fans. You're a great driver and a great guy. You blow a tire, blow an engine, strip a gear, hit a wall or do any one of the thousands of things that can keep you from Victory Lane and you're a nobody. I learned how to win by losing a lot."

BILL LIBBY

76

Drag racer Shirley Muldowney rockets from 0 to nearly 250 miles per hour in less than six seconds.

Shirley Muldowney

by SANDRA HINSON

Shirley Muldowney, one of drag racing's few licensed women and its second-best driver, may become the first female champion of an integrated sport in the U.S.

"I want to be the fastest woman in the world—in a manner of speaking," Shirley half-joked a couple of years ago. She has since been timed at the second-highest speed—249.30 mph—in drag racing history. Now she is trying to beat the records of Don "Big Daddy" Garlits, a 25-year veteran who holds most of the sport's records.

Muldowney is a slight 5'4" and 100 pounds, with nerves of steel and a foot of lead. She gives nothing away to competitor Garlits, 45. "He is like the grandfather of drag racing," she says. "I've beaten him lots of times in the last three years." She also insists she is never afraid, even when rocketing from 0 to nearly 250 mph in less than six seconds. "I'm a professional. I've never driven over my head in my life."

77

Her attitude is all the more remarkable in view of the three fires
that hurt her career—one scorch-
ing her so badly her eyes swelled
shut. "It was like opening a
furnace door in your face," she
recalls. "Before the car stopped it
burned the tires right off." Then
she switched from "Funny Cars"
(shortened stock car bodies with
racing engines in the front) to
safer rear-engine Top Fuelers.
The fastest drag racers built, they
are named after the powerful and
expensive non-petroleum fuel
they require.

Muldowney's fascination
with speed began on the streets of
Schenectady, N.Y. She grew up
driving anything she could borrow
until her first car, a '40 Ford with a
Cadillac engine.

Shirley supported her racing
with jobs as a dental assistant,
typist and waitress. She turned
professional driver 10 years ago in
the face of much resistance,
official and unofficial. One woman
fan was so angry she threw a can
of soda at Shirley. But she
says,"Things started opening up
for me after so many years of
fighting to be accepted." Even
male resistance has decreased.

Last year Shirley pumped
$146,000 into her two cars (one on
each coast) and four-man crew,
logging 80,000 miles during the

racing season. "I've made money, but not a lot," she says. "Plenty of years I didn't have anything left at the end." Prize money and guarantees are 75 percent of her income; sponsors provide the rest for advertising on the car.

On rare occasions she parks her apple-red camper at home in Mt. Clemens, Mich. Here Shirley works with her antique collection and cooks Italian dishes for her son, John, 18, now her mechanic and closest friend. "We kind of grew up together," she says. She plans to start John on his own racing career this year. "It's a sickness," Shirley said. "Either you love it or you hate it. I am probably more comfortable when I get in that race car than I am any other time of the day."

SANDRA HINSON

Rocket Racer

The three-wheeled rocket car screams through the morning air. Its 48,000 horsepower engine hurtles it across the chilly desert, faster and faster...400...500...612 miles per hour! The driver is Kitty O'Neil, trying to break the 627 mile per hour land speed

81

record. She also wants to break the 742 mile per hour speed of sound. She fails!

But Kitty isn't discouraged. She has broken the 308 mile per hour women's record. And soon she will try again to break the world land speed record.

Kitty is determined. She's overcome obstacles before. When she was born, the half-Irish, half-Cherokee girl was deaf. She overcame that. As a teenager she was a top swimmer ready for the Olympics. Then a disease hit. Doctors said she'd never move again. But she did. Now she's a top stunt performer.

Kitty keeps trying. And Kitty—a deaf woman who once could hardly move—will try again.

What's It All About?

1. What do you think were the most difficult obstacles that David Pearson, Shirley Muldowney, and Kitty O'Neil each had to overcome in order to be successful?
2. Why do you think car racing fascinates so many people?

---

1. How did Pearson and Muldowney first become interested in racing? What do you think kept each of their interests alive?
2. What were Pearson's reasons for not giving up when he lost so many races?
3. How did Cotton Owens get Pearson to listen to his advice?
4. Shirley is described as having "nerves of steel and a foot of lead." What does each of these comparisons mean? What facts from the story prove they are true?

PUTTING IDEAS TO WORK

Find someone who has succeeded at something—in sports, in school, in any activity—in spite of obstacles such as illness or other handicap, lack of experience, being male or female, and so on. Interview this person. Write down how he or she overcame these obstacles.

You've probably heard someone say, "The place is so big, you need a map to find your way around!" Well, that is certainly true of large airports.

You Need a Map

The map below gives a simple picture of LAX—the airline code name for the Los Angeles International Airport. Take a careful look at the map. Study the information which gives a key to the symbols. Then read the information on the next page which gives the locations of various airlines and the index of passenger services.

Now turn to page 86 for questions which test your ability to find your way around the airport and to find some of the passenger services.

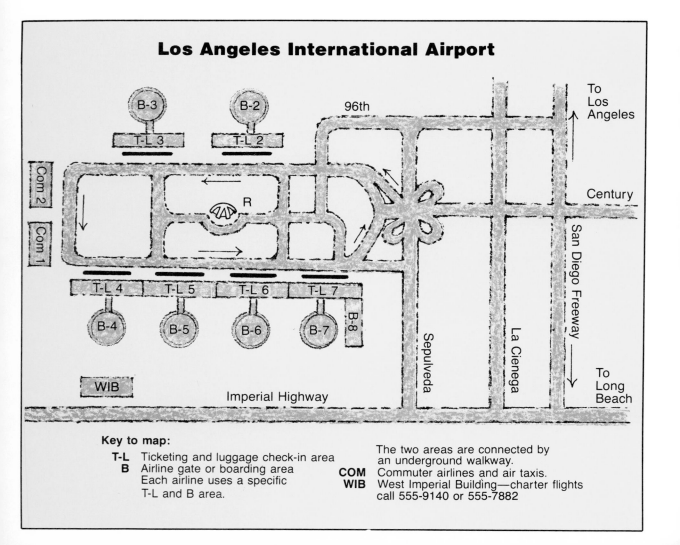

Los Angeles International Airport

Key to map:

T-L Ticketing and luggage check-in area
B Airline gate or boarding area
Each airline uses a specific T-L and B area.

The two areas are connected by an underground walkway.
COM Commuter airlines and air taxis.
WIB West Imperial Building—charter flights call 555-9140 or 555-7882

Airport Guide

Airlines
Building

Aerolineasi Argentinas 2	Golden West .... COM 2
Aeromexico 2	Japan Air Lines 2
Air Canada 2	Lufthansa 2
Air France 2	Northwest Orient 4
American 4	Pan American 2
British Airways 2	Sierra Pacific .... WIB
Charter Flights (most) .... WIB	Swift Aire .... COM 1
China Airlines 2	Texas International 7,8
Continental 6	TWA 3
Delta 6	United 7,8
Eastern 3	Western 5
Ecuatoriana 5	

Passenger Service Facilities
Building

Airport Security ...... Tel. 555-6254	Insurance
Baggage Cart/Stroller Depots .... All	Counters B3,5,6,T-L2,4,7,WIB
Bank .... R	Lost and Found ...... Check Airline
Barber Shop B6	Medical, First Aid ..... Tel. 555-6254
Car Rental Counters .. T-L2,3,4,5,6,7	Newsstands T-L2,3,4,5,6,7,WIB
Change Machines B2,3,4,5,6,7,8	Observation Deck .... R
Food Services	Police Dept. .... Tel. 555-2256
Coffee Shops B2,3,4,5,6,7	Postage Stamps, Mail Drops ..... All
Snack Bars T-L6,7,WIB	Rest Rooms .... All
Restaurant .... R	Telephones .... All
Gift Shops B2,3,4,5,6,7,8,WIB	Travelers Aid T-L2,3,4,5,6,7
Hotel/Motel	Wheelchairs .... Check Airline
Phones T-L2,3,4,5,6,7,WIB	

1. What freeway is near the airport?
2. If you are coming into the airport on Century, which Ticketing-Luggage area do you come to first?
3. Look at the list of airlines. What type of airline most often uses T-L 2 and B-2?
4. If you were picking up friends who are arriving on an Eastern flight, which building would you go to?
5. Which airlines are considered commuter airlines?
6. Which T-L area serves two separate boarding areas?
7. If you were landing at LAX on a Western flight and were transferring to an American flight, what appears to be the fastest way to get to American? (Your luggage is checked to your final stopping place.)
8. Where is the only restaurant located? In what other building can you get a meal?
9. Where can you buy postage stamps? a magazine? a gift?
10. You need help in finding a motel room. Where are some of the places you might get help?
11. You just got off a Delta flight and are waiting in B-6 to take a Continental flight when you discover that you left a package aboard the Delta plane. What do you do and where do you go? (Your Continental flight leaves in 50 minutes.)
12. You have a short time to make a transfer. Would you rather change from Continental to Eastern or from Continental to Delta? Why?

The auto parking information on page 87 is for the convenience of travelers and visitors who use the Los Angeles International Airport. Most large airports have similar lots.

Read the information, then answer the questions below:
1. Which central terminal lot is the least expensive?
2. Ms. Dalton arrives at the airport on January 3. She plans to leave her car in one of the lots, but she has no change. Which lot is the only one she cannot use?
3. Howard is picking up some friends at one of the airlines, but he arrives an hour early. What would it cost him to park in the Central Terminal Lot?

LAX AUTO PARKING

Central Terminal

LOTS 1-7

$ .50 each 2 hours
6.00 each 24 hours

LOT A

$ .50 each 2 hours
4.00 each 24 hours
Fee includes transportation between terminals and Lot A. Take tram marked "Airline Connections— Parking Lot A."

LOT C

$ .50 each 3 hours
2.00 each 24 hours
Fee includes transportation between terminals and Lot C. Take tram marked "Parking Lot C."

VSP LOT

$ .50 first 6 hours
.25 each additional 3 hours
1.50 each 24 hours
Fee includes transportation between terminals and VSP Lot. Take tram marked "VSP Parking."

West Imperial Building

SUMMER MONTHS (cashier booth)

$ .50 each 3 hours
2.00 each 24 hours

WINTER MONTHS (coin operated)

$ .50 entry fee
(two quarters required for coin-operated gates)

Van Nuys Airport Bus Terminal Lot— FlyAway Bus Service
WOODLEY AVENUE AT SATICOY ST.

$ 1.00 entry fee
Non-stop bus transportation to LAX each half hour, 5:30 A.M. to 1:30 A.M.; each 1¼ hours, 1:30 A.M.-5:30 A.M.
$3 one-way, $5.00 round trip fare.
Information: 555-5554, 555-5555

NOTE: Parking rates listed are those in effect in May, 1977, and are subject to change. It is suggested that you check the rates posted at the entrance to each parking lot before entering.

4. Which lot does not provide transportation to the airline terminals?
5. If you did not have this chart, where else might you find information about the parking rates for these lots?
6. The term "live parking" is often used to indicate parking lots used by people who discharge and pick up travelers. "Long-term parking" applies to lots where travelers leave their cars for a few days or weeks while they travel. Which term applies to each lot above?

Taking a Trip?

The Jackson family is taking a trip this summer. They are going to Colorado for two weeks. They are all excited and have lots to do before leaving. Each person is in charge of her or his own clothes and packing. They have lists of things to be done before they leave.

Read the checklists below. How are these items important to the Jacksons' trip? Give reasons for each item.

Home Checklist

1. Stop mail, paper, and milk deliveries.
2. Connect lights to automatic timers or leave a light on.
3. Lock all doors and windows.
4. Remove all leftovers from refrigerator and turn temperature down.
5. Unplug unnecessary electrical outlets throughout the home.
6. Water plants and place them in plastic bags.

Travel Checklist

1. Use sturdy luggage but pack only what is needed.
2. Put identification tags on each piece of luggage.
3. Lock your luggage.
4. Keep important papers with you, not in your luggage.
5. Allow enough time for checking in at station or airport.
6. Claim your bags as soon as you arrive.

Use these checklists on your next trip.

TRAVELERS

Cheryl decided she really cared about track, and she went out to the Prospect Park field to dig in and work—even if nobody paid any attention to her.

RACE TO FAME

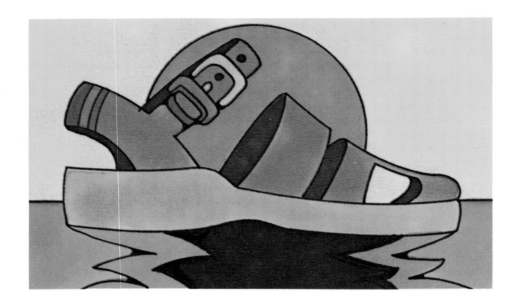

In 1967 a city-sponsored group called Youth in Action held a track meet at the Boys' High School field in Brooklyn, New York. Because she had nothing better to do that day, thirteen-year-old Cheryl Toussaint went to watch the meet. Sitting in the stands with her friends, Cheryl found it all very exciting: the speed of the sprinting girls, the yells and cheers of the spectators, the highly charged atmosphere of noise, tension, and fun.

While the meet officials were arranging the order of final events, an "open" race for girls was announced. That meant that any girl present could come to the starting line and compete even if she didn't belong to a track team. Cheryl loved to run—on the street, in the schoolyard, or in the local playground—and she wanted to enter. Still, she hesitated. The girls she had been watching in the meet looked so fast. Cheryl's friends urged her to give it a try. "Go ahead, don't be chicken," they teased. And when one said, "I dare you," Cheryl accepted the challenge.

She was wearing a dress and a pair of sandals, hardly suitable 90 clothing for a race, so a friend who was wearing sneakers swapped footgear with Cheryl. Of course, the fit wasn't exactly right, but it was the best available. Then another girl, who had changed into track shorts, lent her jeans to Cheryl. "Suited up" this way, Cheryl walked down to the starting line and waited for the race to begin.

"It was a hundred-yard dash," Cheryl remembered, "and I really didn't know what to do. I didn't even know how long a hundred yards was. I just stood at the line in someone's dungarees and someone else's sneakers. I didn't know how to start; I was standing straight up. Then the man said, 'Take your marks . . . Set . . . Go!' and I ran. I got second."

There were several qualifying heats being run, and Cheryl was told that the finals would be held in a while. As she waited, Cheryl began to wonder whether she should enter the finals. "For some reason, I began to hurt right around my hip area, and I didn't understand it. So, I told my friends that I didn't think I'd run. They began the teasing routine again, saying that I was chicken and that I was copping out because I didn't think I was going to win, and that kind of thing. Well, that did

it. I went back on the track, ran the final, and took fourth place. That wasn't bad, but the thing that got me was that the three girls ahead of me were all Atoms. I was so impressed with how fast they were that all I could think of was how I could join the team, too.''

The Atoms Track Club of Brooklyn was an AAU (Amateur Athletic Union) team, made up of local girls who wanted to run competitively. There were many fine runners in the group, and it was beginning to develop into a real track power.

After the meet was over, Cheryl saw some Atoms runners doing exercises on the grass. Screwing up her courage, she walked over to them and asked how she could join the team. They told her that joining was easy: all she had to do was come to the practices every afternoon.

For a while, Cheryl went to Prospect Park in Brooklyn for the Atoms' daily practice. But when no one paid much attention to her, she began to doubt herself and the results of her running. "I thought that because I was putting my whole heart into it, the coach should have done more than tell me to run laps, do exercises, or practice starts," she said.

Cheryl had no way of knowing that Atoms coach Fred Thompson always treated new team members this way. It was his way of testing their willingness to work. Realizing that the tough, time-consuming practice sessions were more than many would endure, he would watch them without their being aware of it. Then, if they stayed with it without any encouragement, he would be sure that they were ready for real coaching.

After two months as an Atom, Cheryl dropped out of the club. The memory of her one race, however, kept coming back to her—the pounding heart before the start, the wonderfully free feeling of running, the excitement of coming in ahead of others. So after six months away from the Atoms, Cheryl Toussaint returned to the club, this time to stay.

Those six months away from track had given the teen-ager time to   93 think about herself, her attitude toward work, and her goals in life. Cheryl decided that she really cared about track, and she went out to the Prospect Park field ready to dig in and work, even if *nobody* paid any attention to her or praised her.

Fred Thompson had missed Cheryl during those six months, and had hoped she'd come back. He had sent a message to Cheryl, telling her she'd always be welcome. The coach hadn't pressed the issue, but he was very pleased when she did return.

The season for cross-country racing (long-distance races over all kinds of terrain) was just beginning, and Fred took the Atoms to a cross-country meet on Long Island, New York. That day Cheryl officially competed for the first time as an Atom, and neither she nor the coach ever forgot it.

"Cheryl had been back training with us for only about two weeks," Thompson recalled, "but I decided to enter her in a one-mile run, just to

give her some competitive experience. Of course, she wasn't really in condition, and I knew it. So, I said to her before the race, 'Don't go out too fast, stay with the pack, and just try to finish.'

"Well, the gun went off, and before I knew it, Cheryl was a hundred yards in front of the whole field and running like a madwoman. I said to myself, 'My gosh, this kid is going to pass out!' But she just kept running. Then, with about a hundred yards to go, the oxygen debt really hit her, and she just about collapsed. She fell down, then got up and started crawling on her hands and knees. It was unbelievable! She stood up, staggered some more, got about twenty yards from the finish line and fell again. She kept on going, crawling, still with nobody near her, and then right at the wire another girl caught up and won.

"Cheryl cried like a baby. I went over and picked her up, tried to comfort her, telling her that she had nothing to be ashamed of. But she just cried. I knew, at that moment, that this girl was going to be

something special. I had never seen anything like that before in my whole life.''

Until Fred Thompson came into her life, nobody had ever thought of Cheryl Toussaint as something special. Shortly after Cheryl's birth on December 16, 1952, her parents separated and Cheryl went to live with her grandmother. Her home was a tenement flat in Bedford-Stuyvesant, Brooklyn. In the crowded ghetto schools she attended, Cheryl slipped further and further behind grade level until, by junior high, she was classified as a ''slow learner.'' She was placed in Corrective Reading and Corrective Math and forbidden to take the courses that would make her eligible for a good academic high school.

Then Cheryl joined the Atoms, and everything in her world, including school, took on new meaning. Fred Thompson assumed the role of the father she lacked at home, demanding that Cheryl do better, scolding her when she let up, praising her when she succeeded. ''Freddy always encouraged me and all the girls to try for good grades,'' Cheryl explained. ''He'd say, 'When those report cards come in, I want to see them!' and he really meant it. He made me feel that he was just as concerned with how I was doing in school as with my running. It was almost as if he were a parent—only having had so much education himself, he really knew what was going on. I couldn't tell him that a C was okay because the teacher had said so—he knew better. My mother and grandmother cared, and were concerned about my schooling, but Freddy knew what each grade meant. There was no snowing him.''

With new motivation, Cheryl set to work. She begged the school authorities to let her take algebra, a foreign language, and more advanced English courses. The teachers seemed certain that Cheryl wouldn't be able to do the work, but she was insistent. Finally, they agreed to let her carry those subjects, in addition to her remedial classes, on a one-year trial. It was grueling, but Cheryl gave it everything she had, and began to learn and do well.

''When I got my report card,'' Cheryl said, ''not only did I feel good for myself in getting good grades, I felt proud having somebody else to show them to, somebody who really appreciated them. Freddy would say, 'Cheryl, that's darn good. Keep it up.' Then he started to talk about college."

Few Bedford-Stuyvesant youngsters go to college, and many don't even finish high school. So to Cheryl, Fred Thompson's mention of college sounded like a wild fairy tale. But she understood, as did all the Atoms, that Fred meant every word he said. He told them that if they were good enough, poverty would never stop them. For example, if they qualified for the Nationals, no matter where the competition was held, he'd see that they got there. An attorney at New York's Madison Square Garden, he would use his own salary, or borrow the money, or beg for it—but the Atoms never had to worry about how they would pay for track equipment, travel expenses, or entry fees.

Her part of the bargain, Cheryl learned, was to succeed in school (flunk and you were off the team) and to work doggedly on the track. And she stuck with the hard, two-hour practice every day. "When I first joined the team," Cheryl remembered, "it was plain exhausting. I'd come home after practice barely able to shower and eat; all I wanted to do was sleep. My grandmother was accustomed to the energetic, bouncy kid I had been, and here I was—collapsing.

"Even though it knocked me out, the running definitely helped me do better in school. I had to be very well scheduled. If I hadn't been running track every day, I'd have been at the nearest park, playing handball or softball, after school. But with those early-evening practices being so tiring, I knew I had to devote afternoons to homework if I wanted to graduate."

As her schoolwork improved, so did Cheryl's performance on the track. She loved the feeling of running and now, with Coach Thompson's faith in her and her own new image of herself, she began turning faster times and winning races. Cheryl had been running for only about a year when she qualified to compete in the U.S. trials for a place on the 1968 Olympic squad.

Looking back at that time, Cheryl later said, "I had been doing fairly well, but at that point I didn't think I was ready for the Olympics. It was enough of a thrill to know that I had made it to the trials. In a way, it was scary for me. I ran and did the best I could, coming in fifth, but I didn't make the Olympic team. I was a little disappointed, but I know now that if I had qualified for the team then, it might have been the ruination of me. Athletes can be thrown, and I've seen it happen to some when they advanced further than their emotional levels could cope with. Success too soon isn't always a good thing. Sometimes people aren't mentally ready for things, and I think I wasn't ready for the Olympics then."

Cheryl was ready to become an outstanding student, however. Fred Thompson had convinced her that she was college material and that with a little more effort she might earn a scholarship. With that goal firing her up even more, the "slow learner" was soon getting A's and zooming to the top of her class.

In June 1970 Cheryl graduated from Erasmus Hall High School in Brooklyn and received an academic scholarship to New York University.

"It might sound kind of boring," Cheryl said of her teen years, "because my life was a round of sleeping, eating, classes, running, studying, and more sleeping. But I was doing what I loved and what I wanted to do."

FRANCENE SABIN

98

What's It All About?

1. How did Cheryl Toussaint become such a successful runner? What important factors made her so good?
2. Toussaint said, "Success too soon isn't always a good thing." What do you think she meant?

1. What made Cheryl Toussaint enter her first race?
2. Why was Coach Fred Thompson so impressed with Toussaint? Why was he so important in her life?
3. How did Coach Thompson treat new team members? Do you think this is a good way to train beginning athletes? Why?
4. How did joining the track team change Toussaint's life? How did it affect her school work?

PUTTING IDEAS TO WORK

Choose a sports figure you admire. Write that person a letter asking how he or she got started in that particular sport.

Make My Bed in the River

"I didn't know then that the river would be a treacherous friend, all soft and warm and friendly, but able to turn on you just when you thought you'd gotten to the buddy-buddy stage."

It's been almost two years now, and there are things I still wonder about. If Jim had a chance to come back, to maybe think it over; if he had another chance to see what all he's been missing, would he do the same thing again? Jim was an awful smart kid, and maybe now, if he was two years older, he'd know better and he wouldn't do that silly reckless thing he did, leaving me alone to wonder and think about it. And yet, somehow, after all this time I've thought about it, I still guess he'd do it, all right. Because that's the way he was.

Tomorrow is my birthday. I'll be seventeen. If Jim was around, he'd give me a hard crack on the back and say something like, "Hey,

Ed, old man. You're going to make a prize fighter yet!'' I know I won't ever be a prize fighter because I only weigh 132½ and I still have to wear glasses. But it would be something nice to hear, if Jim said it.

It was great having Jim for a friend. I guess that summer was just about the best time of my whole life. We did things together, had fun together, that I'd merely dreamed about before. I'm the only kid my folks have, and ever since I can remember there've been times when I'd suddenly come down with a bad attack of asthma. My mother would have me stay home from school, which I never minded anyway, and keep me in bed where I'd read all the books that I had out of the library. The library was like another home to me, sort of, because when I wasn't in school or home, that was where I spent all the rest of my time. But Jim changed all that.

I'd never known our town was so interesting. There were lots of places to go, and things to do, once you knew about them. For instance, can you imagine, I'd never even known that we had a great Chinatown section on the other side of the river. It was beyond the library and, of course, I'd never gone that far. Part of Jim's paper route went through it, and he had friends all over the place. The houses and shops were built right next to each other, just a few steps from door to door. Jim never threw his paper in Chinatown. He always carried it in and laid it gravely down on the counter.

The old men behind the counters would smile and say, "How you today, Jimee?" and sometimes they would give us a piece of pretty good tasting stuff that would turn out to be cocoanut or ginger. Stuff like that.

My parents were glad that I'd finally made a friend of my own and they really approved of Jim. They were always saying to me, "Why don't you invite Jim here for dinner? He could stay overnight too, if he wants."

Jim came from a large family. He had six sisters, three older than he was, and three younger. Can you imagine one guy with six sisters? When I'd go to his house to visit, I'd just sit there open-mouthed and my eyes bugging out behind my glasses to see all these girls swirling all over the place. I'd sit in their kitchen looking at them and wonder what it would be like at my home to have girls around. Then I'd decide that a brother would be better, but since I didn't have any, Jim was the next best thing. I guess a good friend is even better than a brother because I know lots of kids with brothers who fight with them. With Jim and me, now, we never had a fight. Oh, we used to have a lot of arguments. We'd argue about anything that crossed our minds; elections, making lots of money when we got older, school, teachers, other kids. Just anything. Looking back on it now, I can see that I must have filled a kind of empty spot in Jim's life, too, because he had never had a brother either.

That first summer. Boy, that was really a good summer. At first my folks were reluctant to let me be away from home so much because they were used to me being around underfoot curled up with a book. But as they got to know and trust Jim, they let me go with him more and more. Jim was a natural-born wanderer. He'd say to me, "You know, when I'm a man, I'm going to get on a tramp steamer and work my way around the whole world. Maybe I'll become a captain and have my own ship, and go anywhere I feel like. Say, Eddie, why don't we go on down to the river now and fool around on our raft?"

Jim just loved that river. The Turtle flows right through our town, splitting it into two towns almost, with the business section and Chinatown and the older homes all on one side, and the newer homes like mine on the other.

The first few times we went there we just lay around on the banks letting the sun warm us up like a couple of old toads. The cottonwood trees growing along the shore were all leaved out in new green and gold pointed leaves and when the wind shook them a little, it reminded me of a pretty lady in a bright green dress doing a little dance. If you listened hard, you could even hear a sort of soft, murmuring music that she was dancing to.

102   After we'd gone to the river a few times, just lolling around and

killing time, Jim sat up one day and looked intently at the green, curling water. A railroad tie was floating by about ten feet out from shore. He got to his feet, staring at it. "Get a long branch," he said. "Let's see if we can grab it."

We pulled it in with a cottonwood limb, getting our shoes soaked. It was a nice-looking piece of wood.

"What do you want with it?" I asked him.

"If we had about ten more, look at the nice raft we could build," he replied. I thought it was a great idea, and we separated, going up and down the shores looking for more big pieces. In about a week we had enough gathered and pulled up onto our private little beach to start building. I borrowed a hammer from my father's toolbox without saying anything to him, and Jim showed up one day with a bag full of spikes. We put together a great little raft, strong enough to hold both of us, and cut two long poles to use as shovers. From then on we explored the river from our private yacht, going in and out of little creeks, and putting in to small islands to rest. It reminded me a lot of Tom Sawyer and Huck Finn, and one day I told Jim about the book. He looked at me and listened, but then he said, "You can't live out of books, Eddie. Don't you know that? What's wrong with living and doing things, too?"

By this time I knew he was right. It was fun to do things for yourself, so I just shrugged. I hardly went near the library anymore. We worked on the raft all the time, gradually building up the floor boards and putting sideboards on to make a prow. We kept it hidden in a secret little cove where the alder trees grew close together and the grass was long and smelled sweet when we walked over it. My folks would have died if they'd ever seen me on that raft in the middle of the river, floating along and having fun. They didn't even know I could swim, but of course I could. Jim had taught me how and there wasn't anything to it once you learned to stick your head under water and let your breath out slowly. I found the water actually held you up if you kept your lungs full and didn't thresh around in panic.

Jim and I would have a contest. We'd start out floating on top of the water, then when he'd say, "Go!" we'd push all the air out of our lungs and sink to the bottom to lie there stretched out on the soft ooze, holding our breaths and feeling like sleeping mud puppies. It was almost like going to bed, but not quite, because all too soon we'd have to come up, grabbing and gulping at air.

I didn't know then that the river could be a treacherous friend, all soft and warm and friendly, but able to turn on you just when you thought you'd gotten to the buddy-buddy stage.

Jim and I went to different schools then though we were in the same grade. The coming year, when we'd be in High School, we'd be at the same place and we talked about it a lot. We decided we'd both go out for track and basketball and swimming too, if we could make the team. I'd gained a lot of confidence in myself and never even stopped to think about things like "what if I can't make it?"

Jim always said, "Make up your mind what you want. Then go

after it."

The way he said it seemed to mean that there wasn't anything in the world you couldn't have, if you really wanted it, and worked hard enough to get it.

We shared the paper route now which meant that I had to get up at five in the morning to meet Jim at the corner where our papers were dropped. My mother didn't like it one bit and was always protesting. "It certainly can't do a young boy any good to get up at that hour," she'd grouse around at my father.

But my dad was of the old school that felt the Horatio Alger books were the greatest things ever written. "You can see for yourself it isn't doing him any harm," he'd say, looking at me when I'd be gulping my breakfast to get to school in time.

Jim and I had bought ourselves bikes with some of the money we'd earned, and not only did the bikes make our route quicker to handle, but it opened up the whole countryside to us. We would pack ourselves enormous lunches, and on weekends we'd pedal out into the country, going to places we had marked out on a map. There were some tall

buttes about ten miles away and that was one of the first places we decided to explore.

I remember that morning like it was yesterday because on that day Jim Fairchild saved my life. And what can you do for a guy who has saved your life? Nothing, except be proud of him and keep your mouth shut, and hope that someday the chance might come when you can do the same thing for him. And that's what hurts so in telling this story because somewhere along the line I faltered. Oh, I know I did. I live with it every day and every night. It happens to me over and over again, and in my dreams, I'm kicking and threshing, trying to stop the nightmare, but it never stops.

We got out to the buttes about ten o'clock that morning. My legs felt a little weak from all that pedaling, but after we'd rested awhile, they were O.K. We ate part of our lunch and saved some for later. It was Jim, of course, who got the idea for climbing the buttes. I suppose that was really what had brought him out here. I never knew for sure what was on his mind, but I was always willing to go along with him.

"We can do it, don't you think, Eddie?" he said, looking up backwards from where we were lying.

"Sure," I said casually. "Do what?"

"Climb this rock face. It looks like chicken-pot-pie from here."

I tilted my head back and looked up. It seemed pretty straight up in the air to me, but I wasn't about to give any objections if Jim thought we could do it. We left our bikes there at the foot of the cliffs and started up. It was easy at first because there was a lot of rock fall and we just clambered over it until we reached the end. Then the cliff rose steeply, but there were still little ridges and small bushes growing for handholds, so we kept right on going. It wasn't until we were halfway up the cliff face that the accident happened.

I'd been following right along behind him, but in a couple of places where he'd managed to pull himself up by his arms, I'd been a little more careful, searching around for footholds, so he'd gotten about fifty feet ahead of me. I had just taken hold of a small mesquite bush growing

on a little ledge when the place where I'd put my weight suddenly fell away from my foot, and I was left dangling in the air with only my grip on the mesquite holding me. I know I gave a scream because I heard it, bouncing against the cliff and falling off in tiny echoes that showed how far it was to the bottom of the rocks. I didn't want to do it, but my eyes looked down there all by themselves and I could see what a small bundle of rags I was going to look like, falling a couple of hundred feet and smashing on those rocks below. I couldn't look up now, but I heard Jim's voice, "Hold on, Eddie! Hold on! I'm going for help."

Somehow he managed to climb the rest of the cliff by himself, and somehow he got down on the backside where it wasn't nearly so steep. He told me later he'd raced around to the bottom of the cliff where our bikes were and had looked up at me hanging there in space, thinking he'd never make it in time. He jumped on his bike, and bombed off to the nearest house we'd seen, about a mile away. The only person at home was an old, fat farm lady, and Jim saw right away that she wasn't going to be any help, so he asked her for a rope. She gave him one, wanting to know all the time what it was for, and would he be sure to bring it back. Then he pedaled back like he was in a race, and climbed the sloping rear of the cliff again.

Just when I'd gotten to the point where I knew I had to let go, my arms were pulling themselves out of their sockets, and I kept slipping out of the only toehold I could feel, I heard his voice again saying, "Eddie! Grab it!"

The rope came down with a noose at one end and I'll never know how I managed to get it around me, nor how long it took for Jim to pull me up. I remember falling to the ground at the top and grabbing on to the grass and then laughing hysterically while Jim pounded me on the back.

We rode home afterwards silently, and carefully, but every time we looked at each other we'd burst out laughing. The lady got her rope back, but she never did know what we'd used it for.

Sometime in November of that year when we were fifteen, and just going about our own business of studying, getting bigger, growing up, the rains started in our valley. It rained for a whole week, never stopping, sometimes just a gentle patter on the mud puddles lying in all the streets, sometimes pouring down like it was Niagara Falls. The Turtle went into flood, and I knew for sure that our raft must have been carried away. I wanted to go check on it, but the lowland part where we kept it hidden was under water and there was no way to reach the spot.

I met Jim as usual on a Sunday morning to distribute our papers, and when that was done, Jim suggested we ride down to the bridge to look at the river. It was the same bridge where I'd first met him, two years before, when I'd been caught in a fight. I thought of that idly as we splashed through all the water pooled on the bridge and stopped not far from where it had happened.

We leaned our bikes against the railing and got off to watch the black, cold water sliding by just a few feet from the bottom of the bridge. Whole clumps of trees were drifting along with their roots waving in the air like hands beckoning for help, and we saw chicken coops and a perfectly good rowboat drift by, pass under the bridge, and

go on down the river which was five times as wide as it usually was.

While we were standing there, staring fascinated at that mass of
water, Jim suddenly came alert and said, "What's that?"

I couldn't see anything, even when he pointed, so I adjusted my
glasses and peered a little harder.

"It's a dog," Jim said. "A tiny little dog."

Then I could see it. It wasn't any bigger than a rat, and you could
have even mistaken it for one, except that when it got right under us, it
looked up with a despairing fear in its eyes and its tiny paws were
beating at the water, which was just sweeping it along downstream. I
saw Jim hesitate. He turned and looked at me and something in his mind
must have said, "No! I can't. I have six sisters and no brothers. And
Eddie is an only kid."

Just the same, after that one moment of hesitation, he tore off his mackintosh and ran across the bridge. He looked far over the side, then kicked off his shoes and all in one movement, he was over the side of the railing. I was appalled at seeing him go into that black water and ran after him, crying, "Jim! No! Come back!" As if he could. As if he could!

Out of the corner of one eye I saw the little dog get ashore in the backwash from the bridge, but Jim's head didn't come up out of the water for a long time, and when it did, he was way downstream. The water carried him along like one of the tree trunks, turning and rolling, and then he was swept out of sight around the bend the river makes.

I ran for help, forgetting both our bikes on the bridge, but there was no help.

I went over to see Mrs. Fairchild twice. Each time she cried and held me to her breast, and all the little girls were around, crying. After that I didn't go back.

I think of it, but there's no way I know to change things. When Jim hesitated that instant, did he count on me? Did the cliff and the rope flash through his mind? Did the raft loom up in his hopes, tied as it was, should have been, somewhere down below him? Did he know the little dog got out? Did he think of me, standing back there on the bridge, alone, but safe, hollering after him, "Come back!" Did he hear me? Did he care?

JEAN McCord

What's It All About?

1. How did Jim die? How does Eddie feel about his death? What do you think bothers Eddie most?
2. Jim and Eddie had very different backgrounds and interests. Why do you think they became such good friends?

---

1. Why are Eddie's parents at first reluctant to let Eddie be away from home so much?
2. What kinds of things does Eddie do with Jim that he has never done before? How does this change him?
3. Jim always said, "Make up your mind what you want. Then go after it." How does the story show that Jim lived by these words?
4. Knowing the kind of person Jim was, do you think he could have acted differently when he saw the puppy? Why?

PUTTING IDEAS TO WORK

What is a best friend? Make a list of what you think are the qualities of a best friend.

Beyond Expectations

How do people
Move
Beyond expectations?

It was not easy to be a doctor on the Oregon frontier in 1884, but Bethenia Owens-Adair was ready to serve. If she were needed, she would go. Sure enough, one dark and stormy night she heard a pounding at her door.

Pioneer Doctor

When she was forty-four years old, Bethenia Owens remarried. Her husband was a retired army colonel named John Adair. Colonel Adair had invested in a great deal of property along the Pacific Coast southwest of Astoria. At that time, it was mainly a wilderness of tidal flats and forest. Adair was trying to develop the land into a farm and hoped that someday a railroad might pass through his property.

Bethenia, who now called herself Dr. Owens-Adair, moved with her husband into this semi-wilderness. It was here that her life as a frontier doctor really began.

In Portland, Bethenia had taken pride in the fact that she never refused to answer a call from a sick person. She was ready to serve no matter what the time of the day or night, no matter what the weather. This was her attitude in her new practice, though the wilderness was very different from Portland. Storms often flooded the tidal flats and turned them into huge swamps. In the forests, fallen trees and heavy vines often blocked the trails so that not even a horse could get through.

113

Then the doctor would have to walk, sometimes wearing rubber boots that might fill with mud and water.

Bethenia wrote about one of her experiences:

The worst storm that I ever saw took place one dark winter night. It had been raining and blowing hard all day, but that night was horrible! The wind howled and shrieked; the house trembled and shook; the rain fell in sheets. We could not sleep.

"This is just the sort of night someone will come looking for me," Bethenia said. She was only half joking, because such things had happened before.

"Well, this is one night you can't go," her husband said. "I wouldn't let you go out in this weather."

Bethenia said nothing. But she knew that if she were needed, she would go.

And sure enough, at about four in the morning, there was a pounding on the front door. A man's voice could just barely be heard above the howl of the storm.

"I'll see who it is," Colonel Adair said. He got out of bed and lit a lantern. Then he said to Bethenia, "You stay there. Whoever it is, you can't go anywhere until this storm lets up."

She did not answer, but he was hardly out of the room before she was up and getting dressed. She knew that no one would have come for her in this weather unless there was a great need. As quickly as possible, she got on her clothes and went to join her husband.

A big man in a rubber raincoat stood just inside the door. Water dripping from him made a puddle on the floor. Colonel Adair was saying, "—the doctor can't go out in this weather. It's impossible."

"I understand," the man said. "But the lady's awful sick."

"Where is she?" Bethenia asked.

Both men turned, swinging their lanterns. "She's at Seaside," the messenger said.

114

Seaside was fifteen miles away. The road to it was hardly any more than a trail, and much of it would be dangerous if not impossible in this weather. As though he knew what she was thinking, the man said, "I made it, Doctor. I'll admit it took me six hours to get here and the storm was at my back. It'll be much worse going south. But there is no other doctor, and—"

"I'll go," Bethenia said. She turned to her husband. "John, saddle a horse for me while I get my bag."

"No," Colonel Adair said. "I told you. I won't let you go in this weather. It's not safe."

"When I got my medical degree," Bethenia said, "I promised myself that I would always answer the call of anyone who really needed me. I've always kept that promise. Would you stop me now?"

He sighed. "All right. But if you go out tonight, I go with you."

When they opened the front door, the storm almost threw them back into the house. Both men took Bethenia by the arm. Bent far over, they fought their way across the porch, down the steps and across the yard to the barn. Colonel Adair saddled the horses, then took a blanket and cut a hole in the center of it. When Bethenia was on her horse, he pulled this blanket over her head and tied the corners to the saddle. He did this so that the storm would not blow her off the horse.

It was still pitch black. The road at first led through the forest. The wind screamed in the trees. Branches tore loose and flew past in the darkness. Before Bethenia and the men had gone a mile, they came to a place where two trees had fallen and completely blocked the road.

Colonel Adair had brought axes. He and the messenger got off their horses and battled the fallen trees while the wind battled them. They finally hacked out a path and the three moved on.

There was no sunrise, only a gray misty light that seemed to be a part of the storm itself. By the time they could see as much as a hundred yards ahead, they were out of the forest and on the tidal flats. They now felt the full, head-on force of the storm. Bethenia's horse kept trying to turn and go with the wind, and she had trouble controlling the horse   115 because of the blanket tied to the saddle. But her husband kept his horse close alongside and forced hers ahead.

It took seven hours to cover the fifteen miles to Seaside. There Bethenia found her patient still alive but burning with fever. So now she had a new and different kind of battle on her hands. But finally she won that one, too.

This kind of living was hard on Dr. Owens-Adair's health. She was no longer young, and rheumatism began to trouble her more and more.

Her husband was worried about her. Finally, in the winter of 1898, he got her to move to North Yakima, Washington. Here, in the high mountain air, her health improved rapidly.

But this was still frontier country. And Dr. Bethenia Owens-Adair held to the promise she had made herself never to refuse the call of a person in need. Once, in a pea-soup fog, she started to drive her buggy ten miles to a ranch where a woman was about to have a baby. It was impossible to see the road and she let her horse find its own way. After an hour, she saw dim lights—and found that she was right back in front of the North Yakima stable she had started from. The horse had circled and come home.

There was a stagecoach driver in the stable. Bethenia asked him if he thought he could find the way to the ranch through the fog. "I can drive it with my eyes shut," he said, climbing into the buggy with her.

They finally got to the ranch, but not before even the stagecoach driver had been lost for awhile.

Bethenia once worked for sixty hours with only two hours' sleep during a diphtheria epidemic. During that time, going day and night, she drove her buggy for more than a hundred miles to one ranch after another to visit her patients. Part of the way was through deep snow, and all of it was in below-zero weather. At that time, Bethenia was sixty-four years old.

She lived another twenty-two years, working all the time. Even after she retired from medicine, she kept herself busy, either writing the story of her life, or working for women's rights, or fighting for laws to guard public health. When she died at the age of eighty-six, the words placed on her tombstone were from an article she had written:

Only the brave become pioneers.

Bethenia Owens-Adair certainly had the pioneering spirit. But she had still more than this. She was truly a great pioneer doctor.

WYATT BLASSINGAME *and* RICHARD GLENDINNING   117

Lucinda Matlock

I went to the dances at Chandlerville,
And played snap-out at Winchester.
One time we changed partners,
Driving home in the moonlight of middle June,
And then I found Davis.
We were married and lived together for seventy years,
Enjoying, working, raising the twelve children,
Eight of whom we lost
Ere I had reached the age of sixty.
I spun, I wove, I kept the house, I nursed the sick,
I made the garden, and for holiday
Rambled over the fields where sang the larks,
And by Spoon River gathering many a shell,
And many a flower and medicinal weed—
Shouting to the wooded hills, singing to the green valleys.
At ninety-six I had lived enough, that is all,
And passed to a sweet repose.
What is this I hear of sorrow and weariness,
Anger, discontent, and drooping hopes?
Degenerate sons and daughters,
Life is too strong for you—
It takes life to love Life.

118   EDGAR LEE MASTERS

What's It All About?

1. Why did Dr. Owens-Adair go out on such a stormy night?
2. What made it so difficult to be a doctor on the Oregon frontier?

---

1. Briefly describe Dr. Owens-Adairs's ride through the storm to Seaside. Do you think it was worth the trouble? Why?
2. How did the rough life on the frontier affect Dr. Owens-Adair's health? How did this affect her career?
3. What words are on Dr. Owens-Adair's tombstone? Why are they particularly appropriate for her?

PUTTING IDEAS TO WORK

Have you ever kept on working at something when no one expected you to continue? Tell about a time you or someone you know kept going "beyond expectations."

We agreed that night to meet here again in exactly twenty years, no matter what.

AFTER TWENTY YEARS

The policeman on the beat moved up the avenue impressively. The impressiveness was habitual and not for show, for spectators were few. The time was barely ten o'clock at night, but chilly gusts of wind with a taste of rain in them had well nigh depeopled the streets.

Trying doors as he went, twirling his club with many intricate and artful movements, turning now and then to cast his watchful eye down the pacific thoroughfare, the officer, with his stalwart form and slight swagger, made a fine picture of a guardian of the peace. The vicinity was one that kept early hours. Now and then you might see the lights of a cigar store or of an all-night lunch counter; but the majority of the doors belonged to business places that had long since been closed.

When about midway of a certain block, the policeman suddenly slowed his walk. In the doorway of a darkened hardware store a man leaned, with an unlighted cigar in his mouth. As the policeman walked up to him, the man spoke up quickly.

"It's all right, officer," he said, reassuringly. "I'm just waiting for a friend. It's an appointment made twenty years ago. Sounds a little funny to you, doesn't it? Well, I'll explain if you'd like to make certain it's all right. About that long ago there used to be a restaurant where this store stands—'Big Joe' Brady's restaurant."

"Until five years ago," said the policeman. "It was torn down then."

The man in the doorway struck a match and lit his cigar. The light showed a pale, square-jawed face with keen eyes, and a little white scar near his right eyebrow. His scarfpin was a large diamond, oddly set.

"Twenty years ago tonight," said the man. "I dined here at 'Big Joe' Brady's with Jimmy Wells, my best chum, and the finest chap in the world. He and I were raised here in New York, just like two brothers, together. I was eighteen and Jimmy was twenty. The next morning I was to start for the West to make my fortune. You couldn't have dragged Jimmy out of New York; he thought it was the only place on earth. Well, we agreed that night that we would meet here again exactly twenty years from that date and time, no matter what our 121 conditions might be or from what distance we might have to come. We figured that in twenty years each of us ought to have our destiny worked out and our fortunes made, whatever they were going to be.''

''It sounds pretty interesting,'' said the policeman. ''Rather a long time between meets, though, it seems to me. Haven't you heard from your friend since you left?''

''Well, yes, for a time we corresponded,'' said the other. ''But after a year or two we lost track of each other. You see, the West is a pretty big proposition, and I kept hustling around over it pretty lively. But I know Jimmy will meet me here if he's alive, for he always was the truest, staunchest old chap in the world. He'll never forget. I came a thousand miles to stand in this door tonight, and it's worth it if my old partner turns up.''

The waiting man pulled out a handsome watch, the lids of it set with small diamonds.

''Three minutes to ten,'' he announced. ''It was exactly ten o'clock when we parted here at the restaurant door.''

''Did pretty well out West, didn't you?'' asked the policeman.

"You bet! I hope Jimmy has done half as well. He was a kind of plodder, though, good fellow as he was. I've had to compete with some of the sharpest wits going to get my pile. A man gets in a groove in New York. It takes the West to put a razor-edge on him."

The policeman twirled his club and took a step or two.

"I'll be on my way. Hope your friend comes around all right. Going to call time on him sharp?"

"I should say not!" said the other. "I'll give him half an hour at least. If Jimmy is alive on earth he'll be here by that time. So long, officer."

"Good-night, sir," said the policeman, passing on along his beat, trying doors as he went.

There was now a fine, cold drizzle falling, and the wind had risen from its uncertain puffs into a steady blow. The few foot passengers astir in that quarter hurried dismally and silently along with coat collars turned high and pocketed hands. And in the door of the hardware store the man who had come a thousand miles to fill an appointment, uncertain almost to absurdity, with the friend of his youth, smoked his cigar and waited.

About twenty minutes he waited, and then a tall man in a long overcoat, with collar turned up to his ears, hurried across from the opposite side of the street. He went directly to the waiting man.

"Is that you, Bob?" he asked, doubtfully.

"Is that you, Jimmy Wells?" cried the man in the door.

"Bless my heart!" exclaimed the new arrival, grasping both the other's hands with his own. "It's Bob, sure as fate. I was certain I'd find you here if you were still in existence. Well, well, well!—twenty years is a long time. The old restaurant's gone, Bob; I wish it had lasted, so we could have had another dinner there. How has the West treated you, old man?"

"Bully; it has given me everything I asked it for. You've changed lots, Jimmy. I never thought you were so tall by two or three inches."

"Oh, I grew a bit after I was twenty."

"Doing well in New York, Jimmy?"

"Moderately. I have a position in one of the city departments. Come on, Bob; we'll go around to a place I know of, and have a good long talk about old times."

The two men started up the street, arm in arm. The man from the West, his egotism enlarged by success, was beginning to outline the history of his career. The other, submerged in his overcoat, listened with interest.

At the corner stood a drugstore, brilliant with electric lights. When they came into this glare each of them turned simultaneously to gaze upon the other's face.

The man from the West stopped suddenly and released his arm.

"You're not Jimmy Wells," he snapped. "Twenty years is a long time, but not long enough to change a man's nose from a Roman to a pug."

"It sometimes changes a good man into a bad one," said the tall man. "You've been under arrest for ten minutes, 'Silky' Bob. Chicago thinks you may have dropped over our way and wires us she wants to have a chat with you. Going quietly, are you? That's sensible. Now, before we go on to the station here's a note I was asked to hand you. You may read it here at the window. It's from Patrolman Wells."

The man from the West unfolded the little piece of paper handed him. His hand was steady when he began to read, but it trembled a little by the time he had finished. The note was rather short.

> *Bob:*
> *I was at the appointed place on time. When you struck the match to light your cigar I saw it was the face of the man wanted in Chicago. Somehow I couldn't do it myself, so I went around and got a plain-clothes man to do the job.*
>
> *Jimmy*

O. HENRY

What's It All About?

1. Who is Bob waiting for? Why is he waiting?
2. Does the reunion turn out as Bob expected it to? Why?

1. What kind of person is Jimmy? How does Bob describe him?
2. What kind of person is "Silky" Bob?
3. What do you think Jimmy was thinking as he spoke to Bob?
4. Do you think Jimmy should have turned Bob over to the other police officer? Why? What might have happened if he hadn't?

PUTTING IDEAS TO WORK

Resolved: We should stand by our friends no matter what they do. Do you agree or disagree with this statement? Take a position and plan an argument for it.

When summer comes around, the scramble for work begins.

Advertising for a Summer Job

Often there are places such as supermarkets, local drugstores, community centers, and the local paper, where young people can advertise for work. Persons wishing to employ young people can list the jobs that are open, at the same places. Many times these "Jobs Available" and "Positions Wanted" are posted in some convenient place—to help both employees and employers.

On the next page are six jobs that are available and six persons who want jobs. Try to match up the jobs with the persons. Which person is best for each job? Be ready to explain why you made the "matches" that you did.

1. Which two positions do not match up with anyone?
2. Which people will have to look elsewhere for work?
3. What are some of the problems with Wanda Stevens' information card?

Write up the description of a job you would like to have. Then write up your "Position Wanted" card. Are you qualified for the job? Why?

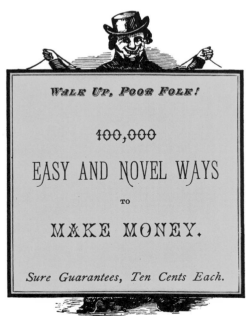

WANT ADS

GENERAL WORK

Laborer: Canning factory
Phone: 491-4906
Requirements: Strong, hardworking
Hours: 35-45 hrs/wk
Pay: Minimum Wage

Filling Station/Pumper
Phone: 910-1455
Requirements: Previous Experience
Hours: Open
Pay: Open

Ad Delivery
Phone 646-7115
Requirements: bicycle must know city well
Hours: Flexible
Pay: $5.00/10 deliveries

Child Care
9 month old girl
phone: 461-7932
Requirements: Like children, able to care for a baby.
Hours: 9AM-3PM weekdays
Pay: Depends on age, experience.

Walk & Groom 3 dogs
Phone: 692-7717
Requirements: Animal lover
Hours: 2 hours/day
Pay: $1-2.50/hr.

GENERAL HOUSEWORK
Phone: 641-7600
Requirements: Experienced, pleasant, hardworking
Hours: 9-12 noon, 6 days/week
Pay: open

POSITIONS WANTED

Jerome Ritter
PHONE: 642-8912
POSITION: Gardening
EXPERIENCE: 2 summers as caretaker, carhop Burger Place
COMMENTS: Hardworking

Salina DeMott
Phone: 969-0592
Position: Child Care
Experience: Many bros. and sisters, 1 yr. of part time babysitting
Comments: Will need transportation, Can start immediately.

Jose Pintura
Phone: 862-6773
Position: Waiter
Experience: Bus boy; Chef, Kitchen helper; know food business
Comment: Prefer starting between 4 and 6 PM.

WANDA STEVENS
Phone: 691-7605
Position: Fashion Designer
Experience: None
Comments: Cannot work weekends, before 9 AM or after 5 PM.

Angela Londa
Phone: 469-1434
Position: Anything W/cars
Experience: Part time attendant gas station; cashier, carwash
Comments: Interested in mechanics or car sales.

Alex Salazar
Phone: 496-9246
Position: Anything!
Experience: Delivery Boy, Stock Boy, animal care, gardening
Comments: Must work 40 hrs/wk; any location.

When you borrow money from any lending institution, you are in fact "renting money". A finance charge or interest must be paid on the amount of money you borrow. So, you in fact pay back <u>more</u> than you borrow.

So Easy to Borrow . . .

The ad makes it all sound so easy and it is. But look at the chart below. This is a chart of the National Atlantic Bank's typical loans and repayments.

NATIONAL ATLANTIC BANK

LOAN PAYMENTS

Amount Borrowed	Monthly Payment	Term	FINANCE CHARGE	Total Payment
$ 5,000	$ 88.26	7 yrs	$2,413.84	$ 7,413.84
5,000	71.74	10 yrs	3,608.80	8,608.80
7,500	132.40	7 yrs	3,621.60	11,121.60
7,500	107.60	10 yrs	5,412.00	12,912.00
10,000	176.53	7 yrs	4,828.52	14,828.52
10,000	143.47	10 yrs	7,216.40	17,216.40

ANNUAL PERCENTAGE RATE: 12%

When you call the bank and get their brochure with the loan application, this is what you find out. Now how easy does it look?

Discuss the ad and the loan repayment chart with your class. How many advantages can you think of for "renting money"? disadvantages?

Opening a Savings Account

Here is a new account form that has been filled out by an applicant. Read the instructions on the form. Study the information and form carefully. Answer the questions below that will help you summarize what you have learned.

New Account Application

New Account Form Pass Book Savings Account

Please fill out this form and mail it with your check to any Westview Federal Office. Your account will be opened promptly. The pass book will be mailed to you.
Or bring the form and your check and/or cash to the nearest Westview Federal Office.

Open an account for:

Social Security No. *496-16-4975*

Mother's Maiden Name *NEWTON*

Mr.
Ms. *JAY BROWN*

Place of Birth *MINNESOTA*

Address *2159 BROADWAY ISLE MASSACHUSETTS 02166*
Street   City   State   Zip

Signature *Jay Brown*
(As you will use it for each deposit and withdrawal)

Amount enclosed *25 00*   Phone No. *691-5212*

1. Are you invited to send cash by mail? How do you know? Would sending cash by mail be a good idea?
2. Why would your telephone number be useful?
3. Why would your signature be needed each time you add or take out money?
4. For tax purposes, the federal government keeps a numbered account for each person that shows the interest paid on savings accounts. What information is given to help the government do this?
5. How does your mother's last name—before marriage—and your place of birth help if someone tries to take money from your account?
6. Why is the pass book—a small booklet which has a record of what you have added and taken out of your account—needed each time you use your account?
7. What new terms have you learned?
8. Do you know of any other ways to open a savings account?

Buck was a remarkable dog, thoroughly devoted to Thornton, the man who had saved his life. Now it was Buck's turn to save Thornton.

For the
LOVE
of a Man

Buck, a broad-breasted dog, white-fanged and long-furred, adored John Thornton. This man had saved his life, which was something; but, further, he was the ideal master. Other men saw to the care of their dogs from a sense of duty and business. Thornton saw to the care of his as if they were his own children, because he could not help it. And he saw further. He never forgot a kindly greeting or a cheering word. To sit down for a long talk with them was as much his delight as theirs. He had a way of taking Buck's head roughly between his hands, and resting his own head upon Buck's, of shaking him back and forth, the while calling him names that to Buck were love names. Buck knew no greater joy than that rough embrace and the sound of murmured words.

Buck's love for Thornton seemed to grow and grow. Thornton, alone among men, could put a pack upon Buck's back in the summer traveling. Nothing was too great for Buck to do, when Thornton commanded. One day the men and dogs were sitting on the crest of a cliff which fell away, straight down, to naked bedrock three hundred feet below. John Thornton was sitting near the edge, Buck at his shoulder. A thoughtless whim seized Thornton, and he drew the attention of Hans and Pete to the experiment he had in mind. "Jump, Buck!" he commmanded, sweeping his arm over the cliff. The next instant he was struggling with Buck on the extreme edge, while Hans and Pete were dragging them back to safety.

"It's unbelievable," Pete said, after it was over and they had caught their speech.

Thornton shook his head. "No, it is splendid, and it is terrible, too. Do you know, it sometimes makes me afraid."

"I don't want to be the man that lays hands on you while he's around," Pete announced, nodding his head toward Buck.

It was at Circle City, before the year was out, that Pete's fears were realized. Bad Burton, an evil-tempered man, had been picking a quarrel with a man at a table, when Thornton stepped good-naturedly between. Buck, as was his custom, was lying in the corner, head on paws, watching his master's every action. Burton struck out, without warning, straight from the shoulder. Thornton was sent spinning, and saved himself from falling only by clutching the edge of a table.

Those who were looking on heard what was neither bark nor yelp, but a something which is best described as a roar, and they saw Buck's body rise up in the air as he left the floor for Burton's throat. The man saved his life by throwing out his arm, but was hurled backward to the floor with Buck on top of him. Buck loosed his teeth from the flesh of 131 the arm and drove in again for the throat. This time the man succeeded only in partly blocking, and his throat was torn open. Then the crowd was upon Buck, and he was driven off; but while a surgeon checked the bleeding, he prowled up and down, growling furiously, attempting to rush in, and being forced back by clubs. A "miners' meeting," called on the spot, decided that the dog had just cause, and Buck was discharged. But his reputation was made, and from that day his name spread through every camp in Alaska.

Later on, in the fall of the year, he saved John Thornton's life in quite another fashion. The three partners were taking a long and narrow poling-boat down a bad stretch of rapids on the Forty-Mile Creek. Hans and Pete moved along the bank, snubbing with a thin Manila rope from tree to tree, while Thornton remained in the boat, moving it downstream with a pole, and shouting directions to the shore. Buck, on the bank, worried and nervous, kept his eyes on his master.

At a particularly bad spot, where a ledge of barely submerged rocks stuck out into the river, Hans cast off the rope. While Thornton poled the boat out into the stream, Hans ran down the bank with the end in his hand to snub the boat when it had cleared the ledge. This it did, and was flying downstream in a swift current when Hans checked it with the rope and checked too suddenly. The boat flirted over and snubbed into the bank bottom up. Thornton, flung clear out of it, was carried downstream toward the worst part of the rapids, a stretch of wild water in which no swimmer could live.

Buck had sprung in on the instant. At the end of three hundred yards, in a mad swirl of water, he reached Thornton. When he felt him grasp his tail, Buck headed for the bank, swimming with all his splendid strength. But the progress shoreward was slow; the progress downstream amazingly rapid. From below came the fatal roaring where the wild current went wilder and was torn in shreds and spray by the rocks which broke through like the teeth of an enormous comb. The suck of the water as it took the beginning of the last drop was frightful, and

Thornton knew that the shore was impossible. He scraped furiously over a rock, bruised across a second, and struck a third with crushing force. He clutched its slippery top with both hands, releasing Buck, and above the roar of the churning water shouted, "Go, Buck! Go!"

Buck could not hold his own, and swept on downstream, struggling desperately, but unable to win back. When he heard Thornton's command, he reared out of the water, throwing his head high for a last look, then turned obediently toward the bank. He swam powerfully and was dragged ashore by Pete and Hans at the point where swimming ceased to be possible and destruction began.

They knew that the time a man could cling to a slippery rock in the face of that driving current was a matter of minutes. They ran as fast as they could up the bank to a point far above where Thornton was hanging on. They attached the line with which they had been snubbing the boat to Buck's neck and shoulders, being careful that it should neither strangle him nor interfere with his swimming, and launched him into the stream. He struck out boldly, but not straight enough into the stream. He discovered the mistake too late, when Thornton was abreast of him and a bare half-dozen strokes away while he was being carried helplessly past.

Hans promptly snubbed with the rope, as though Buck were a boat. The rope thus tightening on him in the sweep of the current, he was jerked under the surface, and under the surface he remained till his body struck against the bank and he was hauled out. He was half drowned, and Hans and Pete threw themselves upon him, pounding breath into him and water out of him. He staggered to his feet and fell down. The faint sound of Thornton's voice came to them. Though they could not make out the words of it, they knew that he was near death. His master's voice acted on Buck like an electric shock. He sprang to his feet and ran up the bank ahead of the men to the point of his previous departure.

Again the rope was attached and he was launched, and again he struck out, but this time straight into the stream. He had misjudged once, but he would not be guilty of it a second time. Hans paid out the 133

rope, permitting no slack, while Pete kept it clear of coils. Buck held on till he was on a line straight above Thornton; then he turned and with the speed of an express train headed down upon him. Thornton saw him coming, and, as Buck struck him like a battering ram, with the whole force of the current behind him he reached up and closed with both arms around the shaggy neck. Hans snubbed the rope around the tree, and Buck and Thornton were jerked under the water. Strangling, suffocating, sometimes one uppermost and sometimes the other, dragging over the jagged bottom, smashing against rocks and snags, they headed in to the bank.

Thornton came to, belly downward and being violently pushed back and forth across a drift log by Hans and Pete. His first glance was for Buck whose limp body lay nearby. Thornton was himself bruised and battered, and he went carefully over Buck's body, when he had been brought around, finding three broken ribs.

"That settles it," he announced. "We camp right here." And camp they did. Not until Buck's ribs healed did they continue their travels.

JACK LONDON

The Fastest Sledder in Alaska

Nome, Alaska

Rick Swenson kneeled on Front Street yesterday and hugged his dogs just before leading them across the finish line to victory after more than 16 days in the 1049-mile Iditarod sled dog race.

"It sure is good to be here," the trapper from Manley Hot Springs called out to the hundreds of spectators who cheered him on. "It was a long way."

The town's fire siren roused residents at 1:27 A.M. and sounded for two minutes each time a musher approached. Spectators wore furs, parkas and mukluks in the 21-below-zero morning temperature.

"I feel pretty good, but I'm tired. And I want to get these icicles off my face," Swenson said.

Swenson finished tenth last year during his first effort at the Iditarod, which follows an old gold rush trail from Anchorage to Nome.

His face was red and was wreathed with icicles after a final drive to the finish that began at Unalakleet 250 miles away 48 hours earlier.

Swenson said he owed his victory to Jerry Riley of Nenana, who was close behind for the last 50 miles. Riley won the race last year and finished second this year, four minutes behind Swenson.

Top prize was $10,000, and second place brought $6,000.

During the race the mushers had to make at least one 24-hour stop for rest and had to report to checkpoints along the route. Whenever a dog tired it would be left at a checkpoint, but to qualify at the finish the teams had to have a minimum of seven dogs.

Dog food, usually frozen in ice, was cached along the trail and the mushers had to chop it out with axes.

The only non-North American in the race, Stein Havardfiestad, 22, from Stang, Norway, lost his ax.

Swenson said he knew he had Riley beaten "when I passed Jerry and he couldn't keep up." Swenson's official time for the race was 16 days, 16 hours, 27 minutes and

13 seconds. The record for the run is 14 days and 14 hours.

Right behind Swenson and Riley was Warner Vent of Musha, who pulled in ten minutes later.

"That's the first time this has ever happened. For a race this long, that was a photo finish for all intents and purposes," said Albro Gregory, publisher of the Nome Nugget.

Swenson arrived with 11 of the 12 dogs that began the race March 5th.

Swenson, Vent and Riley traded the lead during the last 77 miles of the race. "It was tough," Swenson said. "Riley never quits."

Swenson was led to the finish line by a police car from a roadhouse three miles outside this Bering Sea community of 2700. The last 100 yards of the race is through a chute surrounded by snow fences. It keeps the dogs from getting near the crowds.

And despite the hour and the temperature, close to 1000 persons, including children, were there for the finish. Forty-seven members started the race and 33 were on the trail early yesterday morning.   ASSOCIATED PRESS

What's It All About?

1. How does Buck prove his devotion to Thornton? Name three incidents.
2. Some people seem to get along unusually well with animals. What do you think it takes to gain the trust of an animal?

1. How do you know that Buck is a somewhat "wild" dog?
2. Why does Thornton command Buck to jump over a cliff? Do you think Thornton should have done this? Why?
3. Why is Buck not blamed for his attack on "Bad" Burton?
4. How does Buck's rescue of Thornton at Forty-Mile Creek show that the dog's devotion is unusually strong?

PUTTING IDEAS TO WORK

Write a "telegram" message that tells about Buck's rescue of Thornton in ten words or less.

Would it be possible for a young woman to travel around the world in less than eighty days? In 1889 it would be incredible!

NELLIE BLY sets a record

Nellie Bly was at sea when the story broke into headlines in the *World*:

A CONTINUOUS TRIP WHICH WILL GIRDLE THE SPINNING GLOBE

NELLIE BLY TO MAKE AN UNEQUALED RAPID-TRANSIT RECORD

NOW 30,000 MILES IN A RUSH

CAN JULES VERNE'S GREAT DREAM BE REDUCED TO ACTUAL FACT?

The World *today undertakes the task of turning a dream into reality. . . . Nellie Bly, so well known to millions who have read of her doings, as told by her captivating pen, will set out as a female Phileas Fogg and if nothing prevents . . . will report back . . . in just 75 days.*

The crossing of the Atlantic was a ghastly one, storm tossed and terrifying. Passengers were too ill to get out of their staterooms, except for the hardy few. Nellie wasn't ill but the effort of trying to keep her

138

feet on a deck that slid and pitched and tossed her around like a tennis ball was too much. She was glad when the ship docked at Southampton.

It was two-thirty in the morning and a carriage was waiting. Her train ticket for London was held for her at the station. The connections planned in New York were clicking along smoothly. At her London hotel were further instructions brought along by the London correspondent for the *World*.

"You are to sail tomorrow for Italy," he told her.

But she wasn't listening. Among the shower of letters and telegrams of encouragement and praise and commendation was one from Jules Verne, inviting her to visit him in France.

"I can't miss that opportunity!" she explained to her London co-worker. "It would make too good a story. We'll just have to arrange the trip a little differently."

He was shocked. "It can't be done! One side trip like that and you'll lose the race—you'll never make it in seventy-five days."

Her mind was made up, however. Hunting frantically, the two of them found a packet boat leaving England immediately; they read train schedules and found one that would leave Calais, France, in time for her to meet the boat at Brindisi. It would mean split-second timing, otherwise all the tour arrangements for transportation would be cancelled and the trip itself a failure. It would mean sitting up in boats and trains without sleep for two nights. To Nellie it was well worth it. Jules Verne had written the book, famous throughout the world, which had given her the whole idea; his hero Phileas Fogg was her opponent in this race.

Though it was early when she left London, she had her first taste of the excitement which her trip was spreading throughout the world. People lined up in front of her hotel to cheer her, and dockworkers crowded around to see her off.

The trip to Amiens, France, where Verne lived was something Nellie never liked to recall afterward. She spent sleepless nights, one of 139 them aboard a rickety old boat crossing the channel, the other on a jolting ride by train to Amiens. She was exhausted when she arrived.

The sight of Jules Verne and Mrs. Verne at the railroad station to meet her pleased her. She had not expected such kindness. It was a proud and happy moment and her tiredness left her magically. They went on treating her with the same tender thoughtfulness—this "child" who was so brave, so courageous, so little. They drove her to their beautiful, luxurious home where a fire was burning in the velvet-hung sitting room, and a tea tray sat on the low table in front of the fire.

When Nellie explained that she must leave immediately to catch

her train to Calais, they were horrified. She had had no sleep, no rest!—at least, she must sit awhile and talk to them. This is what she wanted. She was a reporter; she wanted to squeeze every possible moment out of this visit—to talk and to listen.

They talked of America, of France, of Jules Verne's books and, of course, of her trip. Kindly Jules Verne warned her: "I do not think you can make it, but you must not be downhearted by that. You will have made the try. And some day it will be done." Mrs. Verne teased her a little about perhaps catching a husband on the trip. After all, she was a romantic figure, this little Nellie Bly—was there no romance in her life?

"None," she answered firmly. "I'm just too busy to think about romance, not with trains to catch and boats to think of."

This reminded them that time was running out.

She raced for the station, barely making her train. That night she found she must sleep in the same compartment with twenty-two other passengers. In other circumstances she might have been too modest; but utter exhaustion made her indifferent. All she cared about were a pillow and a mattress and sleep.

At Brindisi the train was two hours late.

This was disaster. Connections between it and the steamer had had to be figured in minutes. Now she was two hours late. And it had been her own headstrong, reckless decision to see Verne that had brought her to this failure. How could she go back and face Pulitzer? Remembering that little crowd of cheering workers at the dock in England, she felt physically sick with frustration and disappointment.

Her hired carriage finally came in sight of the Brindisi docks. She stared for a moment with unbelieving eyes, then, to the amazement and the scandal of the carriage driver and the porters, the American girl gave a wild whoop of joy, threw a handful of coins into the box of the driver, lifted up her skirts with one hand, her satchels with the other and ran, pell-mell, down to the docks. The *Augusta Victoria* was still in port! It had purposely waited to make connections with the mail train. 141

Now at last on board, she felt that she was finally off on her journey into the unknown.

All over America, people were following her journey with a tremendous interest that grew and grew. The *World* was not exaggerating when it said "The whole civilized world is watching Nellie Bly." Even though other New York newspapers laughed at the idea that she could actually make it in less than eighty days, nevertheless they could not ignore her. Their readers, too, demanded to know every day just where Nellie was—how far along she had traveled—what was happening to her.

Her cables arrived regularly. The people she met, the places she visited, the sights she saw were all subjects for the stories she cabled to the *World*. In between times the newspaper ran stories on the countries her boat was passing, of storms that other ships had encountered in that area, of customs aboard ship—nothing seemed too trivial or too small to be hungrily read by Nellie's fans.

The voyage through the Mediterranean, through the Suez Canal, through the Red Sea—was delayed by weather conditions. December 14th found her in Colombo, Ceylon, a little behind schedule. She worried, but since there was nothing to be done about it, she scampered over the island enjoying herself, filling her cables with the odd, the picturesque, the grand and the trivial. Her stories made the reader feel all the breathless astonishment and delight she herself found in each new discovery—whether it was the magnificence of the harbor and the mountains behind it or the habits of the English there who lived lives of lazy luxury, the women in smart frocks reading novels, the men in their white tropicals smoking cigars and lounging on hotel verandas. What a contrast they made to the Ceylonese people who wore so little and worked so hard!

She rode a bicycle on the island. She had one unusual experience: a midnight drive during which she was pulled by bullocks, those great oxen of the East. She also had her first jinrikisha trip. She talked to

142 merchants, to priests—and the only time she regretted her lack of a

wardrobe was when she had to refuse an invitation to a dinner because her own muslin dress was unsuitable. On the whole, the two dresses were holding up well, though it meant constant cleaning and pressing and watchfulness if they were to clothe her decently for the whole trip.

America marveled. Such words as these—temple priests and jinrikishas—had come out of the pages of dusty encyclopedias and were now part of their own experience—through her eyes.

From Colombo she went to Canton, China, and on to Singapore.

Singapore had plenty of material for her stories. Just as at home, Nellie went everywhere—into slums, into office buildings, into spacious residential areas, into hospitals and churches and dock wharves and factories. She even bought a monkey. Then, en route to Canton, China, the ship ran into a terrific storm. Badly shaken as she was, when they landed she went off sight-seeing immediately.

At Yokohama, she was exactly fifty days from her starting time. There were only twenty-seven days left—to catch a ship, to cross an ocean and then a continent. In those days, when ocean travel was figured in weeks, not days, this was not very much time. In spite of that, her spirits were raised by the reception she received in Japan. It was her second hint of the international interest in her. The Jules Verne interview had been translated into Japanese and printed in their papers; the correspondent there for the *World*, a Japanese, had fed the national press story after story on Nellie Bly. She was met by Japanese officials,

escorted proudly around the city by important men, and her arrival was heralded by the blowing of steamship whistles in the harbor. As she was driven through the streets, the train of carriages and carts following her became an impromptu parade; when she stopped, people came pressing forward to touch her strange American dress, to stare at the spectacle of this amazing girl traveler, and to wish her well in the strange foreign tongue, the words of which she couldn't understand but the meaning of which was clear.

On January 7th, the steamship *Oceanic* sailed out of the harbor for home. As Nellie arrived at the dock, the band struck up "Hail, Columbia," and she wanted to cry out loud with the surging pride in that dear, familiar song and with the homesickness it brought her. Then the band switched to "The Girl I Left Behind Me." She noticed a huge sign printed on the side of the ship—"For Nellie Bly—We'll win or die!" She wasn't alone! It wasn't only she who was running this race; this whole ship and its officers and passengers were pulling for her, hoping and praying for her.

It was a moment of high emotion as the ship sailed slowly out, to the haunting music of "Home, Sweet Home."

From the first day out the ship was in trouble. And on the third day the storms hit. The small ocean liner was tossed about by the high, heavy waves, the pouring rain, the winds that screamed along the decks and tore the ship from its course, sending it plunging and rolling through day after day of dark horror.

The passengers were terrified. Even the crew was frightened. The voyage went on. The storms lightened a little, but just the same it was two weeks before the *Oceanic* saw land—the harbor of San Francisco.

But even as she could feel the land almost underneath her foot, a new hazard arose. A rumor of smallpox on board threatened to quarantine all passengers and prevent them from landing. This was one delay she would not tolerate. Sweeping all objections away, overriding all arguments, she demanded to be put ashore. And she was—in a small tug that landed her, her monkey and her baggage onto the San Francisco dock, alone of all the *Oceanic* passengers.

Quickly a doctor examined her. She was passed. Gathering up her luggage she looked around his small office for the door. But the doctor stopped her.

"Just one moment." He took off his gown. "Now! Miss Bly, will you permit me . . . ?" He gave her his arm and motioned to an attendant to pick up her luggage. "This way, please."

They walked out to the waiting room.

And then came the uproar, confusion, shouts, crowds. Nellie stood, unbelieving. The wharf was thronged, jammed with so many people that nothing could be seen but the masses of thousands of human bodies, nothing could be heard above the roar of thousands of voices screaming, "Nellie! Nellie Bly! Hurrah for Nellie!"

If the whole of America had been waiting for her, San Francisco was not to be outdone. As the carriage drove her to the railroad station, it seemed to her that everyone in the city was in the streets filling every curb to see her go by. The shouts were a roar that swelled with each moment.

They cried for a speech and she tried to speak:

"There's no place like home," she told them through happy tears. "For sixty-eight days I've been dashing around the world and am once again back in America. The saddest sounds were the farewells from the Hoboken pier—the sweetest sounds the words of welcome and applause in San Francisco."

It is doubtful if many heard. But they were satisfied to see her and to claim her as their own, their Nellie Bly. Ahead of her carriage marched a strong band of women suffragists with their banners flying. Behind her were carriages and bands and marchers that made a parade blocks long.

As Nellie rode the train east, ranchers, farmers, sheepherders and cowboys rode hundreds of miles just to stand at a way station and see her train go by. City railroad depots were mobbed. The train itself 145

carried great pennants with her name on them. She was impatient for that train to go on, make good time, but there were many unscheduled stops along the tracks, where they found seas of people drawn from every village, every town, every farm within a hundred-mile radius. Nellie spoke, shook hands and was cheered and loved and applauded.

In Kansas suffragists pleaded with her to come back and run for governor of the state.

In Chicago she was carried off the train on the shoulders of members of the Press Club.

But when her train steamed into Jersey City, where she was to debark for the final estimate of the days and minutes of her journey, then the celebration really began to let off steam. She touched the soil of New Jersey exactly seventy-two days, six hours and ten minutes from the time she had left that soil at Hoboken.

And at that moment, at 3:15 P.M. on January 26th, the race was won. Not only had she equaled the record of Jules Verne's hero; she had bettered it. She had gone around the world in less time than anyone else ever had; she had proved that the world was no longer a place divided—in travel at least. Three stop watches, her own included, registered the fact.

146   IRIS NOBLE

What's It All About?

1. Why was it so difficult to go around the world in less than eighty days in 1889?
2. The New York *World* newspaper wanted Nellie Bly to go around the world as a publicity stunt. Her articles would attract readers. Why do you think Nellie Bly herself wanted to go?

---

1. Where did Nellie Bly get the idea for her trip?
2. How did the readers of the *World* feel about the trip?
3. What do you think was the best part of Nellie Bly's trip? Why?
4. How did Nellie Bly feel when she first caught sight of San Francisco? How did the city greet her?
5. What kind of person was Nellie Bly?

PUTTING IDEAS TO WORK

Choose any of the fascinating places Nellie visited—the home of Jules Verne, Ceylon, Canton, Singapore, Yokohama, San Francisco. Write one of the news stories that she might have sent to the *World* from this place.

THE HUNGRY WINTER

Father Robillard, a storyteller in the old tradition, passes the evening with a tale.

When the launch which was to take him out to the hinterland of northern Canada failed to show up, Spencer Scott felt stumped. There was apparently nothing for him to do but wait. Father Robillard, a priest living in the small village, offered him hospitality which he gladly accepted, for there were, of course, no regular accommodations for visitors in so small a place.

Time passed quickly. The priest was an entertaining old man, always ready with a story.

One evening the two men were sitting in front of the fire when the Indian who looked after the priest brought in an armful of wood.

"Thank you, Uncle."

"Why do you call him that?" Spencer asked as soon as the man had left the room. It seemed an odd way for the priest to address a man so much younger than himself.

"Oh, everyone does. He's a great favorite around here."

Spencer looked thoughtful. "Well, what's the yarn tonight?"

The priest smiled. "What would you like? The North has something to fit every mood. A humorous story, perhaps?"

Spencer shook his head. He did not want to be amused. Already the regret he felt at leaving this country was deepening into nostalgia. No, definitely he did not want a funny story.

Uncle reappeared, this time bearing a pot of tea which Spencer knew from experience would be blacker than tar and strong enough to float metal. He set it down on a table, together with two glasses, then silently disappeared.

The priest hitched about in his chair, making himself comfortable. "Have I told you about Jules Frenelle? I first knew him when, as a young man, I was sent to the Chipewyan country, a good deal north of here around Great Slave Lake. He was fourteen at the time, a bright boy, obedient and mannerly. He learned his catechism so well he could have recited it backward, and he was a great help to his family. He not only cut their entire winter supply of wood, but furnished a large portion of their food as well; he was an excellent hunter.

149

"I tried to persuade him to go south to school—there are good ones in Edmonton—but he always refused to do so. Not only did his people depend on him, but he himself could not bear to leave the North. This country, you know, is like that; once you've become accustomed to it, you can't do without it; you can't bear to live anywhere else."

Spencer understood perfectly. A single summer had been sufficient to convince him of the truth of this statement.

"You have never been here in the winter," Father Robillard went on. "Ah! Then the North is truly magnificent. Then is when she really lays her hold on you.

"But not all winters are good ones. There are the lean years. I can recall winters when it seemed there were no animals alive in the entire North. Even rabbits, which are taken for granted, sometimes die of some obscure disease by the thousands. But the worst of all are the winters without caribou. It is about one of these that I am going to tell you.

"The men of our village, about twenty of them, went out as usual in the fall to hunt the caribou which migrate each year from the Barren Lands. But this particular year the hunters could not find them. The caribou, you know, travel in a large herd, an immense solid mass of creatures which has been estimated at over a million. If the hunters miss this herd they can seldom kill enough meat to last out the winter.

"How well I remember the day the men returned! They were gaunt, exhausted, their eye sockets red from loss of sleep. But worse than all was the resignation expressed in their drooping bodies; they were men without hope; they knew death was not far from them and their families.

"Jules detached himself from the group and came to me.

" 'Father, I know where there is a cache.'

"At once I knew he had made it. On one of his hunting trips he must have laid by food, drying it and caching it so it would be safe.

" 'Is it a big one?' I asked him.

150   " 'Pretty big,' he said.

" 'I think we should wait awhile yet,' I told him. 'We still have some food. We will make it last as long as possible, and in the meantime something may turn up.'

"But nothing did. By mid-January everything edible was gone, even the dogs to pull the sledges. I imagine it is difficult for you to realize our predicament. You are probably thinking, why didn't they go to some other village? Why didn't they send out for help before it was too late? But we were extremely isolated. Besides, it was almost certain that the famine was general. If the migration of caribou was so erratic our hunters could not find it, it was improbable others had succeeded where we had failed. Thus no one would have more food than we, nor, if they had, could they spare it. Even if we had saved the dogs, by the time a trip could have been made to the outside the few provisions the teams could haul had been brought back, all our people would be dead.''

"When all the food was gone, I went to Jules.

" 'Now we will go to your cache.'

"I shall never forget that trip. The entire village set out on snowshoes. The distance was not great, but when your stomach is drawn together like a pouch with a drawstring pulled, and your legs are like boiled macaroni, when your eyes are blurred and watery, even a mile seems interminable. To make matters worse, the weather turned very cold. We were, you must remember, close to the Barrens where temperatures of seventy below are not at all uncommon. And in addition a blizzard overtook us, lashing our faces with icy particles until they were raw. It is impossible to describe our sufferings.

"I am not sure how long we traveled, but at last we came to the shore of a small lake and there, exactly as Jules had promised, was the cache. It was made of rawhide bundles lashed to a platform, raised on poles off the ground so marauding animals could not reach it. A shout of joy went up from all of us.

"Eagerly the men brought down the bundles and tore them open. Alas! they had already been opened; they were empty. Someone else 151 had visited the cache. A different cry arose, one of rage and anguish. Even the children, infected with their elders' grief and despair, sobbed unrestrainedly.

"We sat down in the snow, and even I, who should have known better, wept as bitterly as the rest. But Jules did not weep. When I became calmer, I noticed that he stared fixedly at the frozen lake, and instantly I divined his thought: under the ice there must be fish.

"Now the cache, for all it was devoid of food, did contain some fishhooks. We baited some of these with pieces of rawhide, having nothing else for bait, and dropped them into the water through holes chopped in the ice. We waited and waited, but nothing happened. The fish refused to bite. That night, at my suggestion, the men lighted torches of spruce knots to attract the fish to the holes, lying in wait with knives fastened to poles. Still no fish appeared. Our efforts came to nothing.

"Morning dawned at last. All around us as we sat on that desolate shore were the dark, enclosing trees laden with snow. The wind, rising slowly, moaned across the ice, and the spruces took up its mournful voice. Above us the sky was ominous and heavy; a new storm was brewing. Soon we must inevitably die, every one of us. Now, I had often watched individuals await death, but never an entire community. It defies description. These people ceased to be separate persons; they became a group, a single fused body of humanity. Even their silence was a unit, expressed by the many into a single whole. It was as if they planned to die in a group rather than singly, exactly the opposite of those who go off alone to die. It was frightening. I fell on my knees and commenced to pray. The people joined me; I could hear the low murmur of their voices, slowly strengthening, swelling, till it drowned out the voice of the wind.

"Suddenly Jules rose and ran to one of the open holes. In a way, I think we resented his action; his abrupt movement destroyed the unity we shared. And yet we watched him.

"He sat down on the ice and removed a moccasin and legging. Then, before we guessed what he was about, he had pulled out his knife

153

and had cut a strip of flesh from his own leg. Aghast, we saw him bait a hook with this still living tissue, and fling it into the open hole."

Father Robillard ceased speaking. In spite of the crackling flames in the fireplace, Spencer knew he dwelt on that frozen shore. He himself shivered sympathetically. To break the spell he asked a question.

"Obviously you survived the winter. Was it because Jules caught a fish?"

With obvious effort, the priest returned to the fireside. "Yes, the lake was full of them. After the first, we always had bait. There was never any more trouble. We spent the rest of the winter there, and fortunately spring came early that year. Nature showered us with food. There were quantities of small game and swarms of ptarmigan. It was like a miracle. Naturally, I have my own explanation of it."

Spencer knew he referred to his religion.

"Well!" Suddenly the priest reverted to his usual jovial self. "It's quite a good story, don't you think?"

"A very good story." But in Spencer's mind, a doubt lurked. In a way he believed the yarn; in a way he did not. He suspected that the events just related might have happened to someone else, and the priest, with the license of old age, had merely appropriated them to his own use. Or the story might have no factual basis, but have arisen from a legend or myth. His face must have betrayed his skepticism.

"I don't think you believe my little tale," Father Robillard smiled. "No matter. It is not important. But come, we haven't touched our tea. It must be stone cold. I'll have Uncle bring in some fresh."

When the Indian entered the room, the priest called to him.

"By the way, how is that bad ankle of yours? May I take a look at it?"

He leaned over, lifting the bottom of the Indian's trouser. Spencer saw, as he was sure he was meant to, a long depressed area, a puckered whitish scar, extending up the man's leg for more than four inches.

154   ELIZABETH H. MIDDLETON

What's It All About?

1. What was the main hardship that faced the villagers in Father Robillard's story? How did Jules Frenelle solve the problem?
2. Who is Uncle? Why do you think he is called ''Uncle''?

1. What made the winter that Father Robillard tells about particularly difficult?
2. Why couldn't the villagers purchase food from traders or other villages?
3. What did the villagers do to try and stay alive?
4. How does Father Robillard convince his visitor that his tale is true?

PUTTING IDEAS TO WORK

Imagine you are a villager in ''The Hungry Winter'' and are making the trip to Jules Frenelle's cache. Write about your experience.

155

Does buying the larger size of a product mean that you are getting more for your money?

The Large Economy Size

Look at the items, prices, and sizes below. Decide which size of each product is the best buy. Is it always better to buy the large ''economy'' size?

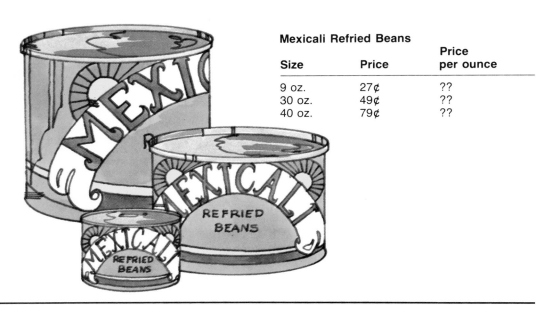

Mexicali Refried Beans

Size	Price	Price per ounce
9 oz.	27¢	??
30 oz.	49¢	??
40 oz.	79¢	??

Stay-Brite Tooth Paste

Size	Price	Price per ounce
1.5 oz.	40¢	??
3.0 oz.	67¢	??
9.0 oz.	$1.17	??

Quick Laundry Detergent

Size	Price	Price per ounce
3 lbs. 3 oz.	$1.31	??
6 lbs. 4 oz.	$2.44	??
13 lbs. 3 oz.	$5.33	??

1 lb. = 16 oz.

Frosty Cool Soda

Size	Price	Price per ounce
32 oz.	32¢	??
6 pk of 32 oz. bottles	$2.10	??
6 pk of 12 oz. cans	$1.53	??

1. For which one of these products is buying bigger, buying better?
2. Check sizes and prices of your favorite products. What do you learn about the large economy size?

Doing several errands at once can save time and energy. Many towns have neighborhood areas with shops and stores where people can do their errands in one place.

One-Stop Shopping

One job everyone riding in the car can share is reading maps and signs accurately to cut down on wasted time and gas. Study the map and the list of stores listed for Village Plaza. Then answer the questions that follow.

1. If you were on U.S. 151 heading south, what direction would you turn to get to the corner of Winford Ave. and Oaks Rd?
2. How would you get to the same place if you were on Highgate headed east? if you were on U.S. 151 headed north?
3. If you were shopping at Village Plaza, where would you find these things?
   a. groceries
   b. latest record albums
   c. fresh fish for dinner at home
   d. Japanese dinner
   e. patterns and fabric
   f. an airline ticket
   g. CB radio
4. Where could you get help with the following?
   a. opening a savings account
   b. finding an apartment
   c. getting your clothes washed
   d. sending a package
   e. getting a hair cut
   f. getting a prescription filled
5. Which store is about to have a competitor? What effect on prices might this have?

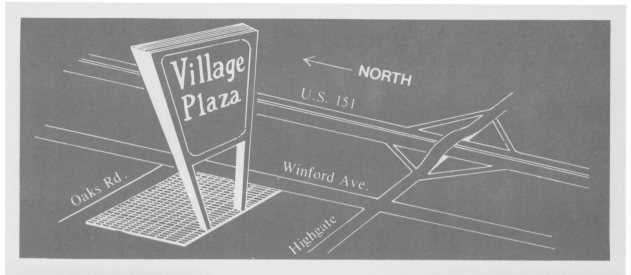

BUENA VISTA SAVINGS BANK

FIESTA REALTY

PEARSON'S Travel Agency

The **TAPE MEASURE**
Fabric Center

OSAKA'S HIBACHI
Japanese-American Food

Top o' the Charts
Record
Tapes
Sheet Music

Free Dry **Launderland**
50¢ Wash **Coin-Op**
Laundry

TWEETERS, OHMS & AMPS
Records
Tapes
Sheet Music

TEDD'S SEAFOOD
Market & Restaurant

HAIR DESIGN, INC.
Hair Design
for
Men & Women

KING'S FOODLAND

U.S. Post Office

WHITEHALL PHARMACY

Orders to Go
Pasquale's Pizzeria

WELLER'S Donut House

Coming Soon:
The Sew and Sew
FABRIC SHOP

When you go shopping, do you wander from one end of the plaza to the other and back again? Or do you plan your shopping needs and save steps and time? Study the Village Plaza directory on the next page and answer these questions.

1. If you are at Whitehall Drug, what is the closest place to get something to eat?
2. You have just started your wash, and now you want to check on the new records. What direction do you go? What stores would you pass?
3. What stores might have paperback books and magazines? Are they close together?
4. Which two stores are the greatest distance apart?
5. If you were going to have your hair cut, would it be handy to pick up a dress pattern on the way? Why or why not?
6. If you found the Pizzeria closed, where is the nearest place to get lunch?
7. Make up some additional questions which will test your classmates' ability to use a directory.

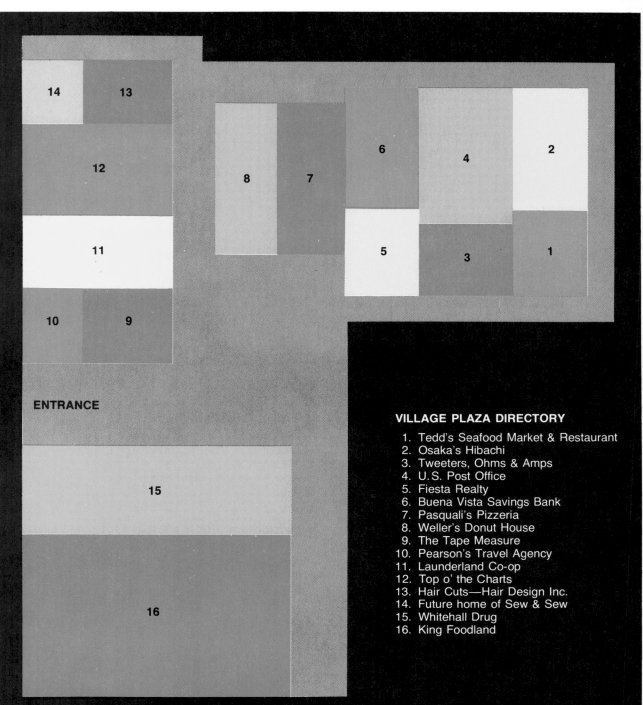

ENTRANCE

VILLAGE PLAZA DIRECTORY

1. Tedd's Seafood Market & Restaurant
2. Osaka's Hibachi
3. Tweeters, Ohms & Amps
4. U.S. Post Office
5. Fiesta Realty
6. Buena Vista Savings Bank
7. Pasquali's Pizzeria
8. Weller's Donut House
9. The Tape Measure
10. Pearson's Travel Agency
11. Launderland Co-op
12. Top o' the Charts
13. Hair Cuts—Hair Design Inc.
14. Future home of Sew & Sew
15. Whitehall Drug
16. King Foodland

As the plane lands, your pilot says "It is sprinkling and the temperature is 35° Celsius." What kind of weather do you expect?

Going Metric: Hot or Cold?

If you are just getting used to the metric system of temperatures, you may wish to use one of these conversion methods.

Conversion Line

To convert Fahrenheit to Celsius or Celsius to Fahrenheit, find your reading and move from one side of the scale to the other.

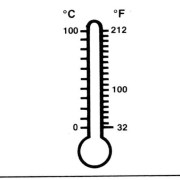

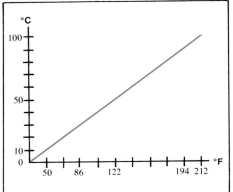

Conversion Graph

To convert Fahrenheit to Celsius:
1. Find Fahrenheit reading on bottom scale.
2. Move straight up to the red line.
3. Move straight across to Celsius scale.

To convert Celsius to Fahrenheit:
1. Find Celsius reading on side scale.
2. Move across to the red line.
3. Move straight down to the Fahrenheit scale.

Conversion Formula

To convert Fahrenheit to Celsius, subtract 32° from Fahrenheit reading and multiply by .556.
To convert Celsius to Fahrenheit, multiply Celsius reading by 1.8 and add 32°.

1. Of the three conversion methods, which do you find easiest?
2. Which conversion method can be used in any situation?
3. If the pilot says the temperature is 35° Celsius, what temperature is that on the Fahrenheit scale?
4. When using the formula, which conversion is easier, Celsius to Fahrenheit or Fahrenheit to Celsius?
5. Which scale has fewer degree marks?

from Ode on a Grecian Urn

. . . When old age shall this generation waste,
Thou shalt remain, in midst of other woe
Than ours, a friend to man, to whom thou say,
"Beauty is truth, truth beauty,"—that is all
Ye know on earth, and all ye need to know.

JOHN KEATS

Defiantly disregarding margins and doubtful spellings, Jeanie let her pen dig into the paper as she began to write.

BEAUTY IS TRUTH

At 125th Street, they all got off, Jeanie and her friend, Barbara, and a crowd of other boys and girls who went to the same downtown high school. Through the train window, Jeanie thought she saw the remaining passengers look at them with relief and disdain. Around her, the boys and girls pressed forward with noisy gaiety. They were all friends now. They were home again in Harlem.

A tall boy detached himself from a group, bowed low and swept his cap before him in a courtly salute.

"Greetings, Lady Jeanie. Greetings, Barbara."

Jeanie bit her lip. Frowning, she pulled her coat closer and shrugged. Barbara smiled and

dimpled, pleased for her friend.

"I told you he likes you," she whispered. "Look, he's waiting. Want me to go on ahead?"

Jeanie really was wasting an opportunity. Norman was keen. Barbara saw Jeanie's head, slightly bowed and thrust forward. It was no use. She was an odd girl, but Barbara liked her anyway. The boy swung gracefully back to his group.

"Coming to the show tonight?" Barbara asked.

"No. I can't. I'm so far behind in my homework. I'd better try to do some before they decide to throw me out." Jeanie still frowned.

"Want a Coke or something?" asked Barbara as they passed the big ice-cream parlor window, cluttered with candy boxes and ornate with curly lettering. They could see the juke box near the door and some boys and girls sitting down at a table. It looked warm and friendly.

Jeanie shook her head, one brief shake.

"I think I'll stop in. I'm awful thirsty," said Barbara.

Jeanie shrugged.

"So long then."

"So long."

She walked along the busy street, aimlessly looking in the store windows, turned the

corner, and walked the few blocks to her house. Though it was chilly, each brownstone or gray stoop had its cluster of people clinging to the iron railings. Some children on skates played a desperate game of hockey with sticks that were not hockey sticks. When a car approached, they did not interrupt their game until it was almost too late. Amid shouts from the driver and wild jeers from the children, the car passed, and the game was resumed in all its concentrated intensity.

Her little brother Billy was playing in front of the stoop with three or four other kids. They were bending over something on the sidewalk, in a closed circle. Pitching pennies again, she thought with repugnance. She was going to pass them, and started up the three stone steps to the doorway. A window on the ground floor opened, and Fat Mary leaned out.

"Now you're going to catch it, Billy Boy. Your sister's going to tell your mamma you been pitching pennies again."

Jeanie did not pause.

Billy sprang up. "Hi, Jeanie. Jeanie, gimme a nickel. I need a nickel. A nickel, a nickel. I gotta have a nickel."

The other little boys took up the chant. "A nickel, a nickel. Billy needs a nickel."

She threw them a furious glance and went in. Two little girls sat on the second landing, playing house. They had a set of toy dishes spread out on the top stair, and held dolls in their laps. She stepped over them, careful not to disturb their arrangements.

The kitchen smelled dank and unused, and the opening of the door dislodged a flake of

green-painted plaster. It fell into the sink, with a dry powdering. A black dress someone had given her mother lay over the chair before the sewing machine. It reminded her that her sleeve had torn half out, dressing after gym. She really should sew it, but the sight of the black dress waiting to be made over made her dislike the thought of sewing. She would just have to wear her coat in school tomorrow. Lots of kids did. She did not like her shape anyway, so big and hefty.

She hung her coat on a hook in the room she shared with her mother, and stood irresolute. Her mother would be coming in soon and would expect to find the potatoes peeled and the table laid. She caught sight of a comic book and, unwillingly attracted by the garish colors, read one side. "Ah!" she thought in disgust, "Billy!" She thought of her homework. She was so far behind in Social Studies that she could probably never make it up. It was hardly worth trying.

167

Mercantilism. The rise of the merchant class. She would probably fail. And gym, all those cuts in gym. Miss Fisher, her grade adviser, had called her down yesterday and warned her. "Ah!" she said again. Miss Fisher was all right. She had even been encouraging. "I know you can do it," she had said.

She sat down on the bed and opened her loose-leaf notebook at random. A page fell out. She was about to jam it back in, when the freshly inked writing caught her eye. Today's English. Some poem about a vase, and youths and maidens. Miss Lowy had brought in some pictures of vases with people on them, dressed in togas or whatever they were, spinning and reading from scrolls. Why did everybody get so excited about the Greeks? It was so long ago. "Wonderful! Wonderful!" Miss Lowy had exclaimed. How could anybody get so stirred up over a poem? She meant it too. You could tell from her expression.

"Listen, boys and girls. Listen." A lifted arm enjoined them.

" 'Beauty is truth, truth beauty,' —that is all Ye know on earth, and all ye need to know."

There it was, copied into her notebook. Caught by something in the lines, she tried to find the poem in her tattered anthology, not bothering about the index, but riffling the pages to and fro. John Keats, at last—*On First Looking into Chapman's Homer.* More Greeks. Here it was—*Ode on a Grecian Urn.* The poem, all squeezed together in the middle of the page, looked dry and dusty, withered and far away, at the bottom of a dry well. She saw, not so much words, as an uninteresting, meandering pattern. The big THOU at the opening repelled her. She turned the page to find that the poem went on. Recognizing the last lines, she heard them again, falling so roundly, so perfectly, from the lips of Miss Lowy. She turned back to the beginning. Why "Grecian," why not "Greek"? With an effort, she began to dig the poem out of its constricted print.

"Thou foster child of silence and slow times," its soft susurrus carried her on. She read the poem through to the end, trying to remember her teacher's cadences.

"Write about beauty and truth. Write about life," Miss Lowy had said.

She tore a page out of her notebook and opened her pen. Pulling over a chair, she rested her book on the sooty window sill. She stared out at the dusk falling sadly, sadly, thickening into darkness over the coal yards.

A crash of the kitchen door caused a reverberation in the window sill. The notebook slipped out of her hands.

"Where'd you get that bottle of pop?" she heard her mother's voice, hard and sounding more Southern than usual.

A high-pitched, wordless whine came in reply.

"I asked you. Where'd you get that pop? You better tell me."

"A lady gave me a nickel. A lady came down the street and ask me—"

"You're lying. I know where you got that money. Gambling, that's what you were doing."

"I was only pitching pennies, Ma. It's only a game, Ma."

"Gambling and stealing and associating with bad friends. I told you to stay away from those boys. Didn't I? Didn't I?" Her mother's voice rose. "I'm going to give you a beating you're not going to forget."

Billy wailed on a long descending note.

Jeanie could hear each impact of the strap and her mother's heavy breathing.

"I want you to grow up good, not lying and gambling and stealing," her mother gasped, "and I'm going to make you good. And you aren't going to get any supper either. You can go now. You can go to bed and reflect on what I told you."

He stumbled past her, whimpering; fists grinding into his eyes, and into the dark little alcove which was his room. Jeanie heard the groan of the bed as he threw himself on it. She felt a pain in her fingers and saw them still pressed tightly around the pen.

Her mother appeared in the doorway. She wore her hat and coat.

"Come help me get supper, Jeanie. You should have got things started." Her voice was tired and tremulous, and held no reproach.

"I don't want any supper, Ma."

Her mother came in and sat down heavily on the bed, taking off her hat, and letting her coat fall open.

"I had a hard day. I worked hard every minute," she said. "I brought you something extra nice for dessert. I stood on line to get some of those tarts from Sutter's."

Jeanie rose and silently put

her mother's hat on the shelf. She held out her hand for her mother's coat, and hung it up.

Together they opened the paper bags on the kitchen table. She set the water to boil.

As they ate in silence, the three tarts shone like subtle jewels on a plate, at one end of the chipped porcelain table. Her mother looked tired and stern.

"You better fix your brother up a plate," she said, still stern. "Put it on a tray. Here, take this." And she put on the tray the most luscious, the most perfect of the tarts. "Wait." She went heavily over to her swollen black handbag, took out a small clasp purse, opened it, and carefully, seriously, deliberately, picked out a coin, rejected it, and took out another. "Give him this." It was a quarter.

After the dishes were washed, Jeanie brought her books into the kitchen and spread them out under the glaring overhead light. Billy had been asleep, huddled in his clothes. Tears had left dusty streaks on his face.

Her mother sat in the armchair, ripping out the sides of the black dress. Her spectacles made her look strange. *"Beauty is truth,"* Jeanie read in her notebook. Hastily, carelessly,

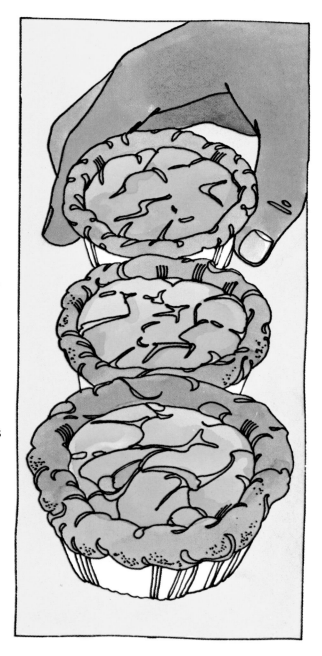

defiantly disregarding margins and doubtful spellings, letting her pen dig into the paper, she began to write: "Last night my brother Billy got a terrible beating. . . ."

Scramble to borrow the Social Studies homework from a girl in her homeroom, say hello to Barbara, undress for gym, dress again, the torn sleeve, bookkeeping—a blot, get another piece of ledger paper. "This is the third I've given you. You might say thank you." Get to English early. Slip her composition in under the others, sit in the last seat. Don't bother me. I am in a bad mood. Rows and rows of seats. Rows and rows of windows opposite. She could even read the writing on some of the blackboards, but who cared? A boy leaned far out of the window before closing it. Other heads turning. Would he fall? No, he was safe. Heads turned back. A poem about a skylark. From where she sat, she could see about a square foot of sky, drained of all color by the looming school walls. Miss Lowy read clearly, standing all alone at the front of the room in her clean white blouse and with her smooth blond hair.

Miss Lowy, maybe you see skylarks. Me, I'd be glad to see some sky, she thought and nearly uttered it. Around her, students were writing in their notebooks. Miss Lowy was about to speak to her. Better start writing something. Sullen, Mr. MacIver had called her last week. She felt about for her notebook and pen. It had been a mistake to write as she had done about her brother's beating. They would laugh if they knew. Shirley, who was the class secretary, and Saul, with the prominent forehead. No, he would not laugh. He was always writing about spaceships and the end of the world. No danger, though, that her story would be read. Only the best manuscripts were read. She remembered keenly the blotched appearance of the paper, the lines crossed out, and the words whose spelling she could never be sure of. Oh, well, she didn't care. Only one more period and then the weekend. "Lady Jeanie's too proud to come to our party. Jeanie, what are you waiting for? Jeanie's waiting for a Prince Charming with a red Cadillac to come and take her away." If Barbara asked her again, she would go with her, maybe. There was going to be a party at Norma's Saturday night, with Cokes and sandwiches and records and dancing, everybody chipping in. "Jeanie, I need a

171

nickel. Mama, I need a dollar. I need, I need.''

The bell rang, and the pens dropped, the books were closed with a clatter. She slipped out ahead of the pushing, jostling boys and girls.

Monday, Miss Lowy had on still another perfect white blouse.

She stood facing the class, holding a sheaf of papers in her hand. Most of the students looked at her expectantly. Marion, who nearly always got 90, whispered to her neighbor. Michael, who had but recently come from Greece—ah, but that was a different Greece—grumbled and shifted in his seat. He would have to do his composition over. He always did.

''I spent a very enjoyable

time this weekend, reading your work," said Miss Lowy, waiting for the class to smile.

"Seriously, though, many of your pieces were most interesting, even though they were a trifle unconventional about spelling and punctuation." A smile was obviously indicated here too, and the class obeyed. She paused. "Sometimes, however, a piece of writing is so honest and human, that you have to forgive the technical weaknesses. Not that they aren't important," she said hastily, "but what the writer has to say is more significant."

The three best students in the class looked confused. It was their pride not to have technical errors.

"When you hear this," Miss Lowy continued, "I think you'll agree with me. I know it brought tears to my eyes."

The class looked incredulous.

"It's called 'Evening Comes to 128th Street.' " Her face took on that rapt look.

Jeanie's heart beat painfully. She picked up a pencil, but dropped it, so unsteady were her fingers. Even the back of Shirley's head was listening. Even the classes in the other wing of the building, across the court-yard, seemed fixed, row on row, in an attitude of listening. Miss Lowy read on. It was all there, 173 the coal yards and Fat Mary, the stoop and the tarts from Sutter's, Billy asleep with the tears dried on his face, the clasp purse and the quarter.

" 'The funny part of it was, when I woke him, Billy wasn't mad. He was glad about the quarter, and ate his supper, dessert and all, but Mama never did eat her tart, so I put it away.' "

A poignancy of remembrance swept over Jeanie, then shame and regret. It was no business of theirs, these strangers.

No one spoke. The silence was unbearable. Finally Marion, the incomparable Marion, raised her hand.

"It was so real," she said, "you felt you were right there in that kitchen."

"You didn't know whom to feel sorry for," said another student. "You wanted to cry

with the mother and you wanted to cry with Billy."

"With the girl too," said another.

Several heads nodded.

"You see," said Miss Lowy. "It's literature. It's life. It's pain and truth and beauty."

Jeanie's heart beat so, it made a mist come before her eyes. Through the blur she heard Miss Lowy say it was good enough to be sent in to *Scholastic*. It showed talent, it showed promise. She heard her name called and shrank from the eyes turned upon her.

After school, she hurried out and caught the first train, that you could catch only if you left immediately and did not stroll or stop the least little bit to talk to someone. She did not want to meet anyone, not even Barbara.

Was that Billy among the kids on the stoop?

"Billy," she called. "Billy."

What would she say to him? Beauty is truth, truth beauty?

"Billy," she called again urgently.

Billy lifted his head, and seeing who it was, tore himself reluctantly away from his friends, and took a step toward her.

ANNA GUEST

174

What's It All About?

1. What does Jeanie write about? Why does Miss Lowy find Jeanie's composition beautiful?
2. "Beauty is truth, truth is beauty." Do you think truth is beautiful? Why?

---

1. What kind of person is Jeanie? Use facts from the story to support your description.
2. Why was Billy punished?
3. Why do you think Jeanie's mother sends Billy a plate, gives him the best tart, and, in addition, a quarter?
4. Why is Jeanie surprised when Miss Lowy reads her story? Why do you think she hurries home right after school that day?

PUTTING IDEAS TO WORK

Write a true short story about an experience you had. Write it in the third person, that is, refer to yourself as "he" or "she."

Final Exam

What started out as a State Science Fair project
turned into something more terrible than
Doug and Marty ever expected.

The two boys destroyed the Civil War Memorial five blocks away on Main Street at three in the afternoon. At one minute before three they were merely two sixteen-year-olds, bright-eyed and full of noise and eager questions, tinkering on a science fair project in the basement of Doug McAllister's home. At one minute after three they became a world menace, and much later one of them was destined—perhaps—to become a world savior. Fortunately it was a depressingly humid day, with the air above the blacktop of Main Street shimmering in undulating waves of heat. For this reason there were few people about. Otherwise, the damage might have been greater than it was and someone might have been injured.

The nearly invisible beam of energy pierced the foot-thick concrete blocks of the basement, sliced cleanly through five feet of raw embankment around the house, and burned a lilac bush into a crumbling black mass. It gouged a thin streak of char across the bright blue top of a Camaro parked at the curb and arrowed down the street at an angle five degrees above the horizontal. The beam went on until it hit the green patinated statue of some forgotten Union soldier leaning tiredly on his bayoneted rifle. He suddenly glowed bright red, slumped like a wax figure before a fireplace, and then shattered into a thousand sparkling droplets of molten bronze. Even then the boys were fortunate; most of the molten metal went into the heavy growth of hedge around the square. The shrubbery crackled and fumed as it withered in the heat of the droplets.

In the semidarkness of the basement, Doug McAllister slapped the transformer switch and fell back. His lean body shook as paint cracked and flaked from the black, pencil-thin hole in the concrete-block wall before him. Marty Larsen sucked in air audibly, his beet-red face redder than ever; his hand had been a bare two inches from the path of the beam when Doug had activated the device. The heat reflected from the white concrete wall had singed the light blond hair on the back of his stubby fingers. He stood now rubbing his scorched hand against his chino-clad leg, his blue eyes wide.

"Wha—what happened?" Marty asked shakily.

"I don't know," Doug said. The summer tan of his face seemed suddenly pale, making his dark eyebrows unusually prominent. "A laser can't generate a beam anywhere near that intensity or . . . " He crouched down and eyed the device mounted neatly on the three-quarter-inch slab of lacquered plywood. " . . . Or that wide."

He switched off the chugging vacuum pump and said, "Where did the power come from? We didn't put that much into the system."

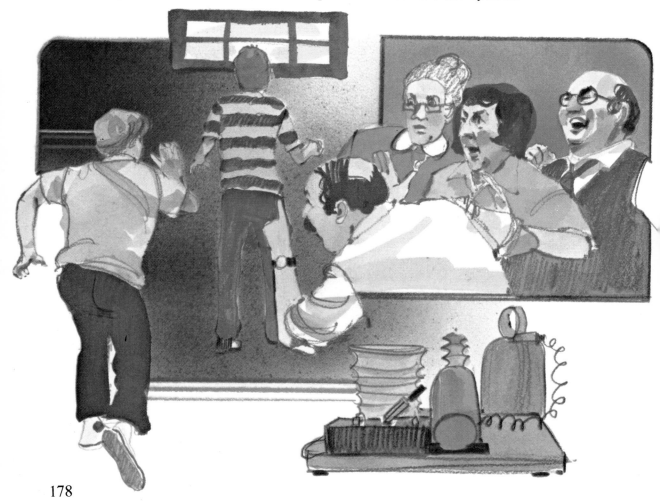

"There was quite a lag before the beam fired," Marty answered. "Could it have been accumulating?"

"Enough to do that?" Doug exclaimed, gesturing at the wall.

Outside someone shouted. Before Marty could answer, a second voice shouted, and in seconds the street outside seemed to fill with people. Doug ran to the high basement window and stood on tiptoe to peer out. A crowd of people—perhaps two dozen of them—were shouting and gesturing in front of the house. As he watched, the crowd grew.

"Brother," he said, turning worried eyes to Marty. "We're in for it."

"It wasn't our fault," Marty said. "We didn't know it would do that."

"Never mind," Doug said. "It did it and we're responsible. Just pray nobody was in the way of the beam."

Marty's eyes darted back from the apparatus on the table to the far corner of the basement. "Maybe we can get out by the back way?"

Doug shook his head. "No, we got to go upstairs and face the music. Come on." He turned and started up the bare timber steps; Marty followed reluctantly. The door at the head of the stairs opened into the McAllister kitchen.

He started through the hall to the living room just as the front door bell rang and rang again. Doug turned resignedly and opened the door. Mr. Renkin stood outside, his finger still on the bell button.

"Close the door and lock it," he told Doug as he pushed through into the hall.

"What have you done?" Mr. Renkin demanded. "How did you do it?" He leaned back against the door as though to keep out the crowd. Mr. Renkin was their high school physics teacher and basketball coach. He was about thirty, six feet tall with longish brown hair and a strong, athletic look. Doug told him what had happened.

"Your State Science Fair project?" Mr. Renkin exclaimed. "I can't believe it. You'd better show me your setup."

The boys led him through the kitchen and downstairs into the 179 basement. "Zap," Marty said enthusiastically. "Just like a death ray, right through the concrete. It just missed my fingers."

"What happened outside?" Doug demanded. "There were an awful lot of people out there." Mr. Renkin told him about the melted blob that had been the Civil War Memorial. "It looks like we're in for it," Doug said dispiritedly. "We didn't mean to, you know? Maybe we can make it up, pay for the damages," he added, his face brightening.

"Boys, I don't think you know what you have here," Mr. Renkin said, bending over their laser setup and checking the construction. "Amazing." He straightened up. "It looks exactly like the plans we drew for the project. Nothing unusual in the setup." He tapped the power source. "An ordinary 12,000-volt transformer. There's simply no reason why this thing should have generated a beam of such power." He shuddered.

"Zap, you know, just like a heat ray," Marty said happily.

"It looks like that's exactly what you have," Mr. Renkin said. "I'm going to ask you not to discuss this with anyone."

"Why?" Doug asked. "What about those people outside?"

"What you have here is a lot more important than you think," Mr. Renkin said. "As for those people, you let me take care of them."

Upstairs the bell rang insistently. Then they heard heavy fists pounding on the front door. Marty ran to the window and managed to peer out over the high sill. "It's a police car," he said. "No, a sheriff's car. They've come to arrest us."

"Let me handle this," Mr. Renkin said, heading for the stairs. He disappeared through the door at the head of the steps before either boy could react. He was gone for a long time. Marty fidgeted silently while Doug walked back to look over the laser setup. He tapped at the silica gel column, accidentally dislodging the glass tube, the hose, and the rubber stopper at the top of the glass column.

Something was odd, he realized, wrinkling his nose. What was the odor? Like quite nothing he had smelled before. He twisted the valve on the carbon dioxide bottle and a sudden cloud of the gas enveloped

180

him, sending him sprawling back, gagging.

"What happened?" Marty exclaimed.

For a moment Doug thought he was going to be violently ill, but he recovered. "The gas. That odor," he managed to say.

"Phew!" Marty said. "It smells like old gym socks and geraniums."

"That's it!" Doug said excitedly. "Don't you see? It's the gas in the bottle. Carbon dioxide is odorless. Someone sent us the wrong bottle."

"You mean some other gas?" Marty asked. "Something that amplified a thousand times as much as carbon dioxide? Wow, we've really hit the jackpot!"

Doug eyed him thoughtfully. "Look," he said, "let's keep this to ourselves for a while."

"Why?" Marty demanded. "Man, this is great. We'll be world famous."

"Look, let's keep it quiet," Doug said. Then he added, feeling somehow dishonest, "We're just a couple of kids. Some grown-up will steal it from us if we shoot off our mouths."

"That's right. There's a lot to what you say." Marty nodded. "Okay, I'll keep my mouth shut until you give the word."

Mr. Renkin came down the stairs and said, "It's all right, boys. The sheriff agreed to post a deputy front and rear."

"A deputy?" Doug said. "Does that mean we're under arrest?"

"Of course not," Mr. Renkin answered. "It's just that you'll need protection until we can get someone down from Washington. I don't think you realize the potential of this thing you boys have built."

"Potential?" Marty said. "See, I told you. We'll be famous."

Doug's eyes fell and he turned away from Mr. Renkin. "What's wrong, Doug?" the teacher asked.

"We didn't set out to build a weapon," Doug said sadly. "There are enough weapons in the world."

"You're right, Doug. But the thing exists now, and you'll just have 181 to face it. Besides, think of the good that can come from such a device. Think of its use in clearing lands and digging canals and a thousand other projects that are important to humanity but just too expensive now.''

"Like the new canal across Panama?" Marty suggested.

"That's right," Mr. Renkin said. "Anyway, I sent a message out with the sheriff. I expect we'll be having a representative in from Washington on the morning plane. Now I suggest you two boys talk to no one until then. Stay home this evening and get a good night's sleep. You'll need it for tomorrow."

Doug nodded slowly, somehow depressed by Mr. Renkin's enthusiasm and even more depressed by Marty's eagerness. The idea of having built such a devastating weapon seemed to please Marty immensely. After Mr. Renkin had said good-by and walked up the steps, Doug asked Marty about it.

Marty shrugged, then laughed. "Well, I guess I don't really want a weapon, either," he said. "It's just that this is the sort of chance that comes along once in a lifetime and anyway. . . ." He walked over and rubbed the charred spot on the concrete. "Anyway, if we hadn't done it, somebody else would have."

At dinner that evening Doug sat silently poking at his food. His mother was preparing dessert in the kitchen and his father, his plate already clean, sat silently drinking his coffee. Several times he looked up to say something to Doug and then thought better of it. Finally Doug spoke.

"Dad? This thing we built. It's our property, isn't it?"

"I think so," his father said.

"I mean, we don't have to give it up if we don't want to, do we?"

His father sighed and leaned back in his chair in thought. "Ordinarily, you would be right," he said at last. "However, I'm not sure that we could prevent the man from Washington from getting a court order and seizing the device. After that it would be a matter of time before they puzzled it out, even though we might want to fight them. Don't you want to give it up, son?"

"No," Doug said slowly. "I don't want to be responsible for providing such a horrible weapon."

"The hydrogen bomb is a much more terrible weapon," his father said.

"That's just it," Doug said. "The bomb is so terrible that no one dares use it. Don't you see? The laser weapon can be controlled in a way a bomb can't. If they built more of them, eventually they would use them. Or some other country would find out and build its own, and eventually the laser would be used against us."

"I'm very much afraid you're right," his father said slowly. He finished his coffee in a gulp and sat silently looking at the empty cup for a long while. Finally he seemed to reach a decision. "Son," he said, "you know we don't have very much money, but if this is the way you feel, I'll hire the best lawyer we can get and we'll try to keep it out of their hands."

His mother had been standing in the background, listening. She came over now, carrying dishes of pudding. She set one in front of Doug's father and impulsively leaned over to kiss him on the forehead. She said, "I was hoping you would say that." Then she turned to Doug and smiled at him. "I'm very proud of you," she told him.

There wasn't much Doug could say. He was suddenly overwhelmed with the strength of his feeling for these two people. He covered up his emotion and said, "Can I have my pudding now, Mom?"

Doug couldn't sleep. He lay in his bed and tossed for an hour. In his mind's eye he saw great cities crumble in flames, their people crisping to black char in the beam of this thing he had built. He saw vast forests turn to flaming ruin as the beam blazed from above. Armadas of ships were blasted to molten ruin in the waters, and mighty air fleets rained in fiery debris from the skies.

Doug had learned a special sense of responsibility from his parents. 183

They had constantly impressed him with the need to consider how his actions affected other people. "There is no such thing as a blameless action," his father had said. "We are each of us a part of the human race and everything we do changes the destiny of the people about us. The effect spreads out like the ripples on a lake when you drop a stone in the water."

Doug lay in the dark. Outside a twig snapped and he knew the deputies must still be patrolling the house. Just before bedtime Mr. Renkin had called to tell him that a Mr. Carruthers from the Department of Defense would be in on the morning plane and wanted to see him and Marty at eleven. Marty had called, his voice excited, but Doug had felt a deeper and deeper sadness at the way things were going.

At long last he rose, donned his robe, and tiptoed down the hall to the kitchen. He descended the stairs to the basement and turned on the worklight over the laser apparatus. Carefully he disconnected the gas bottle and carried it to the rear of the basement. A roll of linoleum

185

leaned against one wall. He raised the bottle, dropped it down inside the roll, and heard the muffled clink as it hit the concrete floor. Then he rummaged around in the storage chest near the work area until he found the exhausted gas bottle that they had removed when the new one was delivered. They would have to return this one to the scientific house for a deposit, but now it served as a good substitute for the bottle he had hidden. Then he reconnected the gas hose and inspected his work. After this he turned out the light and tiptoed up the stairs.

The kitchen was completely dark. He started to move through the hall and then stopped. He thought for a moment he had heard a footstep, but decided that he must be imagining things. He started for his room and then stopped again as he heard the same noise. He stood silently in the darkened hall, listening. When he heard the noise again, it was directly behind him. He turned in alarm, but not quickly enough. A pair of hands from behind pinioned his arms to his sides while another pair of hands held his head. Something smooth with a sweet chemical smell pressed against his mouth and nose. He fought desperately, trying not to inhale. A sudden jolt to his chest made him suck in his breath, and the sick-sweet fumes filled his lungs, pulling him down and down into a red-spotted darkness that closed over his head. He was aware of nothing after this for a long while.

His first reaction was one of nausea. His head throbbed and his stomach churned. His eyes seemed gummed together. He tried to raise his hands to rub his eyes and discovered that he could not move his arms. He realized that he was sitting on a chair and that his arms were tied, albeit somewhat loosely, behind him. His legs were also bound.

He opened his eyes slowly and looked about. He was sitting in one corner of a barren room with walls of rough planking. The floor was woven matting. There were, he saw, two doors set in adjacent walls. On the far side of the room a man in a sport shirt and expensive-looking slacks busied himself at an enameled sink on which stood several amber bottles, half-filled with liquid. Nearby on a low table rested the sheet of plywood with the laser assembly.

"Feel better?" the man asked, turning and smiling. He was small, not more than five-six, and had lean, almost stern features and a high, dark widow's peak.

"Yes," Doug said. "I suppose all this has to do with the laser."

"Suppose we wait until our friends return before talking about it," the man suggested.

"It won't do you any good," Doug said. "I wouldn't give the laser to my own people. Why should I give it to yours?"

"You misunderstand," the man said. "We don't represent any special government. We are—let's say, commercial agents."

Doug was about to answer when the far door opened and another man entered with Marty, who was blindfolded. Behind them Doug saw a darkened passageway, also walled with the crude planking that made up the room.

The second man, who was much taller than the first but had the same stern cast to his features, removed Marty's blindfold. "Is our other guest feeling better, Jera?"

"Much better," the short man said.

"Brother," Marty blurted. "I didn't have a chance. They just scooped me up in the middle of the night and there wasn't a thing I could do."

"Me either," Doug said.

The tall man, who appeared to be the leader, said, "I'm sorry that we had to do it that way, but it was necessary."

"Why necessary?" Doug demanded. The man's manner was strangely friendly and Doug found himself viewing both him and Jera with less alarm.

"We had to get you away, you and your machine, before morning," the tall man said. "You see, we have several ideas on how your device may be used and I think we can promise both of you a great deal of wealth if you help us."

"Wealth and prestige and power," Jera added.

"I'm not interested," Doug said.

187

"Aw, come on, Doug," Marty protested. "I've been talking with Mr. Rill and what he says makes good sense. If we had stayed around there, they'd have taken it off our hands and given us a medal or two and we'd have been out in the cold."

"Your friend is very sensible," Mr. Rill said.

Jera laughed and echoed. "Very sensible."

"Now," Mr. Rill said, "suppose you show us how your device operates."

Marty said, "Well, it's very easy," and walked over to the low table.

"Marty!" Doug cried, straining against his bonds. "Marty, you can't help these men!"

"Why not?" Marty demanded. "I don't want to stay a poor kid all my life. There's plenty in this for both of us, buddy."

"You can't turn a thing like this loose on the world," Doug protested.

"But think of the good one may do with such a machine," Jera insisted.

"That's right," Marty said. "We'll be benefactors of humanity."

"You'll be the cause of the most devastating war in history," Doug cried.

Marty looked at Mr. Rill. "It's pretty violent."

"That's all right," Mr. Rill said. "There's a solid clay hill beyond that stretches a mile." Marty nodded and pressed the switch. They all waited but nothing happened.

"Funny," Marty said and waved his hand in front of the mirror. "It's working just as it was designed to."

He disconnected the power source, opened the dryer column, and sniffed.

"You've replaced the gas bottle," he accused Doug.

"That's right," Doug said.

"What difference does that make?" Mr. Rill asked.

188   "That's the whole secret," Marty said petulantly. "You would

have to analyze the gas to find out how the high-power laser works."

"Then you'll just have to give us the gas bottle," Mr. Rill said to Doug.

"I destroyed it," Doug lied.

"No, you didn't," Marty snapped. "You couldn't. I bet you've hidden it somewhere in your basement."

"That sounds reasonable," Jera said.

"Then we must go back and search for it," Mr. Rill said.

"I'll go with you," Marty said. He turned to Doug and looked apologetic. "I'm sorry, Doug. It's for your own good. Mr. Rill and his friend will know how to use it and I'm sure they'll play fair with us."

"Marty, don't," Doug pleaded, but his friend was no longer listening.

"Let's go," Marty said.

"We'll be back to release you shortly," Mr. Rill said. "Unless you want to tell us where you hid the bottle."

Doug shook his head. Mr. Rill nodded, almost in approval. "Very well," he said. "Let us go."

He and Jera and Marty walked through the door. At the last minute Marty looked back. Then his mouth firmed and he turned resolutely away. The door closed behind them.

Doug began to struggle with his bonds. He had to get away and get back to the basement, perhaps call the police. It was only a matter of 189 time before they discovered where he had hidden the gas bottle and then all would be lost. His nightmare of flaming cities and terrible war would be a reality. He nearly sobbed with anxiety as he tugged at the bonds. Then suddenly they loosened and one hand was free. Quickly he freed the other hand and then his legs. He massaged strength back into his limbs, then stood.

He walked over to the laser apparatus and freed the gas bottle. With its heavy metal body he smashed the plasma tube, splintering the fragile glass with one stroke. Then he systematically demolished the rest of the laser. He threw the bottle to the floor and ran across the room. The door knob twisted in his hand. They had locked the door after them.

For a moment he stood in indecision. There was the other door. He would have to chance it. He walked to it and tried the knob. The door opened slowly to. . . .

To a long metal corridor, softly lighted by overhead panels that glowed with a gentle radiance. The floor was metal, padded with a thick, elastic fabric.

Where was he?

He started along the corridor, his feet sinking into the soft fabric. Ahead a hatchway glowed. He paused, then moved forward and stepped through.

Around him stretched a great circular room with banked rows of lights and strange instruments. The front part of the room was a continuous screen, now black. A man stood facing the screen, hands resting on a wide instrument console.

"Come in, Doug," the man said.

He turned and Doug gasped. It was Mr. Renkin. Only it was Mr. Renkin as Doug and Marty had never seen him before. His lean, muscular figure was clad in an iridescent metallic blue uniform that fit like a second skin. For the first time, Doug realized that Mr. Renkin had somewhat the same somber look that he had seen in Mr. Rill and

190   Jera.

"Where am I?" he demanded.

"This?" Mr. Renkin swept the scene with his hand. "This is the bridge of a Galactic Federation starship, one of thousands that keep the peace in the inhabited galaxy." Mr. Renkin smiled a secret smile. "Is that such a devastating idea?" he asked, seeing Doug's expression.

"I don't understand," Doug said. "What has all of this to do with me? Why have you been playing games with us?"

"That's very bright of you," Mr. Renkin said. "To recognize immediately that it was all a game." He walked forward and put his hand on Doug's shoulder, guiding him over to the console. "Not a game, really, Doug. Call it an examination—your final examination. Look." His hand touched the console and the great screen lit up. A wealth of stars blazed across it like diamonds on crumpled velvet.

"Out there are ten thousand inhabited worlds," he said, "some of them a part of our galaxy-spanning federation, some of them—like Earth—completely unaware of us. The Galactic Service keeps the peace in this great commonwealth of worlds. 'To serve and guard human life'—this is our motto."

"I would never have imagined . . . " Doug said in awe. "It's so vast."

"Members of the Service are recruited from all worlds," Mr. Renkin continued. "They must be superb athletes, and they must have superior minds. Most of all they must have the strongest moral beliefs, for we dare not entrust such power to lesser people. Today throughout the world twelve young people who we felt had these qualities have been tested. You and your friend Marty are two of them. We gave you a moral challenge. Would you give in to self-interest or see clearly the greater good of your race? Only you and a young woman in Hokkaido have passed that test. The rest will forget what has happened and return to their daily lives, none the worse. The weapons we gave you will have disappeared, and even the townspeople will soon forget that anything unusual happened today."

"I?" Doug said. "What about me? I'm nothing special."

"You are one of the two most special people we could find on this earth. If you join us, you must leave your family forever and dedicate yourself to the good of alien people scattered across the galaxy, never seeking gain for yourself."

"Leave my family! I couldn't—"

"Then you will forget everything that has happened and continue your career, undisturbed," Mr. Renkin said. He held up his hand when Doug started to speak. "It's still dark in the outside world. We will return you to your home. Think about it until dawn—four hours. At dawn I will be waiting outside your house. I will wait fifteen minutes and then I will leave. After that you can return to the life you were living."

Doug shook his head, amazed. He felt excitement build in him, but also a great sorrow at the thought of leaving his family and home for those alien stars.

"Come along," Mr. Renkin said. "I will take you back."

They left the ship, which was buried in a great shaft drilled into a
192   mountain in an area Doug could not identify. They boarded a small

silver craft and raced across the still-dark sky. In thirty minutes Doug was walking up his front walk. The house was dark and silent.

He entered the hall and walked swiftly to his room. There he sat by the window and looked up at the stars in the sky. They were such a pitifully small number compared to the vast sweep of stars and worlds he had seen on the ship's screen. He wondered that anyone could have the courage to voyage among them.

He and Marty had dreamed of such a thing. Their early friendship had been based on their enthusiasm for space travel. The thought that in one step he could become a part of that was overwhelmingly exciting. But to leave home—his parents, all that was familiar—forever? To give his life over to a million million beings he did not know, who might be only faintly human to his eyes? He could not do it.

Only, even if they removed his memory, there would always be a faint knowledge, a deep sense of loss. He knew that, and he knew that such sorrow would follow him to his last days.

He glanced at the illuminated clock face on his bureau. It was fifteen to six, and the first light of dawn was showing on the horizon.

Could he do it? Could he *not* do it?

Suddenly he realized that he had made the decision almost at the instant he had seen the blazing stars on the ship's screen. He rose, pulled a small canvas bag from his closet, and packed a few special things—a photograph of himself with his mother and father, the merit badge he had worked so hard for several years ago, a favorite book by Arthur C. Clarke. He turned at the door for one last look at his room, then he stepped into the hall. At his parents' room, he looked in through the partly opened door. He could discern a still form in the near bed. The far bed appeared empty and he wondered where his father was. He tiptoed in and looked down at his mother's sleeping figure. She stirred and turned, her face illuminated by the faint light from the window. She looked tired but peaceful.

His father was waiting for him at the head of the hall. "Dad," he said, wondering what to say.

193

"Never mind, Doug," his father said. "Mr. Renkin told me about it. He says that I'll never be able to tell anyone else, but they feel one of the parents should know."

"Oh, Dad," he said.

"None of that," his father said. "Can you know how proud I am of you?"

They shook hands silently, neither daring to speak.

"Good-by," he told his father.

194   "Good-by," his father said.

He walked through the door. Outside, Mr. Renkin stood in the shadows by the lilac bush, his uniform gleaming in the early light. For a second, Doug hesitated. Then the vision of the stars sweeping across the great screen came to him and he stepped forward.

"I'm ready, sir," he said.

"Come along," Mr. Renkin said, and they walked through the town. Early morning sounds filtered from houses they passed, signaling the beginning of a new day.

THOMAS N. SCORTIA   195

FORTUNES

Chills were hopping in my skin
As I asked for a cup of tea
And my friend gave me also
A bag of fortune cookies.

Not one, not a handful, but a bagful.
That kind of bliss
Which steams from a cup of tea
Steamed to me.

Every probable, every possible,
Every impossible
Fortune from here to Mishima.
It was the world.

I cracked the first cookie, and it said
Do not open more than one
Of these fortunes
At a time.

JOSEPHINE MILES

What's It All About?

1. What is the "final exam"? What is its purpose?
2. A moral challenge is one in which a person must choose between doing something for personal gain and doing something that benefits people in general. Why was it important for Mr. Renkin's organization to give Doug and Marty a "moral challenge"?

---

1. What kind of device do Doug and Marty invent? How is its power demonstrated?
2. What potential does each of the following people see in this device: Doug? Marty? Mr. Renkin?
3. Why does Doug think their invention is more terrible than the hydrogen bomb?
4. What have Doug's parents taught him about responsibility? How do his actions in the story show that he agrees with them?
5. What qualifications does the Galactic Service require? Why does Marty fail the "final exam"?

PUTTING IDEAS TO WORK

What do you think Doug's first day of training with the Galactic Service will be like? Imagine you are Doug. Write a diary entry describing that first day.

Special People

What makes People Special?

There was no way up. We were faced with the nightmare of going down the sheer rock wall—without ropes.

Climbing
Kloochman

When Doug Corpron was nineteen and I was not quite fifteen, the two of us made this climb of Kloochman. Walter Kohagen, Doug, and I were camped in the Tieton Basin at a soda spring. The basin was then in large part a vast rich bottomland. We were traveling light, one blanket each. The night, I recall, was so bitter cold that we took turns refueling the campfire so that we could keep our backs warm enough to sleep. We rose at the first show of dawn and cooked frying-pan bread and trout for breakfast. We had not planned to climb Kloochman, but somehow the challenge came to us as the sun touched her crest.   199

After breakfast we started circling the rock. There are fairly easy routes up Kloochman, but we shunned them. When we came to the southeast face (the one that never has been conquered, I believe) we chose it. Walter decided not to make the climb, but to wait at the base of the cliff for Doug and me. The July day was warm and cloudless. Doug led. The beginning was easy. For a hundred feet or so we found ledges six to twelve inches wide which we could follow to the left or right. Some ledges ran up the rock ten feet or more at a gentle grade. Others were merely steps to another ledge higher up. Thus by hugging the wall, we could either ease ourselves upward or hoist ourselves from one ledge to another.

When we were about a hundred feet up the wall, the ledges became narrower and footwork more precarious. Doug suggested we take off our shoes. This we did, tying them behind us on our belts. In stocking feet we wormed up the wall, clinging like flies to the dark rock. The pace was slow. We gingerly tested each toehold and fingerhold for loose rock before putting our weight on them. At times we had to inch along sidewise, our stomachs pressed tightly against the rock, in order to gain a point where we could reach the ledge above us.

If we got on a ledge that turned out to be a cul-de-sac, the much more dangerous task of going down the rock wall would confront us. So we picked our route with care and weighed the advantages of several choices which frequently were given us. At times we could not climb easily from one ledge to another. The one above might be a foot or so high. Then we would have to reach it with one knee, slowly bring the other knee up, and then, delicately balancing on both knees on the upper ledge, come slowly to our feet by pressing close to the wall and getting such hold with our fingers as the lava rock permitted.

In that tortuous way we made perhaps six hundred feet in two hours. It was late forenoon when we stopped to look over our situation. We were in serious trouble. We had reached the feared cul-de-sac. The two- or three-inch ledge on which we stood, ended. There seemed none above us within Doug's reach. I was longer-legged than Doug, so

200

perhaps I could have reached some ledge with my fingers if I had been ahead. But it was impossible to change positions on the wall. Doug was ahead, and there he must stay. The problem was to find a way to get him up.

Feeling along the wall, Doug discovered a tiny groove into which he could press the tips of the fingers of his left hand. It might help him maintain balance as his weight began to shift from the lower ledge to the upper one. But there was within reach not even a lip of rock for his right hand. Just out of reach, however, was a substantial crevice, one that would hold several men. How could Doug reach it? I could not boost him, for my own balance was insecure. Clearly, Doug would have to jump to reach it—and he would have but one jump. Since he was standing on a ledge only a few inches wide, he could not expect to jump for his handhold, miss it, and land safely. A slip meant he would go hurtling down some six hundred feet onto the rocks. After much discussion and indecision, Doug decided to take the chance and go up.

He asked me to do him a favor: If he failed and fell, I might still make it, since I was longer-legged. Would I give certain messages to his family in that event? I nodded.

"Then listen carefully. Try to remember my exact words," he told me. "Tell Mother that I love her dearly. Tell her I think she is the most wonderful person in the world. Tell her not to worry—that I did not suffer, that God willed it so. Tell Sister that I have acted mean, but I had no malice towards her. Tell her I love her too—that someday I wanted to marry a girl as wholesome and gay and good as she.

"Tell Dad I was brave and died unafraid. Tell him about our climb in full detail. Tell Dad that I have always been very proud of him, that someday I had planned to be a doctor too. Tell him that I lived a clean life, that I never did anything to make him ashamed. . . . Tell Mother, Sister, and Dad I prayed for them."

Every word burned into me. My heart was sick, my lips quivered. I pressed my face against the rock so Doug could not see. I wept.   201

All was silent. A pebble fell from the ledge on which I squeezed. I counted seconds before it hit, six hundred feet below, with a faint, faraway tinkling sound. Would Doug drop through the same space? Would I follow? When you fall six hundred feet, do you die before you hit the bottom? Closing my eyes, I prayed that Doug would get up the wall.

In a second Doug said in a cheery voice, "Well, here goes."

A false bravado took hold of us. I said he could do it. He said he would. He wiped first one hand and then the other on his trousers. He placed both palms against the wall, bent his knees slowly, paused a split second, and jumped straight up. It was not much of a jump—only six inches or so. But that jump by one pressed against a cliff six hundred

feet in the air had daredevil proportions. I held my breath; my heart pounded. Then the suspense was over.

Doug made the jump and in a second was hanging by two hands from a strong, wide ledge. There was no toehold; he would have to hoist himself by his arms alone. He did just that. His body went slowly up as if pulled by some unseen winch. Soon he had the weight of his body above the ledge and was resting on the palms of his hands. He then put his left knee on the ledge, rolled over on his side, and chuckled as he said, "Nothing to it."

A greater disappointment followed. Doug's exploration of the ledge showed he was in a final cul-de-sac. There was no way up. There was not even a higher ledge he could reach by jumping. We were then faced with the nightmare of going down the sheer rock wall. We could not go down frontwards because the ledges were too narrow and the way too steep. We needed our toes, and our heels, on the rock; and we needed to have our stomachs pressed tightly against it. Then we could perhaps feel our way. But as every rock expert knows, descent of a cliff without ropes is often much more difficult than ascent.

That difficulty was impressed on us by the first move. Doug had to leave the ledge he had reached by jumping. He dared not slide blindly to the skimpy ledge he had just left. I must help him. I must move up the wall and stand closer to him. Though I could not possibly hold his weight, I must use enough pressure to slow up his descent and to direct his toe onto the narrow ledge from which he had just jumped.

I was hanging to the rock like a fly, twelve feet or more to Doug's left. I inched my way toward him, first dropping to a lower ledge and then climbing to a higher one, using such toeholds as the rock provided and edging my way crabwise.

When I reached him I said, "Now I'll help."

Doug lowered himself and hung by his fingers full length. His feet were about six inches above the ledge from which he had jumped. He was now my responsibility. If he dropped without aid or direction, he was gone. He could not catch and hold to the scanty ledge. I had little space for maneuvering. The surface on which I stood was not more than three inches wide. My left hand fortunately found an overhead crevice that gave a solid anchor in case my feet slipped.

I placed my right hand in the small of Doug's back and pressed upward with all my might. "Now you can come," I said.

He let go gently, and his full weight came against my arm. My arm trembled under the tension. My left hand hung onto the crack in the rock like a grappling hook. My stomach pressed against the wall. My toes dug in as I threw in every ounce of strength.

Down Doug came—a full inch. I couldn't help glancing down and eyeing the rocks six hundred feet below.

Down Doug moved another inch, then a third. My left hand seemed paralyzed. The muscles of my toes were aching. My right arm shook. I could not hold much longer.

Down came Doug a fourth inch. I thought he was headed for destruction. His feet would miss the only toehold within reach. I could not possibly hold him. He would plunge to his death because my arm was not strong enough to hold him. The messages he had given me for his family raced through my mind. And I saw myself, sick and ashamed, standing before them, testifying to my own inadequacy, repeating his last words.

"Steady, Doug. The ledge is a foot to your right." He pawed the wall with the toes of his foot, searching.

"I can't find it. Don't let go."

The crisis was on us. Even if I had been safely anchored, my cramped position would have kept me from helping him much more. I felt helpless. In a few seconds I would reach the physical breaking point and Doug would go hurtling off the cliff. I did not see how I could keep him from slipping and yet maintain my own balance.

I will never know how I did it. But I tapped some reserve and directed his right foot onto the ledge from which he had earlier jumped. I did it by standing for a moment on my left foot alone and then using my right leg as a rod to guide his right foot to the ledge his swinging feet had missed.

His toes grabbed the ledge as if they were the talons of a bird. My right leg swung back to my perch.

"Are you O.K.?" I asked.

"Yes," said Doug. "Good work."

My right arm fell from him, numb and useless. I shook from exhaustion, and for the first time noticed that my face was wet with perspiration. We stood against the rock in silence for several minutes, relaxing and regaining our calm.

Doug said, "Let's throw our shoes down. It will be easier going." So we untied them from our belts and dropped them to Walter Kohagen, who was waiting at the rock field below us.

Our descent was painfully slow, but uneventful. We went down backwards, weaving a strange pattern across the face of the cliff as we moved from one side to the other. It was perhaps midafternoon when we reached the bottom, found our shoes, and started around the other side of the rock. We left the southeast wall unconquered.

But, being young, we were determined to climb the rock. So once more we started to circle. When we came to the northwest wall, we selected it as our route.

Here, too, is a cliff rising a thousand feet like some unfinished pyramid. But close examination shows numerous toeholds and fingerholds that make the start fairly easy. So we set out with our shoes on.

Again it was easy going for a hundred feet or so, when Doug, who was ahead, came to a ledge to which he could not step. On later climbs we would send the longer-legged chap ahead. And on other occasions Doug himself has used a rope to cross this spot. But this day success of the climb depended on Doug's short legs alone. The ledge to which he must move was up to his hips. There were few fingerholds overhead, and none firm enough to carry his whole weight. Only a few tiny cracks were within reach to serve as holds for him. But Doug would not give up.

He hitched up his trousers and grasped a tiny groove of rock with the tips of the fingers of his left hand, pressing his right hand flat against the smooth rock wall as if it had magical sticking power. Slowly he lifted his left knee until it was slightly over the ledge above him. To do so he had to stand on tiptoe on his right foot. Pulling with his left hand, he brought his right knee up. Doug was now on both knees on the upper ledge. If he could find a good grip overhead for his hands, he was safe. His hands explored the wall above him. He moved them slowly over most of it without finding a hold. Then he reached straight above his head and cried out, "This is our lucky day."

206

He had found strong rough edges of rock, and quickly pulled himself up. His hands were on a ledge a foot wide. He lay down on it on his stomach and grasped my outstretched hand. The pull of his strong arm against the drop of a hundred feet or more was as comforting an experience as any I can recall. In a jiffy I was at his side. We pounded each other on the shoulders and laughed.

My own most serious trouble was yet to come. For a while Doug and I were separated. I worked along a ledge to the south, found easier going, and in a short time was two hundred feet or more up the rock wall. I was above Doug, twenty-five feet or so, and fifty feet to his right. We had been extremely careful to test each toehold and fingerhold before putting our trust in them. Kloochman is full of treacherous rock. We often discovered thin ledges that crumbled under pressure and showered handfuls of rock down below. Perhaps I was careless; but whatever the cause, the thin ledge on which I was standing gave way.

As I felt it slip, I grabbed for a hold above me. The crevice I seized was solid. But there I was, hanging by my hands two hundred feet in the air, my feet pawing the rock. To make matters worse, my camera had swung between me and the cliff when I slipped. It was a crude and clumsy instrument, a box type that I carried on a leather strap across my shoulders. Its hulk was actually pushing me from the cliff. I twisted in an attempt to get rid of it, but it was firmly lodged between me and the wall.

I yelled to Doug for help. He at once started edging toward me. It seemed hours, though it was probably not over a few minutes. He shouted, "Hang on! I'll be there."

Hang on I did. My fingers ached beyond description. They were frozen to the rock. My exertion in pawing with my feet had added to the fatigue. The ache of my fingers extended to my wrists and then along my arms. I stopped thrashing around and hung like a sack, motionless. Every second seemed a minute, every minute an hour. I did not see how I could possibly hold.

I would slip, I thought, slip to sure death. I could not look down because of my position. But in my mind's eye I saw in sharp outline the jagged rocks that seemed to pull me toward them. The camera kept pushing my fingers from the ledge. I felt them move. They began to give way before the pull of a force too great for flesh to resist.

Fright grew in me. The idea of hanging helpless two hundred feet above the abyss brought panic. I cried out to Doug, but the words caught in my dry throat. I was like one in a nightmare who struggles to shout—who is then seized with a fear that promises to destroy him.

Then there flashed through my mind a family scene. Mother was sitting in the living room talking to me, telling me what a wonderful man Father was. She told me of his last illness and his death. She told me of his departure from Cleveland, Washington, to Portland, Oregon, for what proved to be a fatal operation. His last words to her were: "If I die, it will be glory. If I live, it will be grace."

The panic passed. The memory of those words restored reason.

Glory to die? I could not understand why it would be glory to die. It would be glory to live. But as Father said, it might take grace to live, grace from One more powerful than either Doug or I.

My fingers were as numb as flesh that is full of novocain. They seemed detached from me, as if they belonged to someone else. My wrists, my shoulders, cried out for respite from the pain. It would be such welcome relief if they could be released from the weight that was on them.

Hang on? You can't hang on. You are a weakling. The weaklings die in the woods.

Weakling? I'll show you. How long must I hang on? All day? O.K., all day then. I'll hang on. I'll hang on.

I felt someone pushing my left foot upwards. It was Doug. As if through a dream, his voice was saying, "Your feet are eighteen inches below your toeholds." Doug found those toeholds for my feet.

I felt my shoes resting in solid cracks. I pulled myself up and leaned on my elbows on the ledge to which my hands had been glued. I flexed my fingers and bent my wrists to bring life back.

Doug came up abreast of me and said, "We're even Stephen now."

"Even Stephen?"

"Today each of us has saved the other's life."

It was shortly above the point where Doug saved my life that we discovered a classic path up Kloochman. It is a three-sided chimney chute, a few feet wide, that leads almost to the top. There are several such chutes on Kloochman. In later years Cragg Gilbert and Louis Elrich went up Devil's Chimney on the northeast face in a seven-hour nerve-wracking climb with ropes. Clarence Truitt and many others have gone up the chimney chute that Doug and I discovered. Then as now, this chute was filled with loose rock that had to be cleared away. To travel along the chute, we took off our shoes and tied them to our belts. We climbed the chute in stocking feet, pressing our hands and feet against the opposing walls and we kept our backs to the abyss below us. 209

This day we went up the chute with ease, stopping every eight feet or so to measure our progress.

The sun was setting when we reached the top. We were gay and buoyant. We talked about the glories of the scene in front of us. We bragged a bit about our skill in rock work—how we must be part mountain goat to have reached the top. We shouted and hallooed to the empty meadows far below us.

On Kloochman Rock that July afternoon, both Doug and I valued life more because death had passed so close. It was wonderful to be alive, breathing, using our muscles, shouting, seeing.

We stayed briefly at the top. We went down as we came up, in stocking feet. We raced against darkness, propelled by the thought of spending the night on Kloochman's treacherous wall.

It was deep dusk when we rejoined Walter on the rock fields at the base. We put on our shoes and hurried on. We entered the woods at double-quick time, seeking the trail that led toward the South Fork of the Tieton.

WILLIAM O. DOUGLAS

211

Finding a Poem

1
Trail climbing
you have to watch your footing
tricky with fallen rocks and mosses that crumble
leafmold slippery
hold onto a bush
it springs back
scratching your face
your heart is pounding
your legs are ready to cave in
why do mountains have to be so steep
can't they put them in the plain
you can barely discern the ferns and laurel
amid the tangled brush
the evergreens *are* majestic but
sweating you've rubbed a blister
bugs to slap away
a dried-out stream bed
stony stony
until abruptly
light dazzling
you're in the clear
the air is the highest note ever sung
listen you can hear it echoing
all the way down
while here you kingly are
crowning the world
with this view that
is impossible to describe
a poem.

212

2

Where there seems no way to go
go anyway
don't be put off by what you can't see
get up any which way
scramble on hands and knees
ditching your pride
slide along the bottom for a stretch
clutch at roots
and keep going on
once up there you can look back to
the pathway you have cleared
that will make it easier
next time you climb.

3

Climbing often
not just for the music
but for the in between
the lights and darks of greenery
the patterns of touch
make it a ritual
of going round the same trees
sitting on the same lichen benches
pausing for second breath at the same log
a tradition by now
and yet
you can never duplicate the climb
every time is the first anew.

EVE MERRIAM   213

In the Niche of Time

Mountains, like people, have their own particular personalities—each is unique, each different from any other. And so it is with the San Francisco Peaks, near Flagstaff.

Ages past . . . a fiery birth. Molten, white-hot lava from deep within the earth burst forth through tectonic fracture, searing, cremating all life as it spread, radiating and heaping into conic mountain mass with lofty summit towering 13,000 feet above the level of the sea. Then it cooled. Rocks and boulders began to break down into soil, a bed for life . . . the niches.

Glaciers came to gouge . . . freezing, deadly cold. Life nil beneath the giant creeping ice monster, joined by the relentless, dynamic gnawing forces of erosion, breaking the symmetry of crater and cone . . . new niches from which new life could begin, grow and change through time.

Niches are the little places: hollows under rock overhangs sheltered from the elements, crevices which have caught enough soil to support tiny seeds or merely lichens and moss.

The niches harbor the delicate, the brave, the pioneers—and the intimate personality of the mountain. Niches support the miniature: the scarlet primrose blooming gaily in the shadows, columbine laughing in the breeze, the bent and prostrate bristlecone pine, shuddering in the winter wind as it whistles through the boulders above the tree line. Niches are ever present through the seasons. They make up the mountain, where life occurs.

214   The mountain dominates the landscape for many miles with its

singular beauty. No season is the same, as no two years are alike on the mountain. And with the seasons come the many moods and changes. All this happens in the niches.

Spring brings the thaw. The frozen ground oozes as the temperature rises to the call of another season on the mountain. Tiny sprigs of green begin to push their way toward the sun. Aspen, oak and maple explode into patches of new green, awakening from dormancy. Fresh shoots emerge from the bases of the grasses . . . life begins anew.

Summer is the climax of the year on San Francisco Mountain; life is abundant . . . full . . . beautiful. . . . But summer is so short-lived! The first freezing wind blows in too soon. Aspen green turns to yellow . . . then gold.

Whisk! Overnight the autumn gold of aspen turns to winter gray, as the first of the strong winds denudes the trees in unison, strewing the ground below with a carpet of gold. The mountain begins to sleep again. All this happens in the niches.

So it is that life in these little places is dynamic, ever changing.

Once man has experienced these tiny worlds his concept of the mountain may change, so that when he beholds the magnificent profile against the sky, he remembers what it is that, in combination, makes the mountain perfect with perfect beings in perfect balance.

Descriptions of mountains are always inadequate. Perhaps it is the lack of words in languages, or perhaps that mountains themselves defy description. People are hopefully individuals, too. So that one attempt to describe a particular mountain is singular at its outset and singular at its conclusion.

A mountain is an exclusive experience, whether looking up to the mountain from a distant point on the landscape, or living on its slopes in an intimate relationship. People become a real part of the mountain. Their moods reflect the mountain's moods, and they become a part of the mountain and all its quiet little places. This is infinite in itself. It is the ultimate experience.

John Duncklee

What's It All About?

1. How did Doug and William feel about life after they had climbed Kloochman?
2. Why do you think people risk danger to climb mountains?

1. What made William and his friend decide to climb Mount Kloochman?
2. Why is it more dangerous to go down a mountain than to go up?
3. How did William save Doug's life? How did Doug save William's?
4. Why didn't the boys stop trying after their first unsuccessful attempt to climb Kloochman?
5. What qualities do William and Doug have that make them successful in facing the dangers of climbing Kloochman?

PUTTING IDEAS TO WORK

You are preparing a travel booklet to attract visitors to your part of the country. Select one outstanding scenic wonder and write a description to convince people that it is a great place to see. If photographs are available, you may wish to include them with your writing.

It was my grandmother who made me aware of my value, not as her grandson, Carlos P. Romulo, but as a Filipino, the last word in a tremendous saga.

TAPESTRY:
the Islands and the Man

I could not have been more than three years old when my elders decided it was time I learned the alphabet.

The school I attended was the most exclusive in town—I was the only pupil. Classes were held across the street in my grandmother's home, and she was both faculty and principal.

Young as I was, I had firm opinions concerning my natural rights. It seemed an infraction of liberty to be forced to study inside while the other children played out-of-doors. My older brother had suffered this course and was in public school. Sometimes my sister Lourdes accompanied me, but most of the time I went my laggard way alone.

At ten every morning I was forced from my home and across the street, urged on by cries from both houses. I made the crossing last as long as I dared. Scowling, I would enter the big cool room where my Grandmother was waiting, erect and formidable in a straight-backed Spanish chair. Doña Juana Besacruz Romulo was dignified and charming, and I dearly loved her. But how I hated those implements of torture: the "infant" books in Spanish, the pencils, and slate. In one hand she held like a scepter a long-handled, ivory back-scratcher such as all the Chinese stores sold in those days. I dreaded it! If I forgot and let my thoughts wander to the cries of play coming through the windows, down that scratcher snapped on my tender knuckles with the sting of a red ant.

But I knew how loving she could be when I tried to do well, and how precious was her praise!

So, reluctantly, alternating with whacks from the ivory scratcher, I worked my way through the Spanish ABC's, the *Cartilla* (primer), and the *Caton* (maxims). And when I had done well my good grandmother

taught me my infant prayers and the rudiments of our religion in the form of stories of the saints. She also told me the history and legends and folklore of the Philippines and its people—all in Spanish.

Dear Bae (our pet name for her). If I were a fairy godfather and could grant a wish to every child in the world I would wish for each one such a grandmother as mine. I believe in grandmothers for children. The part mine played in helping to shape my life is beyond calculation. I owe her much, and most of all for her enduring patience with one who must at times have been a most exasperating little boy.

I wish now I had listened with greater care and remembered more of all she told me, for in a wonderful way she wove the history of our family into the tapestry of the Philippines.

Actually, comparatively little is known about the origin of the Filipino race, but later, when I studied the anthropological and historical background of my country, I was amazed to remember how much my grandmother had known and how closely her stories, told to a child, adhered to history.

I was not a good listener. I wanted to be out and away. But much that she said stuck in my memory and is with me still. For she was relating to me the origin of that curious small rebel, myself, and history as it relates to his own being can be fascinating even to a very small child.

The Philippines, like the United States, is made up of many kinds of people. The Filipino is a curious creature, a conglomeration of many races and cultures. In direct descent he is the civilized product of the Malayan race.

My grandmother could not tell me from whence her Malayan ancestors came—and neither do the historians know the origin of these sea adventurers who arrived in the Philippines centuries before Christ was born—but she had heard they came from some island far away off the coast of Asia and that they crossed the always savage waters of the China Seas in paraos, small hand-carved boats.

I was impressed by this story. How brave those long-ago relatives had been to cross the unknown waters and start a new race in a strange country!

They were a cultured people, the Malayans, as civilized as any people living at that period in the world. Some were weavers of cloth, others skilled in the making of articles of glass and iron. Many were farmers and planted the rice that would become the basis of the Philippine economy.

But they were not the first people to occupy our seven thousand islands, any more than the Pilgrim Fathers were the first to live in

America. Long before the Malayans came and long before recorded history, so my grandmother told me, the Negritos—who are the original inhabitants as the Indians are those of America—came to our islands from someplace, my grandmother believed, in Asia.

Anthropologists have found Neolithic implements in our islands, and the Negritos are believed to be the descendants of these early citizens of the Stone Age who may have found their way into the Philippines two million years ago.

Following the Malayan, other cultures filtered into our Islands.

Oriental unity is an historic fact. In the eighth or twelfth century there was the Srivijaya-Vishayan Empire. This empire gave way in the thirteenth and fourteenth centuries to a greater one, centered in Java, called the Madjapahit Empire.

A strong infusion of Hindu and Javanese blood followed, and in the fifteenth century Islam was introduced to the Malayans. There are still many believers in Mohammed in our islands.

The most important of these early centuries, to the Philippines and to me, was the sixteenth, for it was at this time, my grandmother told me, that our own family history began.

My ancestors were members of the civilized Malayan group found in the island of Mactan by the Spanish explorer Magellan when he landed there in 1521 carrying the cross. He fought a duel with swords with Lapulapu, the Malayan chief, and lost, and is buried on the island.

221

But before dying, Magellan had introduced into the Philippines the Spanish blood, culture, and religion that were to play such a strong part in the future of the Filipino people. And it was the Spanish who named the Moslems, who had grouped together mainly on the Island of Mindanao, "the Moros (Moors)."

Then, as now, the Filipinos were gentle, friendly, and eager to learn. Spanish speech came into the many dialects. Spanish blood mingled with blood from the Orient. Filipinos became proud of their Spanish blood, without giving up their pride in the Malayan.

My grandmother had no Spanish blood, but she made me proudly aware of the Spanish blood I had inherited from my mother's side. And somewhere far back, she told me, Grandmother had a Chinese ancestor.

Is it a distorted childhood memory that I believe this ancestor to have been Limahong, the great Chinese adventurer who attacked our coasts in the sixteenth century and was known as "The Pirate"?

Piracy is a matter of whose privacy is disturbed. If Limahong had been Spanish he would doubtless have been known as "the Conqueror" and Hispanic history would have praised him.

At any rate, he was the leader of the Chinese adventurers who in 1574 beached their small ships—which had both oars and sails—in Lingayen Gulf (where four centuries later the Fil-American forces would fight their delaying action against the Japanese) and attacked the city of Manila, which had been founded by the Spanish only three years before.

They failed to take the city, but Limahong and his crews of Chinese Vikings did not return to Cathay. They settled along the Lingayen Gulf and married into Malayan families, and among them was perhaps the unknown forefather of my grandmother. Pirate or no, he was one of my earliest heroes.

By 1600 the Spanish held nearly all our islands. They had become our teachers, our religious instructors, and our conquerors. Some were 222 our ancestors.

Meantime, in this same sixteenth century, a great deal more was happening. The Island of Luzon had been Christianized, whereupon groups of Moslems from the island of Mindanao turned to piracy and made flying raids on our island. They were making surprise attacks on Manila as late as 1837.

Civilization brought the Philippines enemies from every side. Portugal was challenging Spain's hold on the islands. England realized a rich prize had escaped her hands. Sir Francis Drake and Thomas Cavendish—heroes in England, pirates to us—prowled and attacked our coastal towns, causing reproving shakes of the royal crown in Madrid. In 1762 a British expedition made a sneak attack on Manila and captured it.

"Did they keep it?" I asked, worried, for my childish sympathies were far more Spanish that British even though my father had only recently been involved in our revolt against Spain.

But my grandmother told me, no, Manila had been returned to Spain within two years following the terms of the Treaty of Paris.

And after that, she told me, in her beautiful, musical Pangasinan, there had been peace in the Philippines until the very end of the nineteenth century, when the Americans came.

That was where I came in. I knew about the Americans and my father's part in the fight against them. In the Spanish prayers taught me by my grandmother I had prayed that his life be spared and the Americans driven out of Camiling.

That was the only unwelcome chapter in the dramatic story of my country as told me by my grandmother, as I, only half-listening, half-remembering, realized the history of our country was also in a way the story of myself.

What a curious pattern was my ancestry in that foggy past. Later I would try to untangle the many races and rovings, the ambitions and explorations and greed and wars, the cultures and the religions that had merged in one small boy. In my veins was the blood of the dedicated and the venturesome, the pious and those brought to these islands by 223

greed. Malayan and Spanish, Aryan and Oriental, and far back—and my secret favorite—that swashbuckling Chinese pirate.

When I learned to study maps I would look from the Philippines to east and west, south and north, and know the world had swept in from all sides to merge in the Philippines. We were the meeting place, the melting pot of the nations, the bridge upon which rested the four corners of that world.

It was lodged early in my childish mind that the Philippines stood in the exact center of the world, and the thought placed a strange burden on me. I was a Filipino—heir to a multicolored, glowing past. The memory of that background must never be permitted to tarnish. A Filipino was in a position of trust. He had to hold his head high and always show his best side to the world.

Somehow my grandmother drummed that point of view into my wondering mind. She made me aware of my value, not as her grandson and the child of my parents, but as a Filipino, the last word in a tremendous saga. The long adventuring and striving must not be wasted.

I grew in importance as I grew in years because I was a Filipino. To do my best, to increase and never lessen my country's pride was behind

all I might attempt. To that end I had flung myself into sports and studies, into the debating clubs and journalism. I had to be outstanding, to make the greatest effort to win, to prove I was capable not in spite of having been born a Filipino but because I *was* a Filipino.

This has been the driving force of my life. It has also been a restraining force. There were many times I might have given way to loss of temper or dignity, and would not because I am a Filipino.

As one of the new generation of Filipinos under American authority I had the advantage of the new educational and governmental methods America introduced. It was up to me and the others to show the Americans that we had profited. America had promised us our independence. It was up to my generation to prove worthy, to prove that all they had done for us and all we were doing to aid our own self-development was worthwhile.

Someday the Philippines would be free, like America. It rested upon my generation to be ready when that time came and show the world what we could achieve.

CARLOS P. ROMULO

226

What's It All About?

1. Why did Carlos Romulo admire his grandmother so much? Why do you think she took charge of his early education?
2. Why did Romulo feel he had to be outstanding?

1. As a child, how did Romulo feel about his grandmother's teaching? How did he feel about it as an adult?
2. Who are the ancestors of the present-day people of the Philippines? Why do you think so many different people came to live there?
3. Who was Limahong? Why was Romulo so interested in him?
4. What was the chief goal of the Philippines when they were under United States authority?

PUTTING IDEAS TO WORK

Interview the oldest person in your family to find out as much as you can about your family history. Write up or tape-record the interview. Preserve this record for your family's use.

About one order in ten sent to mail order houses is incorrect in one way or another. This causes problems.

Getting It Right the First Time

Many mail orders are delayed or must be returned because they are filled out incorrectly. Careful reading of directions and making out the order form slowly will help solve this problem. An accurate reading of information about the product being purchased helps, too.

    Read the section taken from a catalogue below. Then look at the order form on the next page. The form is completed and ready to be mailed off. But just a minute! The form has eight errors. What are they?

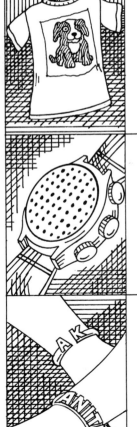

Individualize your T-shirts. Send us your favorite photo (black and white or color). We'll print it on one of our 100% cotton T-shirts. All shirts are white with red collar and cuff trim and are machine washable. Indicate size S, M, L, XL. All photos returned intact.
70227—Photo T-Shirt . . $4.99

Wrist strap radio lets you hear music, news, sports wherever you are! 2½″ diameter AM radio with control dials that look like watch stems. Uses only one penlight battery for hours of enjoyment. Money back Guarantee.
19863—Wriststrap Radio $13.99

What a gift for a special someone! Sterling silver cuff bracelets are ½″ wide with up to seven letters for a first name or two initials. Allow 3 to 4 weeks for delivery.
65717—First Name Bracelet . . . $15.99
65718—Two Initials Bracelet . . . $10.99

Protect your racket with this vinyl waterproof cover. Personalize it with your name written across the cover. All covers done in white vinyl with red vinyl stripes and black lettering. (wipes clean)
10330—Tennis Racket Cover $2.99

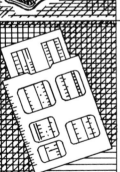

Make conversion to the metric system easy and quick with this convertible rule. There are nine conversions — ounces/grams, pounds/kilograms, inches/centimeters, etc. Large windows for viewing equivalent measurements. Rule measures 6″ by 8″.
87961—Metric Conversion Rule $2.99

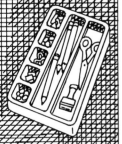

Supply organizer. Keep your desk in order. Places for all items needed for homework or letter writing. Fits in most any drawer, out of sight. Measures 8½″ wide x 11″ long. Made of sturdy smoke-colored plastic. ON SALE—was . . . $4.99
16793—Supply Organizer . . $2.99

ORDER BLANK

Hadley House

2973 Adams Wagon
Landing, Colorado 80012

Name _James Anderson_
Please Print
Address _1433 West Bluff_
City _Pines_ State _Colorado_ Zip _11_

Please print all personalizing instructions clearly						
Catalog Number	How Many	Name of Item (&Personalization)	Size	Color	Price Each	Total Price
65718	1	First Name Bracelet	—	—	15.99	15.99
		"SHIRLEY"				
87961	2	Metric Conversion Rule	—	—	2.99	2.99
70227	2	Photo T-Shirt	—	—	4.99	9.98

4906	1	Bonus-Free Mystery Gift (One with any order over $15.00)

Figure shipping charges with this chart		
If your order costs	Total cost Merchandise	29.95
Up to 2.50—add .50 Up to 12.00—add 1.50 Up to 8.00—add 1.20 Over 12.00—add 1.80	Colorado Residents add 3% sales tax	.80
	Shipping Charges	1.80
	Total Cost of Purchase	31.66

*Reading the fine print is always important. You should always exam-
ine all the facts before purchasing a product or agreeing to join any
kind of club through the mail. Know exactly what you're getting and
what it will cost you.*

Bargains Can Be Expensive

Study the ad on the opposite page. Read all the details. Then answer
the questions about the M&C Record Club.

1. Do those ten records really cost $1.58?
2. What is the obligation involved?
3. About how much will your membership have cost you in two
   years, not counting shipping and handling? Does the ad tell you?
4. Why do you think the detailed information about the club is in
   small print?
5. How does the ad attract your attention?
6. Make a list of your favorite performers. Create your own record
   club ad which will be effective in getting your friends to join. At
   the same time, give *all* the information needed so that those who
   sign up will know the exact cost without having to search for it.

Here are the hits!

Perry Wyns *Far Away and Blue* 9687
The North Hill Gang *A Cowboy's Trail* 4156
Jean E. Speranza *Sing Toward Home* 1789
Doris Capray *Helping You, Helping Me* 1999
Dolly Miles *Great River to Cross* 8476

Jenny Ray *Sky, Rags, and Blue Stones* 1239
Bill Towns *Beyond, So Near* 1050
Mary Brite *Favorites* 1997
Mr. Brown and the Avalanche *Missing you* 9684
The Best of Linda Wallace 1786

Let yourself make music!!
Have fun! You deserve it!

Billie Williams *Lost at Home* 4208
Sara Simpson *The Way I Am* 3246
Liverpool Quartet *Down in the Islands* 5719
Eddy Coy *Tunes of the West* 1679
Helen Bay *Where are You?* 1976

ANY 10 RECORDS* ONLY $1.58
(plus shipping and handling)

M&C Record Club wants to welcome you to our family of music lovers. You can do that by selecting 10 records from the wide selection above for only $1.58 plus $2.95 for shipping and handling. So for $4.53 you will receive 10 albums! That's less than the retail price of one album at your favorite record store. In exchange, for the next two years, you agree to buy 10 more records at our regular club prices. We'll mail you an ad card each month informing you of the selection of the month. If you want it, do nothing. We'll send it to you with a bill for it plus postage. If you don't want it, say so by mailing the card back to us, or by selecting an alternate selection. It's that simple. You have a choice of records at $5.98, 8-track tapes at $7.98, or cassette tapes at $9.98 plus shipping and handling. After that time you may cancel your membership. Act today!—Mail the handy coupon and save!

*If you join now and agree to buy 10 more records in the next two years.

M&C Record Club
1718 Market Street
West Bend, Indiana 47825

Here is my check or money order for $4.53 for my first 10 selections. In the next two years, I'll buy at least 10 more selections at the great prices of the M&C Record Club.

I PREFER:

( ) records
( ) 8-track
( ) cassette

Here are the numbers for my 10 selections

Name _____

Address _____

City _____ State _____ Zip _____

Grandmother loved to read the lost and found advertisements, but she had never found anything herself—until she found a beautiful and expensive lavalier.

I'LL GIVE YOU LAW

When I read the newspaper, there is always a must section in it that I never pass by. This is the lost and found advertisements usually buried in the back pages. I picked up this habit from my grandmother. She always took a keen interest in who had lost what, and who was honestly reporting on items found. She could people a whole colony from just a couple of advertisements.

"Lost—one black puppy with a white patch around its eye. Answers to the name 'Spot.' Please call Beaver 6-5000. Reward."

From this my grandmother would draw for me a picture of a bereft household, of a child sobbing itself to sleep at night, of parents out searching the

232

streets anxiously, calling in hopeless voices. "Spot. Here, Spot. Come on, Spot. Here, boy."

The picture was so visual to both of us we used to sit there with tears in our eyes, willing Spot to answer, wanting the child to cry with joy and not in sorrow.

"Lost—a white platinum ring, inscribed 'To J. from W., forever thine.' Ring not valuable but of sentimental value. Reward."

My grandmother would analyze the situation for me.

"What kind of a woman is she to lose a ring like that?" Grandma would cry sternly. "In the first place, how could it fall off her finger?"

"Maybe it was loose?" I would suggest helpfully.

"Loose? Why should it be loose?" Grandma was not going to accept any of my flimsy excuses. "She didn't have a little string in the house she could wind around the ring so it could fit? Don't give me such stories."

"Maybe she took it off in a washroom when she was washing her hands and then forgot it," I would then suggest.

"A ring like that you don't take off, and if you take it off, you don't forget it. I'm only

sorry for that W., whoever he is. A bargain he hasn't got in her, believe me."

"But, Bubba, how do we know that J. is a woman and W. is a man? Maybe J. is the man and W. is the woman, and *she* gave *him* the ring."

My grandmother was openly amused at such naïveté.

"A lady to give a man a ring?" Absolutely out of the question. My grandmother wouldn't accept it even as a premise.

"Maybe it was a wedding ring," I argued. "Sometimes people have double ring ceremonies."

For the sake of argument, Grandma would concede.

"All right. So J. is the man. So it was a wedding ring. So what kind of a man loses his wedding ring? A good-for-nothing loafer. So what does she need him for? She should let him go with the ring together."

In no time at all, my grandmother would get into a rage at the perfidy of this man, who thought so little of his marriage vows that he didn't have the decency to hang on to his wedding band.

We speculated about all the lost items with equal interest. We wondered about the found

items as well, visualizing the happy claimants, and the honest finders handsomely rewarded. At such moments, God was in Heaven, and all was right with the world.

Then one day, we moved swiftly from the land of fantasy to a world of realities. My grandmother found something!

"What is it? What is it?" I asked, hopping with excitement.

"A lavalier!" My grandmother was absolutely overwhelmed. She had never found anything in her life, and now, here in her hand, was this magnificent lavalier.

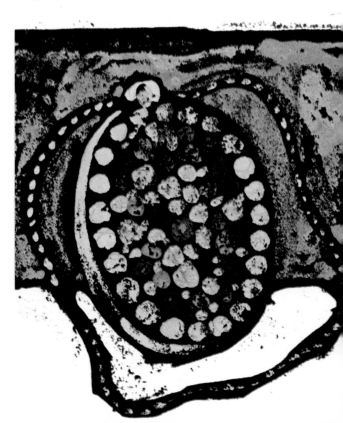

234

"It must be very expensive," I said, running my fingers over it.

"A fortune," my grandmother said positively. She held it up against her. "A regular fortune," she breathed.

"Are you going to keep it?" I asked.

She gave me a sharp look. If the thought entered her mind, she wasn't going to admit it to me.

"Am I going to keep it, she asks. Such a question." She threw her shawl over her head.

"Where are you going?" I asked. "Can I go too?"

"I'm going to the police station. Let them worry about it. You can't come," she added firmly. "A police station is not respectable."

At the police station, the property clerk informed her politely that if the lavalier was not claimed within ninety days, the police department would turn the jewelry over to her, and she would be its rightful and legal owner. He took her name and address and wrote it down. They would let her know, he said indifferently.

"Oh, I hope nobody claims it," I said fervently. "Oh, Bubba, I hope whoever lost it doesn't even know they lost it."

Such a dilemma for my grandmother. If ever she yearned for anything, it was for this lavalier. On the other hand, her active imagination conjured up such tearful scenes that she couldn't wait for the loser to come and claim her property.

She could not compromise with her stern standards. She advertised in the local paper, running the advertisement for three days. Then she had to abandon this, because money spent for anything but food was both wasteful and sinful. During that three-day period, we waited literally with our hearts in our 235 mouths. Every time there was a knock at the door, we could see the lavalier leaving us forever. Meanwhile, my grandmother took to haunting the police station and the property clerk. She would first observe all the amenities. How are you, she would ask, and how is the family? In the beginning he would dismiss this with a curt fine-we-haven't-heard-don't-call-on-us-we'll-let-you-know attitude. But my grandmother began to take a personal interest in the policemen at the precinct. After all, she visited them daily. It wasn't like they were strangers, she would tell me. She knew their names and the names of their wives and the names of their children. She knew at any given moment what child was suffering from what childhood disease, how hard it was to make ends meet on a policeman's salary, what policeman was going to night school to study law and improve his station in life, what policeman was smarting at being passed over when promotions were handed out. Only the property clerk held out. When he would look up and see my grandmother, he would mutter and groan.

"Mrs. Ostrow," he would say, "don't you have anything to do at home?"

"Why don't I have something to do at home?" my grandmother would regard him scornfully. "You think I like to come here day after day?"

"So why do you come?" he would ask logically.

"To see what I have to see," she would tell him cryptically. And then she would demand to see the lavalier with "my own eyes." And then she would subject him to a searching interrogation. Who had come today, and what had they claimed, and wasn't it possible that the lavalier had belonged to one of the people who had come, and had he told anybody about it, and if he was keeping it such a big secret, how could anybody know he had it in the first place?

As fervently as I prayed that no one would show up, he prayed that someone—anyone—would.

"Ninety days," he would cry, clutching his hair. "I'll never survive it."

I never knew that ninety days could last so long. But eventually the ninetieth day arrived, bringing with it much excitement and expectation. My grandmother and I dressed as though we were going to a party. She was going to allow me to go with her for the presentation. On the way we discussed her immense good fortune.

"When I die," she said to me, "I want you to have it."

"Please, Bubba," I said, uncomfortably. It seemed like a grim note to inject in an otherwise cloudless day.

"No," she insisted seriously. "I want you to have it. It will be like a—what is the word I want, Malkele?"

"An heirloom?"

"That's the word." She pounced on it with satisfaction. "And when you die, your children will have it."

In two sentences, my grandmother had disposed of us both.

At the police station, my grandmother was greeted with happy smiles, even from the property clerk. I should say, especially from the property clerk. It was the happiest day of his life.

When my grandmother finally held the lavalier in her hand, her eyes misted over. She couldn't speak, but she nodded her head tremulously at the policemen.

"Don't be a stranger," they urged her. "Don't wait till you find something before you drop in."

"Such nice boys," my grandmother said, as we left the station. She touched her eyes with her handkerchief. "Such good boys, even *him*," she said, referring to the property clerk. "He had his eye on it, but out of respect, he didn't touch it." I believed my grandmother. I didn't see how that property clerk could have looked at that lavalier for ninety days and so nobly fought off temptation.

When we got home, my grandmother promptly put the lavalier on.

"I'll wear it night and day," she vowed. "I'll never take it off." For a week she was as good as her word.

Then one day there came a knock at the door, and tragedy swept in, escorted by an embarrassed and harassed property clerk from the police station.

"Where is it?" cried the woman he had brought to the door. She looked at my grandmother. "My lavalier she's wearing," she cried in horror, pointing to my grandmother.

My grandmother looked at both of them, appalled. Her hand went up automatically to clutch the lavalier.

"It's mine," she said. "You told me, after ninety days . . . "

"That's right," the property clerk said promptly. "Legally it is yours. That's what I've been trying to tell this lady. She didn't

237

claim it in ninety days, and the law says . . . "

"I'll give you law," the lady shouted, vigorously pounding him on the arm. "Does the law ask me where was I the past ninety days? Does the law say after ninety days thieves and murderers can do whatever they want? Law! I'll give you law!"

"Please, lady," the property clerk pleaded. "Let's try to be calm."

"Calm!" she took up the cry. "I'll give you calm!"

My grandmother entered the fray briskly.

"So much commotion," she said. "You want the neighbors to think we're killing you on the doorstep? Come inside." She urged them in and closed the door. "So if you'll stop talking and tell me where you were," she said, guiding the distracted woman to a seat, "we'll listen and we'll be the same good friends."

"Where was I?" the woman said, shaking her head. "My daughter was having her baby, so she says to me, 'Ma,' she says, 'if you don't come, I won't have it, that's all.' Scared to

death with the first child. Wait till she's had six, like me.''

"I had eleven," my grandmother topped her quietly.

"Eleven! So I don't have to tell you," the woman continued. "So I had to go to Scranton yet—a husband takes it into his head to make a living in Scranton," she added in a parenthetical note of disbelief. "With all the children I had to go. One month in advance, just in case. And then, with God's help, the baby comes. Now she's afraid to hold it, it might break. And she's afraid to wash it. It might come apart in the water. And

she's afraid to feed it. It throws up on her. One month. Two months. Finally I say to her, 'Rebeccah,' I say, 'enough is enough already. Whatever you'll do, you'll do.' "

My grandmother was already making tea for everybody, bustling about the kitchen, putting crackers and jam on the table.

"The young people today," she commented, sympathetically.

"So when I come back, I first realized my lavalier is gone. I'm not hung with jewelry, and between you and me and the lamppost," she added confidentially to my grandmother, "I need a lavalier like I need a hole in the head. But when I need a little extra money in an emergency, that lavalier saves my life."

"How does it save your life?" I asked, intrigued.

She made a face, lifting her eyebrows eloquently to the grown-ups present.

"I bring it to the pawnshop and whatever few pennies he gives me . . . "

"The pawnshop!" I was indignant. "She doesn't even *wear* it, Bubba," I said passionately. "Don't give it back. You don't have to. The law says you don't have to."

"That's right," the property clerk said instantly. He was on his second cup of tea and using my grandmother's jam as if the jar had an endless bottom.

The woman opened her mouth to protest, but my grandmother forestalled her by holding up her hand for silence.

"Malkele," she said gently, "there is a law here, too." She laid her hand tenderly on my heart. "Look in your heart and tell me. Suppose it was your lavalier. Suppose you lost it and somebody else found it. Ninety days, a thousand days . . . how would you feel?"

"I would want it back," I answered honestly, "no matter how."

She spread her hands out eloquently.

"So?" she asked me.

"That's not fair," I burst out.

"Fair? Who said anything about fair?" She reached up and took off the lavalier. She fondled it for a moment, and then handed it over to the woman.

"Why should I complain?" she asked no one in particular and shrugged philosophically. "For three months I lived in a dream, and for five days I lived like a queen. Is that bad?"

240

MOLLY PICON

What's It All About?

1. This story presents two views of the law—the law "on the books" and the law "in the heart." What is the difference between these two views? How do the two views conflict in the story?
2. Why does Grandma give up the lavalier after waiting for it for so long?

---

1. Why is Grandma so excited about finding the lavalier?
2. Why does Grandma give the lavalier to the police and advertise for the owner even though she wants to keep it?
3. What reason does Grandma give for visiting the police station every day? What do you think her other reasons might be?
4. What reasons does the owner of the lavalier give for not claiming her property within ninety days?

PUTTING IDEAS TO WORK

Opinions often differ about the value of things. Person "A" lost a favorite possession or pet, and Person "B" finds it, but doesn't think it's very valuable. Write a "Lost" ad for this item from A's point of view, and then write a "Found" ad from B's point of view. Use different descriptive words to show the different values.

The three people whose lives Shirley especially admired had two things in common: they were fighters, and they were women.

The Three Heroines of Shirley Chisholm

Shirley went to Junior High School 178 on Herkimer and Saratoga and then on to Girls' High. She was beginning to have a social life. She and her sisters loved to go to parties where there was dancing.

Shirley discovered that she was very good at dancing. Sometimes when she and her partner were on the dance floor the others would gather around and clap their hands and watch.

"It's funny," she thought, "how I seem to come alive on the dance floor. I know just what to do with my hands and body. I just have to see a step once and I can do it."

A dance called the lindy was popular at the time, and Shirley mastered the steps easily. Her friends would buy some records and they would all get together at each other's homes and lindy and jitterbug. Shirley's favorite dances, she soon discovered, were the Latin ones, especially the rumba and the conga. The whole nation seemed to be in a Latin music craze just then and Shirley was no exception. She could rumba all night, making up her own steps as she went along.

Mrs. St. Hill was horrified by her teen-age daughters' new craze for dancing. "Where will it all lead?" she would say sternly to Shirley 243 and her sisters. "All this fooling around with the boys at your parties will get you into trouble. No nice girl would do those wild dances."

Shirley and her sisters tried to argue that all American teen-agers danced to records, but Mrs. St. Hill wouldn't listen. Rumba-ing and conga-ing was not the way she was brought up in Barbados.

"If the children like music so much," Mrs. St. Hill told her husband one evening, "I think I'll get them a piano. Maybe that will get them off the wild dancing."

Mr. St. Hill just smiled. He had learned long ago that when his wife got something on her mind, there was no stopping her until it was accomplished.

Sure enough, it was just a matter of time before Mrs. St. Hill had purchased a secondhand piano and had it hauled up into the apartment through a window. Shirley did like playing the piano as it turned out. She spent many pleasant hours practicing. But the piano didn't stop her from dancing. She had a lot of energy to get rid of, and dancing was the best way to do it. Besides, she was so good at dancing now that she had even won some prizes at local dance competitions, and winning was a very good feeling.

Mrs. St. Hill particularly disapproved of the big dances the girls loved to go to—the ones that the local boys' social clubs would hold on Saturday nights. When the St. Hill girls were invited to a Saturday night dance, they were allowed to go only if they promised to be home before midnight. "Mother must think we're little Cinderellas," Shirley said to her sisters.

It always happened that Shirley was on the dance floor with her favorite partner when her sister Muriel came rushing over to point frantically at her watch. Shirley never got over being embarrassed that the St. Hill girls were always the first to leave every party. "We must be the laughingstock of the neighborhood," she told Muriel as the girls walked home from a dance one night.

Shirley never let her prizes at the dance competitions turn her away

from her first love, reading. Ever since the days of Granny Scales's farm, when she had read her schoolbooks far into the night by the light of a kerosene lamp, Shirley had adored all kinds of books. She was a fast reader, sometimes going through a book a night. Often the mention of an interesting-sounding person in her American history class would send her to the library to learn more about that person. Since those early days when she had to stay after school to do extra work, Shirley had become a serious student of American history. She was fascinated by the lives of those who influenced the course of American politics.

The lives of three people especially interested her. Not surprisingly, all three were women. They had one other quality in common: they were fighters. The three women that the teen-age Shirley most admired were Harriet Tubman, Susan B. Anthony, and Mary McLeod Bethune.

In the life story of Harriet Tubman, Shirley discovered an important chapter in American history that was only touched upon in her classes. Harriet Tubman, herself an escaped slave from a Maryland plantation, repeatedly risked danger and death to bring slaves North to freedom during the years before the Civil War.

Shirley felt that there was nobody else like Harriet Tubman in American history. The tiny, tough black woman always carried a pistol on her trips down South to the slave plantations. The pistol was for use against betrayers or slave hunters, but Harriet Tubman never had to use it. She was too clever. The slave hunters could never catch her, and none of her own people ever betrayed her.

Dressed in men's clothes to be less conspicuous, Harriet would arrive at a plantation under the cover of night. When she got within shouting distance of the plantation, she sang a song that the slaves knew—like "Follow the Drinking Gourd"—to reveal her presence to those who were expecting her. She led her parties of escaped slaves through woods and swamps to the free states of the North by following the North Star in the sky—the "Drinking Gourd" was a code for the stars that formed the Big Dipper which pointed to the bright North Star.

When she got her parties of escaped slaves up North, Harriet would take them to the homes of freed black men and white abolitionists for sleep and food. That was the Underground Railroad, the secret network of friends and sympathizers that "conductors" like Harriet Tubman relied on.

Harriet Tubman's reputation became legend in the South. Her code name was Moses. The white slaveholders put a price on her head. They wanted her captured, dead or alive. But the slaveholders couldn't believe that "Moses" was a woman. One slaveholder even offered a reward of $40,000 for the capture of "the escaped male slave known as Moses."

Shirley devoured every scrap of information about Harriet Tubman. She learned that Harriet fought as a soldier in the Union Army during the Civil War. She led a troop of three hundred Negro soldiers in one of the most successful raids of the war—against the Confederate forces in South Carolina.

Shirley also learned, with bitterness, that after the war, the U.S. Government for many years refused to give Harriet Tubman a soldier's pension, to which she was entitled, because she was black and a woman.

One day in school, a white boy in Shirley's class had insulted her. They were comparing grades on their test papers. Shirley had gotten the higher mark, and the boy had said, "When I graduate from high school I'm going on to college, but I guess you're not. Negroes don't go to college, do they?"

Shirley had burned. Stiffly she told him that her mother and father expected all four of their children to go to college, and that since her grades were always higher than his, she would have an easier time getting into college too.

The boy was taken aback by Shirley's fast answer, but he wouldn't let the conversation drop. "So what if you get good marks," he went on. "It's much more important for a boy to go to college than a girl. Girls never do anything. They just become housewives. When I grow up I can be President of the United States."

"This girl is going to do something when she grows up," Shirley shot back.

"Oh yeah?"

"Yeah. Or rather, *yes*. My mother taught me to say yes, not yeah. I guess your mother never taught you manners." That ended the argument, and Shirley felt she had won it, but the things the boy had said to her bothered her more than she cared to admit to him.

She knew her American history well enough to know that no black man and no woman—black or white—had ever been elected President. "Why *not?*" she said to herself. "Why *not?*" The girls in her class were just as bright as the boys, and some were even brighter. Why didn't the country let them use their intelligence and education to the fullest?

Was it because, as some people hinted, women didn't want to make anything of themselves? It couldn't be that, Shirley reasoned. That's what people used to say about Negroes. But Shirley knew that white people had always kept black people down. So it must be, she said to herself, that men also wanted to keep women from getting ahead—maybe to keep the good jobs for themselves.

Shirley's second favorite heroine, after Harriet Tubman, was Susan B. Anthony. She was a white woman who spent her life fighting for equality for women. Susan Anthony and Harriet Tubman, Shirley discovered through her reading, were born in the same year, 1820. Harriet was born a slave in Maryland. Susan was born to middle-class Quaker parents on a farm in Massachusetts.

In those days in America, women were not allowed to vote or even hold property in their own name. Women who dared to speak out openly and demand a change in the laws were publicly laughed at.

Susan and a few other women organized a powerful women's rights movement by holding meetings and lectures across the United States. Susan even published a weekly newspaper for women's rights. She called it *The Revolution*.

When the women's rights movement first began, few women or men came to listen to Susan B. Anthony speak. And sometimes when they did come, there were riots. But she went on handing out leaflets, collecting signatures on petitions, and organizing meetings in public halls. She developed a lecture called "Bread and the Ballot." It was a ringing plea to give women the vote to better their economic conditions.

Once, as a test case, Susan marched to the polls and actually voted along with her three sisters in the town of Rochester, New York. She was arrested and found guilty and fined in a court trial. The jurors were all men, of course. *Women* weren't even allowed to serve on a jury—as blacks, men or women, were not allowed to serve on a jury down South.

For a few years before the Civil War Susan B. Anthony devoted herself full-time to the antislavery cause. Harriet Tubman once deposited an escaped slave at Susan's house in Rochester for food and clothing before taking the fugitive farther on the Underground Railroad to Canada and freedom. Susan and Harriet often shared the same speaker's platform at women's suffrage and abolition meetings.

There was much in the lives of Susan B. Anthony and Harriet Tubman that the young Shirley could admire. It made her dizzy to think of such powerful, independent women who by organization, speeches, and courageous action overcame fearful odds and helped to change the course of events of the nation.

If Susan and Harriet could do it, why couldn't she? Anything was possible, wasn't it?

Shirley looked around her for examples of modern women who had the courage of Harriet and Susan. All the boys she knew, and most of the girls, had found their hero in Joe Louis, the heavyweight champion of the world. The Brown Bomber, as Joe Louis was called, *was* inspiring. He could lick any man in the world with his boxing gloves. On the night of a Joe Louis fight, everyone she knew sat glued to the radio, waiting for Joe's knockout punch. And Joe seldom disappointed them.

Shirley was as overjoyed as anyone when Joe Louis won a fight. But, she told herself with a laugh, the one thing she certainly wasn't going to grow up to be was a heavyweight boxing champion of the world!

Shirley found her third heroine in Mary McLeod Bethune. Mrs. Bethune was a trusted friend and adviser of President Franklin Delano Roosevelt when Shirley first became aware of her existence.

The fifteenth child of parents who had been born slaves, the young Mary McLeod had grown up on a farm in South Carolina. She had gotten her first schooling at the age of eight at a Presbyterian mission school. In the early years after Emancipation it was still rare for black children to be sent to school and young Mary had to endure the taunts of white children who made fun of her for wanting to learn.

Learn she did, and education became the guiding force of her life. When still a young woman, she founded a school for Negro girls in Daytona, Florida, getting the black and white community to support her effort by cake sales, fund-raising suppers and pleas to sympathetic businessmen for financial support. The school later became known as Bethune-Cookman College and it took in young men as well as young women.

When Shirley was going to high school, she often saw Mrs. Bethune's picture in the newspaper, as the founder and president of the National Council of Negro Women, as a vice-president of the NAACP—the National Association for the Advancement of Colored People—as a special adviser to President Roosevelt for minority affairs, and as the director of the Division of Negro Affairs for the National Youth Administration.

Shirley liked to see the newspaper photos of Mrs. Bethune with Eleanor Roosevelt, the President's politically active wife. And she liked the group pictures of President Roosevelt and his aides with Mrs. Bethune standing tall and proud among them.

And she especially liked the dignity of this stately black woman. Her name even sounded majestic. Mary McLeod Bethune—it had an important ring to it. Shirley wondered if she would ever be photographed with the President of the United States.

Susan Brownmiller

What's It All About?

1. Who are the three heroines of Shirley Chisholm? Describe each one in a sentence or two.
2. Why did Shirley admire these three women?

---

1. What made Shirley become a serious student of American history?
2. What part did Harriet Tubman play in the operation of the "Underground Railroad"?
3. What rights were women denied in the days of Susan B. Anthony that they have today?
4. Why was education so important to the life and work of Mary McLeod Bethune?
5. As an adult, Shirley St. Hill Chisholm was elected one of the first black members of the United States Congress. How do you think the lives of her "three heroines" influenced her life?

PUTTING IDEAS TO WORK

Write a brief biography of the person (famous or not) you think has added most to your understanding of life. Be sure to tell exactly why and how this person has impressed you.

Example

Like the star
Shining afar
Slowly now
And without rest,
Let each man turn, with steady sway,
Round the task that rules the day
And do his best.

JOHANN WOLFGANG VON GOETHE

*That morning Mack's world had been orderly. Now it was in chaos.
He was just fifteen and suddenly he had become head of a household
with a four-hundred-acre farm to run.*

A SPECIAL KIND OF COURAGE

One Saturday morning in the middle of the fourth planting season after the death of their father, Mack walked over to J.C.'s house. Now fifteen years old, Mack was going to help his brother bring home a bull that J.C. had bought. It was about seven-thirty when Mack got there. J.C. still hadn't come outside, so Mack went ahead and started getting his brother's pickup truck ready for the ride.

When J.C. finally came out his front door, he wasn't saying much, and he looked awful.

"What's the matter, J.C.?" Mack was concerned. His older brother, like his father, never complained about any kind of pain or illness.

"I'm not feeling so good." J.C. was pale and perspiring. "Do me a favor and call up Earl Gunter and ask him to go with you to get the bull."

"Sure, J.C."

"I'm goin' inside to lie down on the couch."

By the time Mack and neighbor Gunter got back to the house with the new bull, J.C. was unconscious. His wife and Cleta, his mother, were there, desperately trying to get him to respond by putting cold towels on his face and talking to him. But there was no response.

The same ambulance from Benton that had carried his father three years before now took J.C. to the hospital. Janice and Mack rode with him. There wasn't enough room for Cleta, so she followed closely behind in the family car.

They kept J.C. in the local hospital for only about thirty minutes. It didn't take the staff there long to realize that they couldn't handle his problem. An ambulance left immediately for St. Luke's Hospital in St. Louis, 180 miles away.

At the height of the planting season, J.C., the stalwart, steadfast rock of a young man, had suffered a stroke. He was thirty years old.

Mack and Janice again rode in the ambulance with J.C. His mother had to arrange for the neighbors to come over to the farm and take care of the animals. As soon as she'd done that, Cleta was also going to head for St. Louis in her car.

J.C.'s young wife cried most of the way. Mack did his best to comfort her, but he needed comforting himself. He was in shock. That morning his world had been orderly. Now it was chaos. He was only a

freshman in high school. His mother was fifty-six years old. With J. C. sick, the two of them were charged with the almost impossible task of holding onto and working a four-hundred-acre farm.

"My father had always told us both no matter what happened, hold onto the farm. He told us no matter how rough things might get, never to give it up."

When Mack remembers that time he gets uncharacteristically misty.

"So when I was fifteen years old, I inherited the tradition and the spirit and the feeling that a family farm is a lot more than just a piece of ground. It was our heritage and our way of life, and I didn't know how I was going to keep it together."

For the next two hours Janice and Mack sat on a metal bench 255 outside the Emergency Room, watching, without understanding, all the hustle and bustle of that frightening place, still not getting any word on J. C.'s condition.

Finally Cleta arrived. She had driven to St. Louis with her brother, Clyde Summers. She clutched at Mack's arms as soon as she spotted him, and asked if he knew anything about J.C.'s condition. After the fifteen-year-old confessed that there was no news, she asked for the attending physician.

When they found the doctor, the bewildered family was told that J.C. had suffered a stroke of some kind, that the extent of the damage was unknown, and that it would be at least two weeks before they would know if he would recover.

"Mack," she said, looking straight and hard at her fifteen-year-old, "you're the man of the family now. You got to get home and take care of the farm."

"But, Ma!"

"Don't worry about me, Mack," she said, holding up her hands as if to stop traffic. "You just get on home and take care of things until J.C. and me get back."

Mack made the long, quiet drive back to Thompsonville with his Uncle Clyde. Janice had also decided to stay in St. Louis, at least for the night.

When Clyde pulled the Chevy up into the big dirt driveway in front of the barn, he and Mack saw eight or ten pickups already parked there. They belonged to the neighbors.

Mack jumped out of the car and hurried into the large red barn where he had spent so many happy afternoons as a kid playing in the hayloft. Now his neighbors were there, tending to the livestock and straightening the place out.

When they saw Mack, the group came quickly over and eagerly began asking questions about J.C.'s condition.

"He's about the same as he was when we left here," was all Mack could tell them. He was near tears, despite his efforts to be manly and in

256

charge of himself. His neighbors saw that, but didn't say anything. They only spoke to offer their time and services, helping him with the farm in any way they could.

"I'll help," said one.

"We'll be here," said another. "Call us whenever you need anything."

For the next two weeks Mack worked getting the fields ready. Despite J.C.'s illness, the soybeans still had to be planted. Everything depended on the new crop, and the neighbors, all farmers themselves, realized that and turned out to help.

Men who had spent long, hot days in their own fields spent their evenings and weekends working on the Gaither farm. They used their own tractors and even insisted on paying for their own gasoline.

The women also helped. After they had cooked and cleaned their own homes, they would walk over in the afternoons and take care of the Gaither house. Mack was touched and grateful for all the help, but he wasn't surprised.

"You know, it just comes natural to farmers. When a neighbor is in trouble and needs help, people lend a hand. We sure needed them, and they turned out."

About three weeks later, Mack went back to St. Louis to help his mom bring J.C. home. His brother had regained consciousness, seemed to be in good health, but was weak as a baby.

When they got him back to Thompsonville, J.C. sat on the porch in front of his house. For a few days he watched Mack, at times helped by   257 neighbors, at work in the fields. By the end of J.C.'s first week at home, he was already getting restless. Mack was doing a good job, but there was so much to be done.

By the end of J.C.'s second week at home, he was up and doing light work around the house and in the barn. In three weeks, the big six-footer was back in the fields, despite the protests of his mom and his wife.

He seemed to thrive on work. Suffering no apparent after-effects of the stroke or whatever it had been, he was soon putting in full thirteen- or fourteen-hour days.

The harvest was good, but J.C. decided after it was all in and work around the farm had slowed that he was going to earn a little extra money. He started working in the oilfields about ten miles south of town.

He'd been at it for a month when Janice called Cleta in the middle of the night. J.C. had suffered another stroke. This time it was a massive, crippling cerebral hemorrhage.

They rushed him to Franklin Hospital in Benton. He was there for a week. This time, J.C. did not completely recover. When they brought him home, he was conscious but paralyzed. The handsome young farmer with dark hair and blue eyes could no longer even feed himself.

One night after Dr. Swinney left, telling the family that there would be no change in J.C.'s condition for the foreseeable future, Janice told

Cleta and Mack that she was leaving J.C. She moved out. This time had been too much.

Mack, at twelve, had understood the significance of his father's words about holding onto the farm, no matter what; but the real responsibility for carrying them out had been his big brother's. Now, when he was sixteen, the burden had shifted—this time for good—to Mack.

J.C. was moved back into the main house. His home was closed, and is still sealed shut.

With the help of his amazing mother, Mack put out the crop. He hired another high-school student to help him. Bruce Higginson's family were laborers in the oilfields, so the seventeen-year-old was free to take the job working with Mack.

Mack also got help from his neighbors. Two who turned out, Ernie and Percy Payne, even insisted on bringing their own sandwiches with them. They didn't take a real lunch break. They would just grab a few minutes late in the day and eat out in the fields, standing alongside their tractors. The two brothers didn't want to go into the house for a proper lunch, because they were afraid it would be too much trouble for Cleta.

But the greatest share of the work, and all the responsibilities, were still Mack's. He had become head of both family and farm at an age when most kids are struggling with decisions like whether or not to try out for the freshman football team.

"Most people would have run away from it," says Joe Williams, one of Mack's closest friends. "Mack was just in the ninth grade, but he still made it work."

Kim Blades, another of Mack's friends and former classmates, agrees. "When things really got bad, Mack had to depend on a lot of other people for support, but when it gets right down to it, he relied only on himself."

Alan Patton, his high-school principal, added that Mack was much more than just independent. "He's outgoing and intelligent. He's had to 259

make adult decisions and do a man's work, even though he was only an adolescent. But he's always come through, and that's made him mature far beyond his years.''

His school, Thompsonville High, is small, about one hundred students. Thirty-one were in Mack's class, ''one of the largest classes we've had in years,'' according to Mr. Patton.

In the school, like the town, everybody knew almost everything about everybody else. The teachers and the school administrators were fully aware of what was happening to the Gaither family, but while they were all very sympathetic, Mack didn't receive any special treatment.

''That's not the kind of help he would have accepted,'' says Mr. Patton. ''Mack always insists on being treated the same as everyone else.''

In the four years he was in high school, Mack never missed a day of classes. He was rarely late, and only occasionally left early, and that was during planting or harvesting, or when there was some problem at home. He never asked for an extension on a term paper, the rescheduling of an exam, or any other special consideration. While running the farm virtually on his own, Mack still managed an A average. Unsurprisingly, his classmates fondly rechristened him ''Superman.''

Not satisfied with this burden, Mack refused merely to get by in   261 school. At Thompsonville, for instance, the average course load is four or five subjects. Mack always signed up for seven or eight, and they were always the most difficult. During his entire high school career, Mack never had a single free study period.

Alan Patton was more than just Thompsonville's principal. Doubling as the school's guidance counselor, he forged close relationships with many of his students, and with Mack, especially, he became almost a second father. Recognizing both the boy's need and obvious abilities, Patton spent hours advising, suggesting, and teaching his star pupil.

"Mack always had an unswerving belief and faith that if he kept doing everything he was able to, then somehow things would work out," reflects Patton.

Typically, Mack would get up at about a quarter past five, and for the next hour he would study, completing the schoolwork left unfinished the night before.

By half past six he was out in the barnyard checking on the livestock. He fed and watered them and checked for anything unusual.

Whatever the season, the hours before breakfast were busy ones, and when he had done what he had time to do, Mack would walk back to the house.

Once inside, he would pick J.C. up out of bed and start getting him ready for the day. He would carefully bathe and shave his older brother, get him dressed, into the wheelchair and down to the breakfast table.

After a quick breakfast made by his mom, Mack would be off. During his first two years of high school he'd wait at the crossroads for the bus. When he was old enough, he drove their slightly battered 1967 pickup truck to school.

The schoolday was filled, but the bell ending his final class was just a signal that he was free to go back to work in the fields. Except for those rare occasions when he stayed to rehearse a play or some other extra-curricular activity, Mack went straight home. Cleta would have a late lunch ready, and as soon as he finished that, he'd pick up where he had left off in the fields that morning. To lengthen his working hours, Mack had night lights installed on both the combine and his tractor. That way he could work the fields until nine-thirty or ten o'clock in the evening.

After he washed the day's dirt off, there would be the evening meal. Fighting the accumulated exhaustion, Mack would always tell his mom and brother about his day. They were confined to the house, and he always tried to make them feel part of his life outside the farm.

When J.C. had been put to bed, Mack was finally free to do his schoolwork. Because he was such a hard-working student, that often meant studying until one or two in the morning. Four or five hours later, it would all start over again.

"Most grown men could never have carried that load," says Mr. Patton.

Mack's problems continued to get worse.

On a Sunday morning in April 1974 he got up at about four-thirty. It was earlier than usual, because he had more to do than he usually did. Mack was in the yard by five o'clock. Still below the horizon, the morning sun was just starting to color in the shadows.

Mack began his day, as he customarily did, tending to the animals. He started there, because he could find his way around the barn and the pens in the dark.

From the barn, he moved into the fields, and he was out there when the sun finally broke on the horizon. He worked, cultivating the long bean rows, expecting after some time passed that his mother would be calling him in for breakfast. As was their Sunday custom, they were going to the eight-o'clock church services. That meant he had to be in the house by seven-thirty if he was going to have time to eat and change his clothes.

Mack wasn't wearing a watch, but like most farmers, he carried a clock around in his head. At one point, it just seemed later than seven-thirty.

263

Mack started walking toward the house, but as his apprehension grew, he started running. Frantically he stumbled right through the wet soybeans, soaking his clothes in his headlong rush toward the house. Once inside he called out for his mother. There was no answer. He ran to her bedroom. She was there, in bed, unconscious and breathing heavily.

Mack tried, but he couldn't wake her. Cleta had also suffered a stroke during the night.

"Oh, no! Not again!" he cried out, standing over his mother's bed, but she couldn't hear him.

He called the ambulance in Benton, for the fourth time in four years. As soon as that was done, he called a neighbor to come over and look after J.C. Then, in the few minutes left before the ambulance arrived, Mack got his brother up and dressed, did the same for his mom, and carried her over near the door, so there wouldn't be any delay once the ambulance got there.

Cleta was taken to Franklin Hospital. For the first week, she was only semiconscious. She couldn't recognize anyone or feed herself.

Mack visited her every day on his way to and from school. Worried because the local hospital was understaffed, he made the four-thirty wake-up permanent. That way he was able to do the chores, get J.C. ready for the day, and still have time enough to drive the ten miles out to the hospital before going to school.

He'd feed his mother breakfast, then get on to school by nine o'clock. Mack would leave school at eleven, feed his mother her lunch, then be back in school by twelve-thirty.

"I knew that if it was me in the hospital," he explained, "then she would have always been right there."

For the three weeks Cleta was in the hospital, Mack also had to find time to study for his rapidly approaching senior finals.

While she hadn't been as hurt by the stroke as J.C. had been, Mrs. Gaither still needed constant attention after she finally came home from the hospital. So to Mack's already impossible burden of a large farm, an invalid brother, and a difficult school schedule was added the need to care for his elderly, heartbroken, and crippled mother.

Earlier in the year Mack had made a final decision to go on to college after he graduated from Thompsonville High. Farming was part of his blood, but he wanted to expand his horizons, thinking always that he could come back home after he had earned his degree. Because of his impressive record, he had been offered scholarships to a dozen colleges and universities, among them the Air Force Academy, West Point, and Harvard.

Harvard was his first choice, and when word came that he'd won a scholarship there, it was one of the high points of his life. He talked it over with Mr. Patton, his mom, J.C., and Joe Williams. All of them enthusiastically agreed. Mack would accept the offer; he would be going to Harvard.

The plan was shattered when Cleta suffered the stroke. Now she was unable to care even for herself. Mack wrote to Harvard explaining 265 the situation and requesting more time to think about his future plans. The college, which had offered a $5,250 scholarship, was sympathetic, but needed an answer by the end of May. Mack desperately wanted to go, but with the further collapse of his family situation, it seemed impossible.

While he wrestled with this problem, there was no rest from his daily routine. Actually, things got tougher for him. It was the beginning of the planting season. He was also right in the middle of his final exams.

When Mack had finished disking the fields and plowing one evening, he came into the house for dinner. Several of his neighbors had come over and prepared a meal for him and the family. As Mack ate, everyone silently watched him. He looked up from his plate, conscious that something was going on.

"What's up?"

His mother, whose speech had not been harmed by her illness, answered. She gently explained how both she and J.C. were determined that Mack go to Harvard. They would manage, somehow, if he went. But if he didn't go because of them, it would break their hearts.

It was Alan Patton, the school principal, who came up with the answer several days later.

"Somewhere, somehow," he told a group of Mack's classmates, "we've got to find somebody to help that family and get them some financial aid."

The school newspaper published his remarks, and several students offered to contribute either time or money to help the Gaithers. Mr. Patton also set up the Angus Mack Gaither Trust Fund. Barb Leebens, a reporter for *The Southern Illinoisan* newspaper, heard about the effort and ran a story about Mack's situation. It was later picked up by *Time* magazine and became national news. The response was overwhelming.

From virtually every state in the union, donations and letters of encouragement came pouring into Thompsonville. Paul Hellmuth, of

Boston, gave Mack a thousand-dollar-a-year grant to help pay the medical expenses of Cleta and J.C. A nineteen-year-old senior from a high school in Liberty, Texas, sent five dollars. Mrs. Thomas Leach, of Tulsa, Oklahoma, contributed one hundred dollars a month for a year. Another woman, from Waukegan, wrote asking for Mack's measurements so she could make him some clothes for school, and there were scores of other gifts. Perhaps the most touching came from an eighty-year-old widow in Albuquerque, New Mexico. She sent Mack a little note. "I know how difficult it is to make some decisions. I know how it is to be alone. I would send you everything I have, as your story deeply touched me." Enclosed in the note was a money order for one dollar, made out to the trust fund.

On the last Sunday in May, the deadline set by Harvard, Mack wired that he would be gratefully accepting the scholarship offer. In all, he had received more than six thousand dollars in contributions, enough, at least, for the family to make it through his first year.

"It made me very proud to be an American," he said in his totally sincere way. "Generous people from all across this great country made one of my dreams come true . . . and I'm very thankful."

Mack graduated from high school in June. The exercises were held in the school gymnasium, and he delivered the valedictory speech: "We observe today a beginning, as well as an end . . . a sense of anticipation for the future, a fullfillment in the accomplishments of the past. . . . "

Mack went off to Harvard and scored impressively in his first year there. Both his mother and brother also made great strides in their recoveries. Cleta is up and around again, and J.C. can sit up in his wheelchair and clothe and feed himself.

Despite going off to that fancy college back East, Mack plans to return to the country to live.

"People always come back. They may go away for a while, even a long while, but they always come back. There's something about farming and Franklin County that gets in your blood. It's the tradition, the family thing, and the sense of community. You can never forget it, no matter how far away you go. You always come back."

268

GERALDO RIVERA

What's It All About?

1. What problems does Mack face? What are his personal characteristics that keep him going?
2. How do you feel about Mack's accomplishments?

1. Why did Mack's father want the family to hold on to the farm no matter what happened?
2. How do the neighbors help the Gaither family?
3. What kinds of responsibilities make Mack more mature than most teenagers?
4. Make a time schedule showing how Mack spends a typical day.
5. What makes it possible for Mack to go to college? Why do you think everyone seems to want Mack to go to college?

PUTTING IDEAS TO WORK

Imagine you are writing a letter of recommendation for Mack. You are trying to convince a college to accept him as a student. Write a one-sentence statement about one of Mack's outstanding qualifications, such as his capacity for hard work, his ability to assume responsibility, and so on. Then complete the paragraph with examples, facts about Mack that prove your statement.

Magazines, newspapers, advertising flyers, and the post office all bring us coupons which tempt us to buy.

Coupons! We've Got Lots and Lots of Coupons

Have you noticed the different approaches used to encourage you to buy? Study the collection of grocery coupons below.

1. How many different techniques for influencing customers to buy a product do you see? Name at least three.
2. Which coupon is for a new product?
3. What coupon advertises a savings at first glance but will cost you more money if you purchase the product? Why does it cost you more?
4. Which coupons do you think give the customer the best buys?
5. Design three coupons of your own. Use three special approaches to get the customer to buy your product.

Grill Time
1 qt. Charcoal Lighter Fluid

Ideal for barbecues beach, or picnics. Quick start; burns clean. Saves you 20¢

49¢ CAN REG. 69¢

Limit 1 per coupon, 1 coupon per customer
Valid Wednesday May 19 thru Saturday May 22, 1978

15c 15c
15¢ OFF SCRUB CLEANER

8¢ **8¢**

Fontana's Cheese Ravioli Meat Sauce

IT'S NEW!

To Grocer:
Mail to Fontana's P.O. Box 1752 Clarey, Ohio 62741 or present coupon to our sales representative. Coupon expires December 31, 1980.

8¢ **8¢**

SAVE 15¢
ON ANY TWO VARIETIES OF DOGGONE DINNERS FROM DALMATION

15¢ 15¢

15¢ **STORE COUPON** 15¢

25¢ OFF
MANAGER'S PRICE

one coupon per item of your choice
unless otherwise specified

plus 20¢ OFF
Peterson's Grocery adds 4/5 the value for a total of ▶

45¢ GRAND TOTAL SAVINGS

Hayes "You Get to Choose" coupon from Hayes
ANY 42 oz. OR LARGER
DETERGENT

With this coupon and $5.00 minimum purchase, excluding alcoholic beverages, tobacco, and fluid milk products.
Coupon good Thursday May 15 thru Wednesday May 21, 1980

25¢ OFF

Limit one item per coupon and one coupon per customer.

SAVE $1.50

(with these 12 money-saving coupons)

Inside specially marked cans of BT-AT Coffee, you'll find coupons worth a total of $1.50 for these 12 great breakfast favorites. Coffee has always helped breakfast taste better. Now it is helping breakfast cost less. So look for the BT-AT labels marked "Save $1.50." You'll save money and get the enjoyment of coffee with a rich aroma and flavor. Enjoy Breakfast Time-Anytime Coffee whenever you like. It's always good. Hurry! Supplies are limited.

Save 13¢ on Valley Bottled Grape Juice

Save 17¢ on Lite-Side Cholesterol-Free Egg Substitute

Save 15¢ on Arbie's Hash Brown Potatoes

Save 15¢ on Lumber Jack Buttermilk Pancake Mix

Save 15¢ on Vermont Pancake Syrup

Save 15¢ on Breakfast Time Corn Flakes Cereal

Save 7¢ on Seasoned Pepper

Save 12¢ on Farmer's Brown 'N Serve Sausage (links or patties)

Save 7¢ on Lite-Side Margarine

Save 12¢ on Quick Clean Paper Towels

Save 7¢ on Quick Clean Paper Napkins

Save 15¢ on Lite-Side Granulated Sweetner

1. What must you do in order to get the $1.50 worth of coupons?
2. Are you told how much the coffee costs? The cereal?
3. Do you get your 50¢ refund right away for the cereal?
4. How much money must you spend for a 50¢ refund? Is it clear? How do you claim your refund?
5. Suppose the coffee costs $6.50 per can. If you use all the coupons and subtract their value from the price of the coffee, how much will the coffee cost you in the end? What does the coffee cost if you use only 3 of the 15¢ coupons?
6. When you subtract your 50¢ refund from the price of the cereal ($1.75), how much does the cereal cost in the end? Suppose it costs 25¢ to mail the side panels and value statements, then how much does the cereal cost in the end? Is it worth it? Do you really save 50¢?

Only Five Days

Below is a typical ad that might be found in any local newspaper.
Read it and study all the information it gives.

1. In what ways does the ad attempt to get people to buy?
2. What phrases or words are used for special appeal?
3. What phrases or words are used for urgent appeal?
4. Which item will give the greatest amount of savings? What is the drawback in buying this mattress?
5. How does the ad attempt to get customers to buy the more expensive items?
6. Why do you think the ad reads ''$68.00 each piece'' rather than ''$136 per set''?
7. Find similar ads in your local newspaper. Read them and look for words and phrases that are used for special appeal. Bring them to class for discussion.

ONLY FIVE DAYS LEFT!
Sleep Comfort Super Rest

At one low Price for Twin, Twin X-Long, Full

A Low $68.00 Per Piece

for mattress or spring base
Save 16.95 to 105.95—how much is up to you.
We've made it easy to get the mattress you deserve.

Size	Reg.	Sale
Twin	84.95 ea. pc.	$68 ea. pc.
Twin X-long	94.95 ea. pc.	$68 ea. pc.
Full	104.95 ea. pc.	$68 ea. pc.
Queen	269.95 set	$176 set
King	369.95 set	$264 set

TODAY THROUGH MONDAY

Even greater savings on the queen and king sizes.
Easy Credit terms available

Also available, a limited number of Sleep Comfort Royal Rest with extra, even support. Ask the salesperson. (Not at our Huntington Mall Store)

The Sleep Shop

489 Pendergast Highway
10-6 P.M. Mon.-Fri.

10-5 P.M. Saturdays
1-5 P.M. Sundays

A Most Unpredictable Japanese Lady

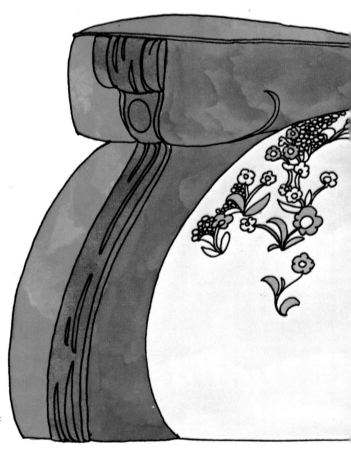

Mother was still glowing with excitement. She looked exquisite and beautiful in her best gown of pale lavender silk velvet. But what party had she attended?

Mother's haphazard way with the English language did not always work against her. I remember once she became involved in a switch of identity and lived for a day like royalty, suddenly swept into high society. It happened when Sumiko and I were rabid fans of Mickey Mouse and members of the Mickey Mouse Club at the Coliseum Theater which met every Saturday morning. We sang Mickey Mouse songs, we saw Mickey Mouse pictures, we wore Mickey Mouse sweaters, we owned Mickey Mouse wrist

watches. Because the club had the endorsement of the Parent-Teacher Association, Father and Mother raised no objections to our latest craze.

One Saturday there was to be a very special party to which we could invite our mothers. There would be a Mickey Mouse drawing contest for the members and refreshments for everyone. Mother said although she would like to be there, she was too busy Saturday morning. Sumiko and I wept.

"But, Mama, everybody else's mother will be there. We'll be the *only* ones without a mother. People will think we're orphans."

Fortunately, a few days before the event, Mother went to a P.T.A. meeting at Bailey Gatzert School at which time Miss Mahon, our school principal, pleaded with the Japanese mothers to go to this particular party with their children. Women of different nationalities would be there and Miss Mahon wanted to see the Japanese represented. Miss Mahon stirred Mother's conscience. Mother decided to go. Sumiko and I knew it was going to be one of the biggest, happiest parties we would ever attend.

That bright Saturday morn-

ing Sumiko and I put on our best red coats and matching red berets. We bounded down the long flight of stairs, clutching our Mickey Mouse sketches and ran all the way downtown. Mother had promised that she would follow later, as soon as she had finished the hotel chores. We had drilled Mother on the location of the theater building. With a thick red crayon, we printed the name of the theater, its address and the name "Pike Street," the block where she was supposed to get off the streetcar, on a big sheet of paper so Mother could not lose it or herself.

Having taken these precautions, Sumiko and I relaxed. At the Coliseum Theater, we pushed our dimes through the box-office window, deposited our drawings in a large chest in the foyer and slid into our seats, breathless with hope that one of us would win a prize. The meeting started off as usual. The same double-chinned master of ceremonies greeted us, shook with laughter at his jokes and raved a great deal about what a wonderful time we were going to have. He introduced a bouncy, Dutch-bobbed five-year-old girl named Patsy who tap-danced and sang for us. Later the lights were dimmed, the words of songs were flashed on the screen and Patsy led us in singing our Mickey Mouse songs. Soon it was time for the judging of the picture contest. Sumiko and I also thought it was time for Mother's appearance. We went to the lounge where we had agreed to meet her. No one was there. Little Sumiko's lips started to tremble. I said, hastily, "She'll be here soon. Let's wait."

We sank deep into the luxurious low sofa and waited silently. Hours seemed to pass and still there was no Mother. We hurried back to our seats to see what was going on, but it was hard to keep our attention focused on the stage. We learned that the pictures were still being judged upstairs. Everyone was getting restless, and two boys started wrestling in the aisle. Soon a team of ushers swooped down the aisles, distributing ice cream in Dixie cups and cookies. While we thoughtfully ate our refreshments, the master of ceremonies suddenly appeared and announced the names of three contest winners. Our spirits sagged when neither of our names was mentioned; and worse than that Mother was lost.

The party over, the auditorium, hallway, and lounge soon filled with chattering boys and girls and their smiling, bright-eyed mothers. We made one last inspection of the theater without success. Maybe Mother was wandering downtown, lost and bewildered. Or maybe she had just decided not to attend.

We headed back home with an ache lodged deep in our throats. How could Mother have failed us, after she had promised us a dozen times? We climbed heavily up the hotel stairs, made our way to our living quarters with a solemn expression on our faces, all set to reprove Mother. The rooms were empty. We scurried through the dim labyrinth of halls until we found Father in the last room at the other end of the hotel. He was busily making the bed. Indignantly I asked, "Papa, where is Mama? Why didn't she come to the party?"

"*Nani?* Why, Mama left about half an hour after you both had gone. I was afraid she would be late so I told her to take a taxi. Where could she have gone?"

We were thoroughly alarmed. Sumiko burst out crying. Father, looking harried, put the finishing touches on the bed, picked Sumiko up and led me out of the room.

"Now, now, don't start that. Mama's all right, wherever she

277

is. She's been downtown before by herself. Maybe she just walked into the wrong place. If Mama isn't home in an hour, I'll call the police."

At the word "police," I started to cry, too. Father sighed and took us into the kitchen where he tried to stifle our sobs with cookies. "Now, why don't you two go back to the parlor and play a while. I have a little more work to do."

No, we didn't feel like it. We wanted to be with him. We trailed after him with wet faces and damp cookies, really feeling like orphans now. As Father pushed the carpet sweeper carefully over the frayed edges of the rug, he asked questions about the party. Between sniffles and bites, we managed to give Father all the boring details. Then all of a sudden behind us, we heard the sweetest voice in the world. It was Mother.

"Ka-chan, Sumi-chan," she said happily, "wasn't that a lovely party?"

Father stopped sweeping. Sumiko and I stared at her, wondering what party she had attended. Mother was still glowing with excitement. She looked exquisite and beautiful, in her best gown of pale lavender silk velvet. Delicate floral patterns were traced in velvet, woven over a background of sheer voile. A huge butterfly rhinestone pin held the drape on the side of the skirt. Mother also wore a close-fitting, beige helmet over her freshly marcelled black hair. The long length of hair was coiled into a low, thick bun at the nape of her neck. She looked pretty and out of place, standing in the doorway near the mop and the laundry pile. She turned brightly to Father, "By the way, what does 'consul's wife' mean?"

"Consul's wife? What in the world . . . why, that's the wife of a *ryoji*. Why do you ask?"

"Arrrah!" Mother shrieked in horror. "A *ryoji's* wife! *Doshima sho.*"

Mother clapped her hand to her mouth, then to her head as if she didn't know what to do next. Sumiko and I jumped all over her, trying to get her attention.

"Mama, Mama, what happened? Where were you anyway? We waited for you all morning."

Mother then burst into hysterical laughter and the only words we could get out of her were, "*Mah, iyayo!* What shall I do? *Tondemo nai kotoyo.*"

We went back to the parlor and waited impatiently for

278

Mother to subside. Father scolded her, "Where were you all this time? The children have been crying all morning."

With tears of laughter in her eyes, Mother told us the whole story. She had gone to our Mickey Mouse party. The taxi driver had delivered her to the front of the Coliseum Theater. Just as soon as she had stepped out of the cab, a suave, beautifully groomed woman pounced on Mother and escorted her into the theater. "We're so glad you could come, Mrs. Saito. We're having quite a party this morning."

Mother felt slightly overpowered with this warm reception, but she smiled politely back at the nice lady as if she were quite used to such cordiality.

"Thank you. I'm late little bit. I'm so sorry."

"It doesn't matter in the least, Mrs. Saito. You're in time for the important part of the program."

Mother didn't completely understand what the woman was saying, but she realized she was being addressed as Mrs. Saito. She corrected her new friend, "I'm Mrs. Itoi."

"Oh? Er . . . you're the Japanese consul's wife, aren't you?"

Mother didn't know what she meant, but she knew very well she should be agreeable at all times. She said, "Yes, thank you."

Obviously, the hostess had been assigned the special task of taking charge of the Japanese consul's wife, Mrs. Saito. The eager hostess had stepped out of the theater door several times and when at last a beautifully gowned Oriental woman had stepped out of a cab she thought the quarry was safe in her hands. The woman trilled to Mother, "Oh, Mrs. Saito, I wonder if you would do us the honor of acting as one of the judges for our Mickey Mouse drawing contest?"

"Yes, yes," Mother answered absent-mindedly, wondering why the woman kept calling her Mrs. Saito. "I'm Mrs. Itoi."

"I beg your pardon, Mrs. Itoi." The hostess paused for a moment, and then began again, "You *are* the consul's wife?" This time she asked the question slowly and loudly. "Yes!" Mother replied, almost snapping. The woman was certainly asking a lot of questions. The hostess finally seemed satisfied with Mother's positive reply.

Just then, a woman walking in front of her stumbled. Her

279

high heel had caught the edge of the carpet and both heel and shoe came off. Mother dove for the torn heel and shoe. She had fixed many a broken heel. The woman with the broken heel said, "Dear me, it would happen now."

"I fix for you," Mother

assured her.

The hostess's eyes widened, "Please, Mrs. Saito, er, Mrs. Itoi, the maid will do that." She turned in desperation to the woman, "I'd like you to meet Mrs. Saito, the Japanese consul's wife."

The introductions were made, but Mother ignored them both, adjusted the heel into the nail holes, kneeled down and pounded it back into place on the marble floor.

"Fixed now, I think." Mother returned the shoe to the pink-faced woman while the hostess made high-pitched sounds.

Mother was led upstairs to a luxuriously furnished room which glittered with mirrors and elegant crystal chandeliers, the like of which Mother had never seen. The room was filled with the subdued murmurs of distinguished-looking guests. The hostess introduced Mother to many gay, enchanting people. Mother caught words like "Swedish . . . English . . . German . . ." and heard the same mysterious expression, "consul's wife" over and over again. Soon everyone was addressing Mother as Mrs. Saito and Mother let it pass good-naturedly. Far be it from her to keep correcting these lovely people. Nobody seemed to mind that Mother hardly said anything except, "I'm glad to meet you," and "Yes, thank you" whenever refreshments were offered to her, and "I think so" when she couldn't understand the topic of conversation.

Mother sipped delicious coffee from a tiny, doll-sized cup and nibbled at dainty sandwiches of all shapes and colors. On the tables were gleaming silver platters of bonbons, cookies and assorted nuts. Mother felt as if she were part of a movie set.

Soon the hostess came up to Mother again and closeted her in a small, adjoining room with three other smartly dressed women who spoke English with heavy foreign accents. No one understood what the other was saying, but somehow they picked the prize pictures of Mickey Mouse. They went back to the reception room again for some more polite chatter and laughter. Half an hour later the party drew to a close. Mother bade farewell to her new acquaintances, the French consul's wife, the English consul's wife, the German consul's wife, and a few more. They all shook her hand cordially, "Goot-by, Mrs. Saito. It was just loavely meeting you. . . . "

What charming manners! What delightful ladies! The same attentive hostess escorted Mother out of the theater, hailed a taxi for her and waved farewell. Mother sank back in the rear seat, feeling positively giddy with the personal attention and hospitality that had surrounded her from the beginning to the end. The cab driver had to ask her, "Where to lady?"

"Yes, please. Oh! . . . 217 Occidental Avenue."

The driver glanced back at her twice. Mother, looking like an Oriental princess of the court, sat fanning herself with her perfumed silk handkerchief and sighing . . . my, my what a grand party it had been and such cultured, gentle people. Miss Mahon will be certainly glad to know I took part and helped with the picture contest. The taxicab sped through the downtown shopping district and plunged into the fish and barnacle atmosphere of the waterfront where our hotel was located.

We have often wondered if the reception committee of the gala Mickey Mouse Club party ever discovered this error. We thanked God that Mrs. Saito, the Japanese consul's wife, had not appeared. Mother might have been hustled out of the theater as an impostor and criminal. Then we thought of something worse . . . maybe Mrs. Saito did attend, but nobody had met her at the door. She would have had to pay an admission fee at the box office to get in and been forced to find a seat for herself in the audience of screaming, squirming youngsters. I wondered if an usher had handed her a Dixie cup of ice cream and a cookie, too. She probably would have resented such shabby treatment and reported it to her husband, the Japanese consul. We saw international complications arise and diplomatic relationships slip a notch between America and Japan. For days after, Mother was not quite herself as she wavered between sudden bursts of laughter and mortified mutterings.

MONICA SONE

What's It All About?

1. Where was Mother, the "unpredictable Japanese lady," supposed to go that Saturday? What did she end up attending? What caused the mix-up?
2. Read the last sentence of the story. How does Mother feel about her experience?

---

1. The story is told by Kazuko Itoi (Monica Sone) who looks back on her childhood in Seattle. How did Kazuko and her younger sister Sumiko feel about the Mickey Mouse Club and this party in particular?
2. Why did Mother decide to attend the party?
3. How did Kazuko and Sumiko enjoy the party? How did their mother enjoy the party she attended?
4. Why did the family worry that Mother was lost?
5. What do you suppose would have happened if the consul's wife had come to the party? What would each woman have done?

PUTTING IDEAS TO WORK

Mistakes may be amusing or embarrassing. They might even be valuable on occasion. Describe some kind of mistake you once made and what happened as a result of it.

"I was no longer just a blind kid competing against other blind kids," said Tom Sullivan. *"I could hold my own in the sighted world."*

On Equal Terms

Like an airliner beginning to move down the runway for takeoff, my whole life suddenly gathered momentum.

Sport now shifted from back-yard games with Sullivan rules into the high adventure of real contest. Wrestling gave me the opportunity I'd been waiting for. It was a chance to test muscle, coordination and self-discipline not only against my Perkins classmates but, on a basis of equality, against those who had no physical handicap.

The man who helped me learn the art of wrestling, and along the way helped ease me out of the eddies of self-pity, was Dick Kamus, the Perkins wrestling coach.

Himself only partially sighted, Dick saw in the gangling kid before him not only a willingness to try hard but a potential to win. Had Dick not been my coach, my first wrestling match against a sighted opponent would surely have been my last.

My first meeting with Dick was when he instructed the boys in my class to report to the gym. There he took each of us by the shoulders and threw us one by one to the floor. The other kids protested meekly, but I responded by getting off the floor and butting the coach in the stomach with my head.

"So you're the one with a temper," said Dick, laughing. "I'm going to teach you a contact sport where you may get hurt. But if you lose your temper you'll be no good."

Dick used two methods to teach us wrestling. First we went through the different movements and holds with him, feeling where his hands and feet were placed and the poise of his body. Then he gave a number to each of the movements. If he called three, for instance, we locked our hands around our opponent's knees. On the call of five we dropped our opponent and got on top of him.

At fourteen, I was the youngest member of the Perkins upper-school team. The hour before my first match I was very nervous. Then my name and weight were called. Rubber-legged, I walked to the mat. Instead of a roar of encouragement, laughter swept through the gymnasium. I learned that I was the object of the laughter when Coach Kamus shouted at me as I got to the mat, "Your uniform's inside out."

In the locker room I had put on my tights and pants with the school colors (red and blue) against goose-pimpled flesh and left exposed to spectators the white fluff of the lining. I must have looked as if I'd dressed to play an Easter bunny. Across my backside flapped a label reading "Machine wash warm—tumble dry."

Shamed and shattered before my friends and rivals and, worse still, before my parents, who . . . had come to see my first match, I turned to run back to the locker room. Then, during a momentary ebb of laughter, I heard Dick Kamus growl, "Quitting, Tom? I thought you were gutsy!" I hesitated, then turned once more toward the mat, thrusting out a trembling hand to a confident opponent. The match was over in thirty-seven seconds. I was thrashed! My humiliation was followed by more pain. I wept alone in the shower. . . .

In my next five matches Mom and Dad heard five referees pronounce my opponents winners. . . .

Before my seventh match, even Dick Kamus told me I had no chance. "Your boy's three years older than you are, Tommy," he cautioned, "and he's never lost. But learn from him, eh?"

A curious effect of the coach's lack of confidence was my total freedom from pre-match nerves. . . . In fact, I was nonchalant as I shook hands with my opponent. No one in the gym was more surprised than I was when I took him down in the first period. In the second, he equaled the points with a reversal. In the third period I "escaped," and

thus chalked up my first match win by a score of three to two.

Although I wasn't to lose again in 384 consecutive wrestling matches (a record that led me to a U.S. national title and an invitation to Olympic trials), this first win was the most exciting sports victory of my life. It dawned on me that I was no longer just a blind kid competing against other handicapped kids. I wasn't a sightless boy for whom rules had to be changed. For the first time I had shown my family and friends, and all those people who had patted me on the head and pitied me, that I could hold my own in the sighted world. I had shown that in a real international sport that did not favor the handicapped, I, Tommy Sullivan, could win.

My blood boiled with exhilaration. Standing alone in the same shower where I had wept after my first match, I now stood, white-knuckled and grinding my teeth, deciding I wasn't going to be merely a wrestler, but a champion.

Now when Dick Kamus coached us, I stopped fooling around and hung on to his every word. I practiced the movements, the holds, the rhythms, the reactions until I could have carried them through in my sleep—and always that important fraction of a second faster than my opponents, real or imagined.

Wrestling was not without its pain and broken bones. Since the match began with both wrestlers in the standing position, I was almost always taken down in the first period, when my sighted opponent had the advantage. But because of my determination to win, I always discovered inner reserves of strength. In one match I was thrown to the second row of the bleachers during the first period. I cracked two ribs, hit my head and suffered a concussion. I still have no recollection of the second and third periods of that match or of the two other matches that afternoon in which I competed and won. . . .

But at the age of fourteen, through wrestling, I wedged my foot in the door to the sighted world, the world that almost everyone else took for granted.

288   Tom Sullivan *and* Derek Gill

JOE ROTH

Joe Roth refused to let his life become a soap opera. He lived well and he died young.

The tragedy is that Joe Roth died in the prime of his life, but the triumph is that he continued to live in the best way he knew how. He lived well and he died young.

It is a tribute to Joe Roth that he chose to live his life as he did, by being Joe Roth, human being, and not Joe Roth, tragic cancer victim. He refused to let his life degenerate into a soap opera.

It was 10 minutes before the start of the Cal-Washington basketball game. The two teams were out on the court, dribbling, shooting, talking idly. Cal's band was there, firing light-hearted insults at the Straw Hat Band.

The Straw Hat Band yelled something back, and then began singing "Happy Birthday" to Cal assistant coach Bill Berry. The mood of the crowd was a happy one—the Bears were going for their fourth straight conference win.

Five minutes later, athletic director Dave Maggard boomed his voice over the public address system. "Ladies and gentlemen, may I ask you to stand, please.

289

This afternoon, after a brief illness, a great California athlete, Joe Roth, passed away. . . . "

James Edwards, Washington's seven-foot center, stood at centercourt. He winced when he heard the news, then his knees gave slightly. Two of Cal's cheerleaders buried their faces in their hands. The crowd moaned.

"I'd like to have a moment of silence for Joe. . . . "

Once Joe Roth talked about his life and his career at Cal.

"I think a lot of people would give their right arm to be in my shoes," Joe said.

What he said then sums up his short but intensely rich life. The way he lived his life was an example of the power of the human spirit.

Joe Roth first had cancer while a freshman at Grossmont Junior College in San Diego. Three years later, the cancer—melanoma—cropped up again after Cal's second football game against Oklahoma.

Joe did not want attention brought to this development, and, along with Cal's coaching staff, he kept it secret. Then the melanoma flared up violently again. And again, on Roth's request, his sickness remained secret until January

1977, when the story became public.

Joe Roth played nearly all of the 1976 football season with the knowledge that he had cancer and could die at any time. All of his football exploits and records became meaningless in comparison with the extraordinary amount of courage and class Joe displayed.

Joe could have easily let the knowledge of his cancer become public. He could have had an overwhelming amount of sympathy. But it is a tribute to Joe Roth that he chose to live his life as he did, by being Joe Roth, human being, and not Joe Roth, tragic cancer victim.

Although weakened by chemotherapy treatments and a loss of weight, Joe refused to let his life turn into a soap opera. He played in the Hula and Japan Bowl games, returned to Cal for the 1977 winter academic quarter, and played on an intramural basketball team.

As late as February 15, 1977, Joe was scheduled to speak at a medical symposium at the Claremont Hotel on life-threatening illnesses. By this time he had been hospitalized, but his desire to help others was as strong as his desire to live life to the fullest.

The last week he was in the hospital, Roth's doctors told him that he wouldn't make it through the weekend. At first they wanted to amputate his legs. But Roth didn't want to die with part of him missing.

Joe had said on several occasions that he would always be grateful for the opportunity he had at Cal, the opportunity not only to play football but to have made the friends he did.

The converse is also true. Joe Roth was a genuinely modest and sincere person. Virtually everyone who knew him came away impressed with Joe as a refreshingly honest person.

Joe Roth was the kind of person it would be hard to imagine as having an enemy. He never bragged about himself or his accomplishments, preferring instead to talk about his teammates. Typically, after he passed for a school record 380 yards against Washington two years ago, Joe praised his receivers for getting open and his offensive line for giving him great protection.

At first, this seemed like false modesty on Roth's part. But it soon became apparent that this was just Joe Roth. He neither basked in deserved glory nor offered hollow excuses in defeat. Football was not Joe Roth's life. Living was.

In this respect, Joe Roth's life was not tragic. He lived as long and as well as his life would permit, and when the time came, he was prepared to meet his fate.

Joe Roth died Saturday, February 19, 1977, at 3:55 P.M. in his Berkeley apartment, sitting up in bed, surrounded by his parents, two brothers, several teammates, and Cal coach Mike White.

The tragedy is that Joe died in the prime of his life. But the triumph is that he continued to live in the best way he knew how, knowing he did all he could, and was fully prepared to die. His courage in the shadow of death is a lesson to us all.

One day several weeks before he died, Joe Roth was back on campus, attending school. On this particular day, he was walking through Sather Gate, laughing softly and talking with Cal water polo player Dave Post. His face showed no concern for his grave condition.

That moment told more about Joe Roth than any number of words can ever hope to. Many millions of words have been written about death and dying, but none are so appropriate as these four that someone once said:

The good die young.

Joe Roth died at 21 years of age. They were 21 good years. He lived well and he died young.

291

Photo by Tobin Spirer

. . . *The moment of silence in memory of Joe Roth was too short. But almost as if on cue, Cal's Straw Hat Band flowed gently into a moving rendition of Cal's alma mater. Everyone who knew the song sang it.*

It was then that knees weakened, lumps quickly lodged in people's throats, and eyes watered. Those who were there will never forget that moment.

JOHN CRUMPACKER
and JON ROCHMIS

292

To
an Athlete
Dying Young

The time you won your town the race
We chaired you through the market-place;
Man and boy stood cheering by,
And home we brought you shoulder-high.

Today, the road all runners come,
Shoulder-high we bring you home,
And set you at your threshold down,
Townsman of a stiller town.

Smart lad, to slip betimes away
From fields where glory does not stay
And early though the laurel grows
It withers quicker than the rose.

Eyes the shady night has shut
Cannot see the record cut,
And silence sounds no worse than cheers
After earth has stopped the ears:

Now you will not swell the rout
Of lads that wore their honors out,
Runners whom renown outran
And the name died before the man.

So set, before its echoes fade,
The fleet foot on the sill of shade,
And hold to the low lintel up
The still-defended challenge-cup.

And round that early-laureled head
Will flock to gaze the strengthless dead,
And find unwithered on its curls
The garland briefer than a girl's.

A. E. HOUSMAN

What's It All About?

1. What difficulty did Tom Sullivan have to live with? Joe Roth? How did each handle his problem?
2. What do you think is the secret of overcoming difficulties, both large and small?

---

1. Why is wrestling a sport that gives blind and sighted contestants an equal chance to win?
2. How successful did Tom Sullivan become at wrestling?
3. What personal characteristics made a winner of Sullivan?
4. Why did Joe Roth want to keep his sickness a secret?
5. Why did so many people admire Roth when he was alive?

PUTTING IDEAS TO WORK

Everyone has difficulties to live with. Write a paragraph that describes a problem you have. Write a second paragraph telling how you would handle it.

295

Worlds in the Making

Where are
Our yesterdays,
Our tomorrows?

A WORLD TO COME

It would be a small meeting. Of the twenty-two original members, many had already left town to avoid arrest by the British. The time had come for men and women to stand up for the rights of good citizens everywhere.

It was fall, and for the last time Samuel Adams told Johnny to call the Boston Observers for eight o'clock that night.

"After this we will not meet again, for I believe General Gage knows all about us. He might be moved to arrest Mr. Lorne. He might send soldiers to arrest us all."

"I hardly think they would hang the whole club, sir. Only you and Mr. Hancock."

Johnny had meant this for a compliment, but Sam Adams looked more startled than pleased.

"It has been noticed that every so often many of us are seen going up and down Salt Lane, entering the printing shop. We must, in the future, meet in small groups. But once more, and for the last time . . . and make us a good punch."

As Johnny went from house to house, talking about unpaid bills of eight shillings, he was thinking of the punch. Not one ship had come into Boston for five months except British ships. Only the British officers had limes, lemons, and oranges these days—they and their friends among the Boston Tories. Miss Lyte had plenty of friends among the British officers. He'd get his tropical fruit there.

Mrs. Bessie, the Lyte's cook, listened to him.

"And who's going to eat these fruits or drink them, if I do give you some?"

"Well . . . Sam Adams for one."

"Don't say any more. Give me your dispatch bag, Johnny." She returned with it bulging.

It would be a small meeting for, of the twenty-two original members, many had already left town to get away from the threat of arrest by the British. Josiah Quincy was in England. Of the three revolutionary doctors only Church and Warren remained. Doctor Young had gone to a safer spot. James Otis was at the 297

Sam Adams

Johnny Tremain

John Adams

James Otis

moment in Boston. Johnny had not notified him, although he had founded this club in the first place. Ever since he had grown so odd, the other members did not wish him about, even in his lucid periods. He talked and talked. Nobody could get a word in edgewise when James Otis talked.

This, the last meeting, started with the punch bowl on the table instead of ending with it. They were talking about how General Gage had at last dared send out a sortie beyond the gate of Boston and, before the Minute Men got word of their plans, they had seized cannon and gunpowder in Charlestown and had gotten into their boats and returned to Boston. Not one shot had been fired, and it was all too late when the alarm had been spread and thousands of armed

Dr. Joseph Warren

Paul Revere

John Hancock

farmers had arrived. By then the British were safe home again. Yet, Sam Adams protested, this rising up of an army of a thousand from the very soil of New England had badly frightened General Gage. Once the alarm spread that the British had left Boston, the system of calling up the Minute Men had worked well indeed. The trouble had been in Boston itself.

"In other words, gentlemen, it was our fault. If we could have known but an hour, two hours, in advance what the British were intending, our men would have been there before the British troops arrived instead of a half-hour after they left."

Johnny had been told to carry letters for the British officers and to keep on good terms with their grooms and stable boys over at the Afric Queen. Somehow he had failed. He hadn't known. Nobody had known that two hundred and sixty redcoats were getting into boats, slipping off up the Mystic River, seizing Yankee gunpowder, and rowing it back to Castle Island for themselves.

299

Paul Revere was saying, "We must organize a better system of watching their movements—but in such a way that they will not realize they are being watched."

Sam and John Adams were standing, and the other members were crowding about them, shaking hands with them, wishing them success at the Continental Congress in Philadelphia. They were starting the next day. Everyone was ready to give them advice—whom to see, what to say, or to prophesy the outcome of this Congress. Paul Revere and Joseph Warren were apart a little, making plans for that spy system, which was needed badly. They called Johnny to them, but he was too intent on listening to a man standing near the Adamses: "But there must be some hope we can still patch up our differences with England. Sir, you will work for peace?"

Sam Adams said nothing for a moment. He trusted these men about him as he trusted no one else in the world.

"No. That time is past. I will work for war: the complete freedom of these colonies from any European power. We can have that freedom only by fighting for it. God grant we fight soon. For ten years we've tried

this and we've tried that. We've tried to placate them and they to placate us. Gentlemen, you know it has not worked. I will not work for peace. Peace, peace—and there is no peace. But I will, in Philadelphia, play a cautious part—not throw all my cards on the table. Oh, no. But nevertheless I will work for but one thing. War—bloody and terrible death and destruction. But out of it shall come such a country as was never seen on this earth before. We will fight. . . . "

There was a heavy footstep across the floor of the shop below. Rab leaped to the ladder's head.

"James Otis," he reported to the men standing about Adams.

"Well," said Sam Adams a little crossly, "no one needs stay and listen to *him*. Still talking about the natural rights of man—and the glories of the British Empire! You and I, John, had as well go home and get a good night's sleep before leaving at dawn tomorrow."

Otis pulled himself up the ladder. If no one was glad to see him, at least no one was so discourteous as to leave. Mr. Otis was immediately shown every honor and given a comfortable armchair and a tankard of punch.

Seemingly, he was not in a talkative mood tonight. The broad, ruddy, and good-natured face turned left and right, nodding casually to his friends, taking it for granted that he was still a great man among them instead of a milestone they all believed they had passed years before.

He sniffed at his punch and sipped a little.

"Sammy," he said to Sam Adams, "my coming interrupted something you were saying. . . . 'We will fight.' You had got that far."

"Why, yes. That's no secret."

"For what will we fight?"

"To free Boston from these infernal redcoats and. . . . "

"No," said Otis. "Boy, give me more punch. That's not enough reason for going into a war. Did any occupied city ever have better treatment than we've had from the British? Has one rebellious newspaper been stopped—one treasonable speech? Where are the firing squads and the jails jammed with political prisoners? What about the gallows for you, Sam Adams, and you, John Hancock? It has never been set up. I hate those infernal British troops spread all over my town as much as you do. Can't move these days without stepping on a soldier. But we are not going off into a civil war merely to get them out of Boston. Why are we going to fight? Why, why?"

There was an embarrassed silence. Sam Adams was the acknowledged ringleader. It was for him to speak now.

"We will fight for the rights of Americans. England cannot take our money away by taxes."

"No, no. For something more important than the pocketbooks of our American citizens."

Rab said, "For the rights of Englishmen—everywhere."

"Why stop with Englishmen?" Otis was warming up. He had a wide mouth, crooked and generous. He settled back in his chair, and then he began to talk. It was such talk as Johnny had never heard before. The words surged up through the big body and flowed out of the broad mouth. He never raised his voice, and he went on and on. Sometimes Johnny felt so intoxicated by the mere sound of the words that he hardly followed the sense. That soft, low voice flowed over him—submerged him.

" . . . For men and women and children all over the world,"

302

he said. "You were right, boy, for even as we shoot down the British soldiers, we are fighting for rights such as they will be enjoying a hundred years from now.

" . . . There shall be no more tyranny. A handful of men cannot seize power over thousands. A man shall choose who it is shall rule over him.

" . . . The peasants of France, the serfs of Russia. Hardly more than animals now. But because we fight, they shall see freedom like a new sun rising in the west. Those natural rights God has given to every man, no matter how humble. . . . " He smiled suddenly and said, "or crazy," and took a good pull on his tankard.

" . . . The battle we win over the worst in England shall benefit the best in England. How well are they over there represented when it comes to taxes? Not very well. It will be better for them when we have won this war.

"Will French peasants go on forever pulling off their caps and saying, 'Oui, Monsieur,' when the gold coaches run down their children? They will not. Italy. And all those German states. Are they nothing but soldiers? Will no one show them 303 the rights of good citizens? So we hold up our torch—and do not forget it was lighted upon the fires of England—and we will set it as a new sun to lighten a world. . . . ''

Sam Adams, anxious to get that good night's sleep before starting the next day for Philadelphia, was smiling slightly, nodding his gray head, seeming to agree. He was bored. It does not matter, he was thinking, what James Otis says these days—sane or crazy.

Joseph Warren's fair, responsive face was aflame. The torch Otis had been talking about seemed reflected in his eyes.

"We are lucky men," he murmured, "for we have a cause worth dying for. This honor is not given to every generation."

"Boy," said Otis to Johnny, "fill my tankard."

It was not until he had drained it and wiped his mouth on the back of his hand that he spoke again. All sat silently waiting for him. He had, and not for the first time, cast a spell upon them.

"They say," he began again, "my wits left me after I got hit on the head by that customs official. That's what you think, eh, Mr. Sam Adams?"

"Oh, no, no, indeed, Mr. Otis."

"Some of us will give our wits," he said, "some of us all our property. Heh, John Hancock, did you hear that?

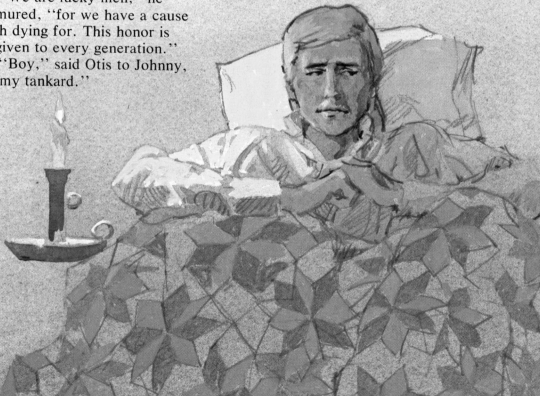

Property—that hurts, eh? To give one's silver wine coolers, one's coach-and-four, and the gold buttons off one's waist-coats?''

Hancock looked him straight in the face, and Johnny had never before liked him so well.

"I am ready," he said. "I can get along without all that."

"You, Paul Revere, you'll give up that silvercraft you love. God made you to make silver, not war."

Revere smiled. "There's a time for the casting of silver and a time for the casting of cannon."

"Doctor Warren, you've a young family. You know quite well, if you get killed they may literally starve."

Warren said, "I've thought of all that long ago."

"And you, John Adams. You've built up a very nice little law practice, stealing away my clients, I notice. Ah, so it goes. Each shall give according to his own abilities, and some—" he turned directly to Rab— "some will give their lives. All the years of their maturity. All the children they never live to have. The serenity of old age. To die so young is more than merely dying; it is to lose so large a part of life."

Rab was looking straight at Otis. His arms were folded across his chest. His head was flung back a little. His lips parted as though he would speak.

"Even you, my old friend— my old enemy? How shall I call you, Sam Adams? Even you will give the best you have—a genius for politics. Oh, go to Philadelphia! Pull all the wool, pull all the strings and all the wires. Yes, go, go! And God go with you.

305

We need you, Sam. We must fight this war. You'll play your part—but what it is really about . . . you'll never know."

James Otis was on his feet, his head close against the rafters that cut down into the attic, making it the shape of a tent. Otis put out his arms.

"It is all so much simpler than you think," he said. He lifted his hands and pushed against the rafters.

"We give all we have, lives, property, safety, skills . . . we fight, we die, for a simple thing. Only that a man can stand up."

With a curt nod he was gone.

Johnny was standing close to Rab. It had frightened him when Mr. Otis had said, "Some will give their lives," and looked straight at Rab. Die so that "a man can stand up."

Once more Sam Adams had the center of attention. He was again buttoning up his coat, preparing to leave, but first he turned to Revere.

"Now *he* is gone, we can talk a moment about that spy system you think you can organize in Boston."

Paul Revere, like his friend, Joseph Warren, was still slightly under the spell of James Otis.

"I had not thought about it

306

that way before," he said, not answering Sam Adams's words. "You know, my father had to flee France because of the tyranny over there. He was only a child. But now, in a way, I'm fighting for that child . . . that no frightened, lost child ever is sent out a refugee from his own country because of race or religion." Then he pulled himself together and answered Sam Adams's remarks about the spy system.

That night, when the boys were both in bed, Johnny heard Rab, usually a heavy sleeper, turning and turning.

"Johnny," he said at last, "are you awake?"

"Yes."

"What was it he said?"

"That a man can stand up."

Rab sighed and stopped turning. Soon he was asleep. As had often happened, it was the younger boy who lay wide-eyed in the darkness.

"That a man can stand up."

He'd never forget Otis with his hands pushed up against the cramping rafters over his head.

"That a man can stand up," as simple as that.

And the strange new sun rising in the west. A sun that was to illumine a world to come.

ESTHER FORBES

What's It All About?

1. Why do the Boston Observers want war? What rights and ideals do they want to protect?
2. Describe the "world to come" that Johnny dreams of. Do you think it has come? Why?
3. Write a brief summary of the story told by the poem "Paul Revere's Ride" on pages 308 to 312.

---

1. Who are the Boston Observers?
2. Why does Sam Adams feel the time has come to fight for freedom?
3. Why does James Otis at first say they should not go to war?
4. Later what reasons does Otis give for going to war?
5. Otis says that we must fight so "that a man can stand up." What does he mean?
6. What will people have to give up in order to gain their human rights in war?

PUTTING IDEAS TO WORK

Imagine you are present at some great moment in American history, just as Johnny was present at the planning of the American Revolution. Write a conversation between two people living at that moment or a report telling about it.

Paul Revere's Ride

Listen, my children, and you shall hear
Of the midnight ride of Paul Revere,
On the eighteenth of April, in Seventy-five;
Hardly a man is now alive
Who remembers that famous day and year.

He said to his friend, "If the British march
By land or sea from the town tonight,
Hang a lantern aloft in the belfry arch
Of the North Church tower as a signal light—
One, if by land, and two, if by sea;
And I on the opposite shore will be,
Ready to ride and spread the alarm
Through every Middlesex village and farm,
For the country folk to be up and to arm."

Then he said, "Good night!" and with muffled oar
Silently rowed to the Charlestown shore,
Just as the moon rose over the bay,
Where swinging wide at her moorings lay
The Somerset, British man-of-war;
A phantom ship, with each mast and spar
Across the moon like a prison bar,
And a huge black hulk, that was magnified
By its own reflection in the tide.

Meanwhile, his friend, through alley and street,
Wanders and watches with eager ears,
Till in the silence around him he hears
The muster of men at the barrack door,
The sound of arms, and the tramp of feet,
And the measured tread of the grenadiers,
Marching down to their boats on the shore.

Then he climbed the tower of the Old North Church,
By the wooden stairs, with stealthy tread,
To the belfry chamber overhead,
And startled the pigeons from their perch
On the somber rafters, that round him made
Masses and moving shapes of shade—
By the trembling ladder, steep and tall,
To the highest window in the wall,
Where he paused to listen and look down
A moment on the roofs of the town,
And the moonlight flowing over all.

Beneath, in the churchyard, lay the dead,
In their night encampment on the hill,
Wrapped in silence so deep and still
That he could hear, like a sentinel's tread,
The watchful night wind, as it went
Creeping along from tent to tent,
And seeming to whisper, "All is well!"
A moment only he feels the spell
Of the place and the hour, and the secret dread
Of the lonely belfry and the dead;
For suddenly all his thoughts are bent
On a shadowy something far away,
Where the river widens to meet the bay—
A line of black that bends and floats
On the rising tide, like a bridge of boats.

Meanwhile, impatient to mount and ride,
Booted and spurred, with a heavy stride
On the opposite shore walked Paul Revere.
Now he patted his horse's side,
Now gazed at the landscape far and near,
Then, impetuous, stamped the earth,
And turned and tightened his saddle girth;
But mostly he watched with eager search
The belfry tower of the Old North Church,
As it rose above the graves on the hill,
Lonely and spectral and somber and still.
And lo! as he looks, on the belfry's height
A glimmer, and then a gleam of light!
He springs to the saddle, the bridle he turns,
But lingers and gazes, till full on his sight
310 A second lamp in the belfry burns!

A hurry of hoofs in a village street,
A shape in the moonlight, a bulk in the dark,
And beneath, from the pebbles, in passing, a spark
Struck out by a steed flying fearless and fleet:
That was all! And yet, through the gloom and the light,
The fate of a nation was riding that night;
And the spark struck out by that steed, in his flight,

Kindled the land into flame with its heat.
He has left the village and mounted the steep,
And beneath him, tranquil and broad and deep,
Is the Mystic, meeting the ocean tides;
And under the alders that skirt its edge,
Now soft on the sand, now loud on the ledge,
Is heard the tramp of his steed as he rides.

It was twelve by the village clock,
When he crossed the bridge into Medford town.
He heard the crowing of the cock,
And the barking of the farmer's dog,
And felt the damp of the river fog,
That rises after the sun goes down.

It was one by the village clock,
When he galloped into Lexington,
He saw the gilded weathercock
Swim in the moonlight as he passed,
And the meetinghouse windows, blank and bare,
Gaze at him with a spectral glare,
As if they already stood aghast
At the bloody work they would look upon.

311

It was two by the village clock,
When he came to the bridge in Concord town.
He heard the bleating of the flock,
And the twitter of birds among the trees,
And felt the breath of the morning breeze
Blowing over the meadows brown.
And one was safe and asleep in his bed
Who at the bridge would be first to fall,
Who that day would be lying dead,
Pierced by a British musket ball.

You know the rest. In the books you have read,
How the British Regulars fired and fled—
How the farmers gave them ball for ball,
From behind each fence and farmyard wall,
Chasing the redcoats down the lane,
Then crossing the fields to emerge again
Under the trees at the turn of the road,
And only pausing to fire and load.

So through the night rode Paul Revere;
And so through the night went his cry of alarm
To every Middlesex village and farm—
A cry of defiance and not of fear,
A voice in the darkness, a knock at the door,
And a word that shall echo forevermore!
For, borne on the nightwind of the Past,
Through all our history, to the last,
In the hour of darkness and peril and need,
The people will waken and listen to hear
The hurrying hoofbeats of that steed,
And the midnight message of Paul Revere.

HENRY WADSWORTH LONGFELLOW

A Gentleman Scientist

Why would a man stay up all night just to look at the stars?

Benjamin Banneker, grandson of an ex-indentured servant and a freed slave, grew up on his family's Pennsylvania farm. In a day when few were educated, Banneker learned to read. He attended school as long as he could and read every book he could find. By the time he reached manhood, he had begun to teach himself advanced mathematics and science. In addition to running the farm after his parents' deaths, Banneker devoted much time to scientific studies and experiments. But for a long time there was no one nearby with whom he could discuss what he had learned.

313

Banneker's life underwent an unexpected change in 1772. In that year, the Ellicott family moved into the Patapsco valley. The Ellicotts were Quakers and members of one of the more well-known Maryland families. They were surveyors and they all had a keen interest in mathematical and scientific matters. Andrew Ellicott was known as one of the more important surveyors in the Colonies.

The Ellicotts had come to the valley to set up a flour mill. It did not take long for the Ellicotts and Banneker to become close friends. Joseph Ellicott and Banneker had much in common. And the Ellicotts encouraged Banneker to expand his scientific work.

When the Ellicotts set up their mill it seemed like a poor idea. Most of the farmers raised tobacco rather than wheat. However, the Ellicotts assured the success of their mill by encouraging the farmers to switch to wheat. The reputations of the Ellicotts contributed to their persuasive powers, and they soon had a successful business. The uncertain political situation also stimulated the change from tobacco to wheat. The possibility of separation from Britain was very real. With that separation, the major market for tobacco would be cut off. At the same time, there was a good domestic market for flour. The mill became the center of the region and soon a village called Ellicott's Lower Mills grew in the area of the mill.

The setting up of the mill was lucky for Banneker in many ways. The Ellicotts and the mill employees purchased fruit and honey from the Banneker farm. More people moved in. This resulted in more sales and prosperity for Banneker and his mother. The major benefit to Banneker was not the sale of more honey and fruit. It was the Ellicotts, who were accomplished mathematicians and fairly active amateur astronomers. Banneker at last had the companionship of people who shared his interests and accomplishments.

As was the custom of the time, Banneker and the Ellicotts visited each other frequently.

The mill became a gathering place for Banneker, the Ellicotts, and
314 other interested villagers. The news-hungry village people hoped to pick

up bits of information from the discussions of Banneker and the Ellicotts. George Ellicott traveled a great deal. When he did he spoke of his accomplished black neighbor. Banneker soon found that his mail increased. More and more people requested mathematical problems and solutions.

Contact with the Ellicotts did indeed encourage Banneker to do more scientific work. But the demands of the farm kept him from doing as much as he would have liked. Banneker was really not interested in farming. He farmed only because he had to do something for a living. He would have much preferred to spend his time on mathematical and astronomical studies, but science is not the kind of thing that lends itself to part-time efforts. Banneker decided to make himself a full-time scientist.

He discussed the problem with his friend George Ellicott in 1783, and Ellicott agreed to buy Banneker's land. Banneker and Ellicott worked out a system of payments. Banneker could live on the land while Ellicott paid him for it. Banneker now had a patron of sorts and a private income. Benjamin Banneker, the grandson of a slave and an indentured servant, was now a "gentleman scientist."

When Banneker sold his land it amazed his neighbors. They could not understand why a man would give up one of the best farms in the entire Patapsco valley. Banneker now settled into a routine which shocked his neighbors. Every clear night he would leave his cabin with a blanket and notebooks. He would lie flat on his back looking at the stars until dawn. Then he would return to his cabin for sleep. Rising at noon he would spend the rest of the day working on his calculations and correspondence.

To the good farmers, sleeping away half the day was nothing short of sinful. Many of the neighboring farmers had some very unkind things to say about this black man who neglected his farm. They could never begin to understand why a man would care to stay up all night just to look at the stars.

Banneker carried out his observations with only his eyes and brain as tools. Since he owned no books on astronomy and no instruments, his observations was severely limited. That situation changed dramatically in 1787. George Ellicott gave him some astronomical books and instruments.

With the aid of the books and instruments Banneker began to organize his observations into information which he would later put into an almanac. The Ellicotts had encouraged Banneker to work on an almanac and had offered to help him get a publisher. Almanacs were in very wide use at that time. Next to the Bible, an almanac was the book most likely to be found in American homes of the period. Farmers depended on them for planning their work. Almanacs contained the times of the rising and setting of the sun, moon, and planets. They also included weather predictions and little articles on various topics. They were the "poor man's encyclopedia."

Before he could do much work on his almanac, Banneker was called on for another task. Politicians had agreed that a permanent site for the nation's capital had to be chosen. Moving about from one place to another did not encourage the people's confidence in Congress. The "residence bill," establishing a permanent federal district, was finally passed in 1790. The bill did not specify the location, but left it to the President to make a choice. Although George Washington was the President, the choice of site was really a political compromise between Thomas Jefferson and Alexander Hamilton.

Hamilton was generally recognized as the spokesman of the North, for strong central government; Jefferson upheld the southern view of more powers for the individual states. Hamilton agreed to get northern support for a southern capital city if Jefferson would encourage Southerners to support a measure which served to strengthen the central government. Thus, a compromise was reached.

The chosen site for the "Grand Columbian Federal City" was a ten-mile square of land on the Potomac River. It was near the town of Georgetown, about forty miles from where Banneker lived. To plan the city, President Washington appointed a "Board of Commissioners."

Chosen to do the actual planning was the engineer and architect, Major Pierre Charles L'Enfant. L'Enfant had come to the United States from France as a volunteer during the Revolutionary War.

L'Enfant had grand visions for the Federal City. He saw it as a city of broad sweeping boulevards and magnificent public buildings. His plan included boulevards radiating out from central points like spokes of a wheel. This design was similar to Versailles, Rome, and other European cities. L'Enfant did not concern himself too much with such details as where people were going to live in this grand city. Nor did he plan necessary services for the population. Although he changed his mind often, he fiercely defended his ideas for the moment that he had them. Since he ignored all suggestions from anyone, he was very difficult to work with.

L'Enfant was asked to produce a map of the planned city. This was very important politically. The Congressmen who were voting the money wanted to be sure that the money was for something real and not imagined. Despite much prodding L'Enfant failed to produce the map. As time went on, Washington and Jefferson were afraid that Congress might give up the whole plan.

Jefferson tactfully suggested to L'Enfant that a surveyor be appointed to assist him. At Jefferson's suggestion, Washington appointed Andrew Ellicott for the job. Upon accepting the appointment, 317

Ellicott asked Banneker to be his assistant. Banneker accepted and Ellicott relayed the information to Jefferson. The official appointment was made by President Washington. Thus Benjamin Banneker became the first black presidential appointee in the United States.

L'Enfant's cooperation with Ellicott and Banneker was grudging and reluctant. Usually there was no cooperation at all. The site swarmed with land speculators who were trying to buy up lots even before the streets had been laid out and the location of the lots decided. Once a politically important person started to erect a house in the middle of where New Jersey Avenue was supposed to be. L'Enfant flew into a rage and had the house torn down. Washington had no choice but to dismiss L'Enfant. L'Enfant left, understandably angry, and took his plans with him.

The commissioners were left with ten square miles of mud, buildings in various stages of non-completion, and curious tracks in the mud which were supposed to be avenues and grand boulevards. And they had no plans with which to bring some kind of order out of the muddy chaos.

Banneker then amazed Ellicott and the commissioners. He reproduced L'Enfant's plans almost exactly as the Frenchman had drawn them. While working on the surveying job Banneker had written down L'Enfant's field notes and used them for practice in map making. His constant efforts to improve his skills had resulted in the saving of Washington City. It is entirely possible that Congress might have withdrawn its support if the commissioners had not been able to present the plans and map.

It did not take long, however, for Banneker and Ellicott to become disgusted. Politicians and speculators, knowingly or not, held the project back. In time, both Banneker and Ellicott left the project—but not before Banneker had become known throughout the new nation as the "Afro-American Astronomer" who had helped to build the city of Washington in the District of Columbia.

318   AARON E. KLEIN

What's It All About?

1. Describe at least three of Benjamin Banneker's interests or talents.
2. What was Banneker's role in the building of Washington, D. C.?

---

1. How did Banneker learn the mathematics he needed in order to do his experiments?
2. How did the establishment of the Ellicott's Lower Mills benefit Banneker?
3. How did the neighboring farmers feel about Banneker's becoming a "gentleman scientist"?
4. How did Banneker's work as an astronomer become important to farmers?

PUTTING IDEAS TO WORK

Suppose you had an opportunity to plan the city or town in which you live. How would you make it different from what it is now? List and describe three main changes you would make.

Do you have items around the house that are coming apart or items that are broken?

Putting It Back Together

If you read the information below about Quik-Set Epoxy glue, you may solve your problems. Or will you? Read the front and back of the package. Then answer the questions below.

1. "Quik Set" claims to be super easy, fast, safe, and sure. Which two of these claims are supported by information on the package?

WES-CO

QUIK-SET ®
BRAND
EPOXY GLUE

Super easy
Super fast
Super safe
Super sure

For Use On:
. Aluminum
. Ceramics
. China
. Copper
. Fiberglass
. Iron
. Leather
. Most Plastics
. Steel
. Wood

Ideal for:
. Hobbyist
. Do-it-yourselfers

Net Wt. 1½ oz. (42 grams)

2. Can the glue be used by following only the pictures on the back of the package? Why? Why not?
3. Does the guarantee seem clear? Is it adequate?
4. What extra information is given in the step-by-step directions?
5. If you were repairing a paper lamp shade, would you use this glue?
6. Why is the warning printed larger than the directions?
7. How much glue is in the kit?
8. How should you treat your hands if they become irritated by the glue?

QUIK-SET ®

BRAND
EPOXY GLUE

Super easy
Super fast
Super safe
Super sure

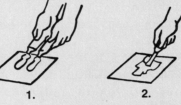

1.   2.

1. Pierce ends of tubes. Squeeze equal lengths of "Quik Set" and hardener onto clean discardable surface. Squeeze with equal pressure from bottoms of tubes. See Picture 1. Diameter of lengths must be the same. Mix well. See picture 2.

2. Thoroughly clean and dry surface to be glued. Apply glue. Glue will harden in about 4 minutes for most repairs. If temperature is below 32°F (0°C), the hardening time is much longer. Roughen the surface before applying glue for improved holding results.

CAUTION

Contains epoxy and resins. May cause skin or eye irritation. Wash with clear water.

Do not take internally.
Keep away from children.

Guarantee: If not completely satisfied, return the unused portion for a full refund.

Wes-Co
2121 North East Main
Valley View, Texas 75118

If your home has dry wall (sheet rock) construction, you can easily install a medicine chest in your bathroom.

Installing a Medicine Chest

If you already have one medicine chest, another might help you organize better. It can be installed with only a few hours work. Read the directions and study the diagrams. There are questions to answer after you read the instructions.

Materials Needed	**Tools Needed**
2—2×4's	Stud Finder
Medicine Chest	Pencil
Screws to fit Chest	Drill—hand or electric
	Keyhole saw
	Screwdriver

Follow the easy steps and the diagrams.

1. After deciding on the general area for the medicine chest, locate the studs. A stud finder uses a magnet to help you locate a row of nails—a stud.
2. Locate two studs that are side by side and 16″ apart. Hold the medicine chest against the wall and have a helper draw an outline of it on the wall. Be sure that the outline is drawn at the very back of the chest and is only as large as the back of the chest. Now you have the location of the chest.
3. Drill a hole in the center of the outline. Using a keyhole saw, saw across to one stud, then saw across to the other. Now cut out the entire outline. The studs will guide you on each side. Be careful at the top and bottom. Make straight cuts only.
4. Cut two pieces of 2×4 just long enough to fit between the studs at the top and bottom of the opening. Nail them in place. You must slant the nails as the diagram shows.
5. Slip the medicine chest in place. Locate the screw holes inside the chest. Insert and drive screws in those holes. That's how easy it is!

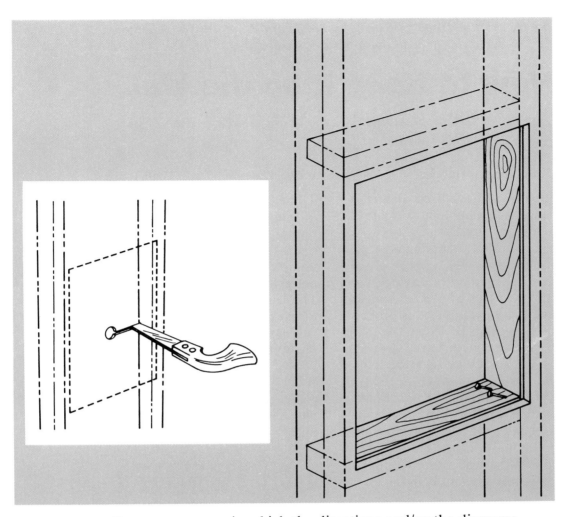

1. Do you see ways in which the directions and/or the diagrams could have been made easier to follow? How?
2. Would it have been a good idea to test the size of the opening after step 3? Why or why not?
3. What parts of the directions aren't really directions but are explanations or comments?
4. What parts of at least two steps seem unclear? Rewrite the steps with clearer directions on another sheet of paper.
5. On another sheet of paper, write directions explaining how to tie your sneakers. Try your directions out on a friend. Are they clear? Do they work?

The information that follows could be helpful to you if you are planning to decorate the walls of a room with pictures, book shelves, etc.

How to Hang It on the Wall

Read the information about each type of wall hanger. Then answer the questions that follow:

Using Picture Hangers

Most of us have used picture hangers to hang light-weight items. Picture hangers are usually rated by the number of pounds they will support. Read the package before buying. There are two types of picture hangers (see the diagrams). A is probably stronger than B. Using two hangers for one picture (see diagram C) is a good way to be certain that the picture stays on the wall and stays straight. Special hint: placing a piece of masking tape over the spot where you pound in the nail will prevent a crack or chip in the wall. Remove the tape after the nail is in place.

Using Plastic or Lead Wall Plugs

To begin to understand this type of hanger, see Diagram D. Wall plugs—especially the plastic ones—are generally used for light items. The plastic plugs work better in wood than in plaster. The lead plugs are generally used to hang something on brick—such as a fireplace. A hole is made in the wall. The hole must be just the size of the plug. When the plug is tapped into place, a screw is driven into the plug. The plug expands and holds tightly to the wall.

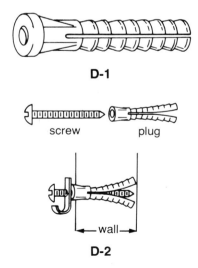

D-1

screw   plug

D-2

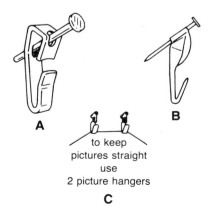

A

to keep
pictures straight
use
2 picture hangers

B

C

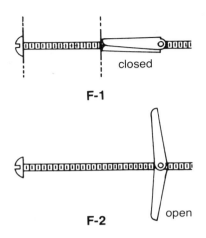

closed

F-1

F-2   open

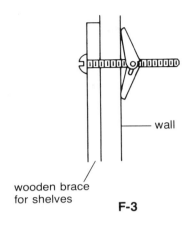

wall

wooden brace
for shelves   **F-3**

Using Toggle Bolts

The toggle bolt is sometimes called the wing bolt. The toggle or wings can be held against the bolt or let loose to spring open. See diagrams F-1 and F-2. Again, a hole is drilled into the wall large enough for the toggle to pass through. The wings are held against the bolt and the bolt is inserted into the hole. Once through the wall, the toggles open up making it impossible to remove the bolt. Therefore, when using a toggle bolt, you first put it through whatever you are attaching to the wall. The toggle bolt is used to attach very heavy items such as hanging book shelves, cupboards, and stereo equipment.

1. Write a brief summary (one or two sentences) to describe each type of hanger.
2. Each hanger has its disadvantages. For each one name one problem you might have.
3. What are the main uses for toggle bolts?
4. For each item below, name the type of hanger you would need to hang it on the wall.

stereo speakers
painting in a heavy frame
a wooden plaque
a school pennant
shelves for a rock collection
an 8″ × 10″ picture without glass
an 11″ × 14″ picture with glass
shelves for a bookcase
kitchen shelves for dishes
piece of fabric stapled to a
    wooden frame

The
DREAM
of the
GOLDEN MOUNTAINS

The discovery of gold at Sutter's Mill in 1848 helped to change the course of California's history. It touched off the world's first great gold rush.

Gold fever swept California. Towns and villages quickly emptied as their inhabitants rushed off to the hills to dig for gold. As a San

Francisco newspaper owner sadly reported: "The majority of our subscribers and many of our advertisers have closed their doors and places of business and left town. . . . " Then, the publisher himself gave in to the hunger for gold and left town to join his former subscribers and advertisers in their search for gold.

In time, the news spread to the eastern United States—and then across the Atlantic to Europe—causing great excitement everywhere. Men by the tens of thousands (the exact number can only be guessed at) hastily left farms, homes, and jobs. They made their way, in one way or another, to the Golden Gate on the Pacific coast. They went to California in such huge numbers during the year 1849 that they have become known as the Forty-Niners.

The news of the California gold find reached China. In villages around the city of Canton, stories were told of a place where gold was just lying around for anybody to come along and scoop it up. (The stories became exaggerated as they were told and retold.) And in these villages, young men began to dream of going to this fabulous place which, in the language of the Cantonese, came to be called *Gum San*— the land of the Golden Mountains.

Late in the 1840s, small numbers of Chinese began arriving in San Francisco. Most of them were not young peasants, however, but merchants who came to set up small businesses of one sort or another. Through hard work and saving, some of them did very well for themselves. They were later able to return to their homeland much wealthier than they had been.

Their stay in California, of course, was during the time of the discovery of gold at Sutter's Mill. And it was believed that they were the ones who carried the exciting news back to China.

The dream of the Golden Mountains had a great effect on the pattern of Chinese emigration. Up to 1850, less than a thousand Chinese had made their way to America. Yet, in 1852 alone, more than eighteen thousand Chinese passed through the Golden Gate.

DANIEL CHU *and* SAMUEL CHU 327

"You are no longer a child, Precious Jade," her mother said gently, as she prepared to send her daughter on a long journey—from China to the Golden Mountains of California.

Precious Jade's Journey

It was only the end of the sixth moon, yet the morning heat brought a wet stickiness to Precious Jade's face. She started to run the back of her hand across her face, but felt her mother's eyes on her and decided to be very carefully proper in her behavior this last day. She stopped the movement of her hand and reached instead for the carefully folded gown that her mother was handing her. She handled it gingerly, with the tips of her fingers lest the salt wetness of her perspiration stain the silk, and laid it gently in the pigskin chest. The chest was small, so small, yet it was to hold everything she would take with her across the sea. She had never liked the color of the chest. It was a deep brownish red, the color of chicken's blood, she often said, after it had been cooked in soup.

"If all is not ready when Uncle Chok comes, he will leave alone." Her mother's voice was soft and slightly tremulous, yet insistent.

Precious Jade looked at her mother then. She had been very careful to avoid her mother's eyes until now, but she had to see, if she could, what feeling would break through into them. She had to see if this woman who rarely revealed any hint of emotion would do so now that her daughter was about to embark on a ship that would carry her thousands of *li*, thousands of worlds away. The thin film of moisture that she saw in the eyes drew from her an anguished wail. She threw her arms about her mother's thin neck and poured forth all her fears and anxieties, all her love and filial devotion in a flood of tears.

Her mother stroked the back of her head and neck gently a few times, and then Precious Jade felt the shoulder under her tears brace itself and stiffen. "You are no longer a child, Precious Jade," her mother said very gently, with a voice that was husky and not quite as firm as usual. "Do not weep as if your mother were dying."

She grasped Precious Jade by the shoulders and pushed her gently away to hold her at arms' length. Precious Jade stifled her sobs with a great effort and raised her eyes to her mother's face. Two wet lines crept down the gaunt cheeks, but the eyes were no longer filmed with moisture.

"The Golden Mountains—they are so far—so far," she wailed.

"A woman belongs to the father of her sons," her mother said. "When you go, remember the father and the mother who brought you to womanhood, but also remember that you are a woman."

"I shall remember. I shall remember." Her voice was hardly more than a whisper.

They finished packing the chest in silence, a warm, comfortable silence that felt as if each were holding the other in an affectionate embrace. Precious Jade held the lid of the chest down tightly while her mother pressed the heavy brass hasp into place, pushed the bolt through, and locked it. "It is done," her mother said, as if she were locking up forever the part of her life in which Precious Jade belonged.

As though he had been awaiting the "click" of the lock for a signal, 329

Uncle Chok called from the outer doorway. "Elder Sister, Elder Sister. Is your precious daughter ready? The boat leaves."

"We come!" cried Precious Jade. Her tears quickly forgotten, she grasped the brass handle at one end of the chest and lifted. It was heavy. Her mother took the other handle, and the two carried the chest unsteadily out toward the room from which had come the voice of Uncle Chok.

They did not get to the door with their burden. Precious Jade's younger brothers and sisters, unable to contain themselves any longer, burst into the room and commandeered the chest. They carried it out, holding it above their heads as if they were in a triumphal procession, laughing and shouting, "Going to Golden Mountains! Going to Golden Mountains!" and deposited it at the feet of the benignly smiling Uncle Chok.

"Are you so happy to be getting rid of your sister, then!" he exclaimed.

There was a sudden shocked silence. Thrilled and excited by their sister's imminent journey to the distant but fabulous land, they had completely forgotten that the great adventure for her meant that they would not see her again for many years. Precious Jade, following close behind them with her mother, was amused by their sudden silence and their turning as one to confront her with a mass of solemn, almost tearful faces. She laughed gaily. She had smiled to herself and wondered about her mother's restraining herself from scolding the children for their noisy demonstration. Now she knew the reason for

the indulgence. Her mother knew that the twinkles of joy in their eyes made an effective dam against the threatening floods of tears.

"Ai yah! Such mournful faces. Is that my coffin you have carried out?" she chided.

"Ai yah!" her mother gasped. "What a thing to say when you go on a journey. It will bring ill fortune. How often have I cautioned you about such words at such times?" Her voice was trembling. Precious Jade was glad to see her father appear in the doorway.

"All is ready?" He ignored Precious Jade, the children, and their mother and addressed himself to Uncle Chok. "If this daughter of little worth does not behave as befits a grown woman, Elder Brother Chok, this person would be grateful if you will give her a few words to guide her."

Uncle Chok smiled his benign smile. "There will be no need for words from me. You have taught her well." He turned to Precious Jade. "It would be well for us to go now. The boatman waits to take us to Hong Kong."

Precious Jade gazed silently at the two men, her father and Uncle Chok, and felt a giant hand within her take hold of her heart and squeeze it. She pressed a clenched fist against her chest, looked dazedly around at her brothers and sisters and then at her mother, then threw her arms around her mother and wept in great wrenching sobs, not noisily as when they had been alone in the other room, but hoarsely, almost silently. For a long time her sobbing was the only sound in the room.

Both her father and Uncle Chok cleared their throats at precisely the same moment. Choking back a sob, she lifted her head from her mother's shoulder and looked at the two men shifting uneasily, searching for words of comfort that they could not find. Despite her tears she had an impulse to laugh at them. So wise they were, and yet a woman's tears baffled them, paralyzed them in thought and in action. She wiped her eyes and wet cheeks with the tips of her fingers. "I am ready," she said.

To her mother she whispered with bowed head, "I go, my mother. Let not your heart be troubled about me."

Her mother patted her shoulder, but her lips were tight against her feelings and she said nothing. Precious Jade turned to go.

"You two eldest may carry the chest." Her father spoke hoarsely, as if there were an obstruction in his throat. The words were hardly out before the two boys were tramping out the door, the chest swinging between them. The other children started to follow, but were stopped short by their father's "Not so. You little ones will stay at home with your mother. It is unseemly that a mob should accompany your sister to the boat." Their faces fell, but they obeyed without a word of protest, turning back from the door to cluster around Precious Jade.

She tried to encompass them all in the circle of her arms and rubbed her cheeks against each of their foreheads. "Be obedient children. Be obedient children," she crooned in their ears.

"We go," grumbled her father, and he started out the door with Uncle Chok. Precious Jade followed, casting but a brief glance at her mother, who was standing quite still, watching her with eyes that were full of the sadness of leave-taking.

The last memory-picture of her village home that Precious Jade took into herself to treasure was that of her mother, framed by the peaked arch that gave into their courtyard, standing surrounded by the younger children. She stood nodding her head slowly, gravely, in response to Precious Jade's jaunty wave.

Monfoon Leong

What's It All About?

1. How do Precious Jade and her mother each react to Precious Jade's departure?
2. How would you feel and act if you were leaving your home for a long time?

---

1. How did news about the discovery of gold in California reach China?
2. Why did the Chinese come to call California *"Gum San*—The Land of the Golden Mountains"?
3. Where is Precious Jade going? Why do you think a family would allow a young person to go so far away?
4. As they are packing, why does Precious Jade look directly into her mother's eyes?

PUTTING IDEAS TO WORK

As one of the merchants in the first selection, imagine you are trying to impress the folks back home over the incredible discovery of gold in California. Using as much exaggeration as you can, write a letter home (to China) telling all about "The Golden Mountains."

April 22, 1889. At the stroke of twelve o'clock noon, one hundred thousand home seekers stood ready at the border to race after the prize of twelve thousand parcels of land. This was the Oklahoma Land Run.

Oklahoma Land Run

"There we were, the girl on my left, the old plainsman on my right. Eleven forty-five. Along the Border were the soldiers, their guns in one hand, their watches in the other. Those last five minutes seemed years long; and funny, they'd quieted till there wasn't a sound. Listening. The last minute was an eternity. Twelve o'clock. There went up a roar that drowned the crack of the soldiers' musketry as they fired in the air as the signal of noon and the start of the Run. You could see the puffs of smoke from their guns, but you couldn't hear a sound. The thousands surged over the Line. It was like water going over a broken dam. The rush had started. . . . We swept across the prairie in a cloud of black

334

and red dust that covered our faces and hands in a minute. . . . Off we went, down the old freight trail that was two wheel ruts, a foot wide each, worn into the prairie soil. The old man on his pony kept in one rut, the girl on her thoroughbred in the other, and I on Whitefoot on the raised place in the middle. The first half mile was almost a neck-and-neck race. The old fellow was yelling and waving one arm and hanging on somehow. He was beating his pony with the flask on his flanks. Then he began to drop behind. Next thing I heard a terrible scream and a great shouting behind me. I threw a quick glance over my shoulder. The old plainsman's pony had stumbled and fallen. His bottle smashed 335 into bits, his six-shooter flew in another direction, and he lay sprawling full length in the rut of the trail. The next instant he was hidden in a welter of pounding hoofs and flying dirt and cinders and wagon wheels. . . .

"The girl and I—funny, I never did learn her name—were in the lead because we had stuck to the old trail, rutted though it was, rather than strike out across the prairie that by this time was beyond the burned area and was covered with a heavy growth of blue stem grass almost six feet high in places. A horse could only be forced through that at a slow pace. That jungle of grass kept many a racer from winning his section that day.

"The girl followed close behind me. That thoroughbred she rode was built for speed, not distance. A race horse, blooded. I could hear him blowing. He was trained to short bursts. My Indian pony was just getting his second wind as her horse slackened into a trot. We had come nearly sixteen miles. I was well in the lead by that time, with the girl following. She was crouched low over his neck, like a jockey, and I

could hear her talking to him, low and sweet and eager, as if he were a human being. We were far in the lead now. We had left the others behind, hundreds going this way, hundreds that, scattering for miles over the prairie. Then I saw that the prairie ahead was afire. The tall grass was blazing. Only the narrow trail down which we were galloping was open. On either side of it was a wall of flame. . . . A Sooner sneaking in ahead of the Run, had set the blaze to keep the Boomers off, saving the land for himself. The dry grass burned like oiled paper. I turned around. The girl was there, her racer stumbling, breaking, and going on, his head lolling now. I saw her motion with her hand. She was coming. I whipped off my hat and clapped it over Whitefoot's eyes, gave him the spurs, crouched down low and tight, shut my own eyes, and down the trail we went into the furnace. Hot! . . . I could feel the flames licking my legs and back. Another hundred yards and neither the horse nor I could have come through it. But we broke out into the open, choking and blinded and half suffocated. I looked down the lane of flame. The girl hung on her horse's neck. Her skullcap was pulled down over her eyes. She was coming through, game. I knew that my land . . . was not more than a mile ahead. I knew that hanging around here would probably get me a shot through the head, for the Sooner that started that fire must be lurking somewhere in the high grass ready to kill anybody that tried to lay claim to his land. I began to wonder, too, if that girl wasn't headed for the same section that I was bound for. I made up my mind that, woman or no woman, this was a race. . . . My poor little pony was coughing and sneezing and trembling. Her racer must have been ready to drop. I kept thinking how, when I came to Little Bear Creek, I'd bathe my little mustang's nose and face and his poor heaving flanks, and how I mustn't let him drink too much, once he got his muzzle in the water.

"Just before I reached the land I was riding for, I had to leave the trail and cut across the prairie. I could see a clump of elms ahead. I knew the creek was nearby. But just before I got to it, I came to one of those deep gullies you find in the plains country. Drought does it—a 337 crack in the dry earth to begin with, widening with every rain until it becomes a small cañon. Almost ten feet across this one was, and deep. No way around it that I could see, and no time to look for one. I put Whitefoot to the leap and . . . he took it, landing on the other side with hardly an inch to spare. I heard a wild scream behind me. I turned. The girl on her spent racer had tried to make the gulch. He had actually taken it—a thoroughbred and a gentleman, that animal—but he came down on his knees just on the farther edge, rolled, and slid down the gully side into the ditch. The girl had flung herself free. My claim was fifty yards away. So was the girl, with her dying horse. She lay there on the prairie. As I raced toward her—my own poor little mount was nearly gone by this time—she scrambled to her knees. I can see her face now, black with cinders and soot and dirt, her hair all over her shoulders, her cheek bleeding where she had struck a stone in her fall, her black tights torn, her little short skirt sagging. She sort of sat up and looked around her. Then she staggered to her feet before I reached her and stood there swaying, and pushing her hair out of her eyes like someone who'd been asleep. She pointed down the gully. The black of her face was streaked with tears.

" 'Shoot him!' she said. 'I can't. His two forelegs are broken. I heard them crack. Shoot him! . . . '

"So I off my horse and down to the gully's edge. There the animal lay. . . . He was done for, all right. I took out my six-shooter and aimed right between the eyes. He kicked once, sort of leaped—or tried to, and then lay still. . . .

"Then something made me turn around. The girl had mounted my mustang. She was off toward the creek section. Before I had moved ten paces she had reached the very piece I had marked in my mind for my own. She leaped from the horse, ripped off her skirt, tied it to her riding whip that she still held tight in her hand, dug the whip butt into the soil of the prairie—planted her flag—and the land was hers by right of claim."

338   EDNA FERBER

the Nez Percé Indians

Nez Percé Indians, *nehz* PURS, are a tribe that lives in north-central Idaho. The rich farmlands and forests in the area form the basis for the tribe's chief industries, agriculture and lumber.

The name *Nez Percé* means *pierced nose*, but few members of the tribe ever pierced their noses. In 1805, a French interpreter gave the name to the tribe after seeing 339

some members wear shells in their noses as decorations.

The Nez Percé originally lived in the region where the borders of Idaho, Oregon, and Washington meet. Prospectors overran the Nez Percé reservation after discovering gold there in the 1860's.

The Nez Percé resisted the efforts of the government to move them to a smaller reservation. In 1877, fighting broke out between the Nez Percé and U.S. troops. Joseph, a Nez Percé chief, tried to lead a band of his people into Canada. But he surrendered near the United States-Canadian border.

See also JOSEPH, CHIEF.

ALLEN P. SLICKPOO, SR.

Joseph, Chief

Joseph, Chief (1840?-1904), was a Nez Percé chief. He became famous for a military retreat he led through Idaho and Montana in 1877. Joseph conducted the retreat so skillfully that he has been called the "Indian Napoleon."

In June, 1877, war broke out between Joseph's band and U.S. troops. The fighting began shortly after government officials had ordered the band to move from its homeland in the Wallowa Valley of Oregon to a reservation in Idaho. The government wanted the land opened to white settlers.

Joseph's warriors won several battles, but he realized that they could not defeat the Army. He ordered a retreat to Canada, where he hoped to join forces with Sioux Indians who had fled there. Joseph conducted the retreat brilliantly, fighting off the troops and leading warriors, women, and children more than 1,000 miles (1,600 kilometers). In October, 1877, he finally surrendered about 40 miles (64 kilometers) from the United States-Canadian border. In 1878, the government sent Joseph and his people to the Indian Territory in what is now Oklahoma.

As a youth, Joseph attended a mission school. He learned much about military tactics by watching soldiers at drill. After about 1885, Joseph lived on the Colville Indian Reservation in Washington. A monument marks his grave in Nespelem, Washington.

CECIL CORBETT   341

HEAR ME, MY CHIEFS

I am tired of fighting. Our chiefs are killed. Looking Glass is dead.
Toohulsote is dead. The old men are all dead. It is the young men who
say no and yes. He who led the young men is dead. It is cold and we
have no blankets. The little children are freezing to death. My people,
some of them, have run away to the hills and have no blankets, no food.
No one knows where they are—perhaps they are freezing to death. I
want to have time to look for my children and see how many of them I
can find. Maybe I shall find them among the dead. Here me, my chiefs,
I am tired. My heart is sad and sick. From where the sun now stands I
will fight no more forever.

342   CHIEF JOSEPH

What's It All About?

1. Who wins the piece of land that narrator is racing for in "Oklahoma Land Run"? How is it won?
2. Compare this fictional account of the Oklahoma Land Run with a United States history text description of this event. What differences do you notice?

---

1. How do the man and the girl keep their lead at the start of the Run?
2. Why does someone set the prairie fire? How does the narrator get through it?
3. How does the girl's horse get hurt?
4. How does the girl get the narrator's horse? Do you think she does this intentionally, or does she just see the chance and take it?
5. Who was Chief Joseph? Why did he and the Nez Perces fight the government troops? Why did he finally give up?

PUTTING IDEAS TO WORK

What do you think happens next? Write a scene that might follow the selection "Oklahoma Land Run."

This barrio was not like the one he had left in Mazatlán, Mexico. Ernesto found himself entering a strange, new world in the barrio of Sacramento, California.

Our Early Days in Sacramento

We found the Americans as strange in their customs as they probably found us. Immediately we discovered that there were no *mercados* and that when shopping you did not put the groceries in a *chiquihuite*. Instead everything was in cans or in cardboard boxes or 344   each item was put in a brown paper bag. There were neighborhood grocery stores at the corners and some big ones uptown, but no *mercado*. The grocers did not give children a *pilón*, they did not stand at the door and coax you to come in and buy, as they did in *Mazatlán*. The fruits and vegetables were displayed on counters instead of being piled up on the floor. The stores smelled of fly spray and oiled floors, not of fresh pineapple and limes.

Neither was there a plaza, only parks which had no bandstands, no concerts every Thursday, no Judases exploding on Holy Week, and no promenades of boys going one way and girls the other. There were no parks in the *barrio*; and the ones uptown were cold and rainy in winter, and in summer there was no place to sit except on the grass. When there were celebrations nobody set off rockets in the parks, much less on the street in front of your house to announce to the neighborhood that a wedding or a baptism was taking place. Sacramento did not have a *mercado* and a plaza with the cathedral to one side and the Palacio de Gobierno on another to make it obvious that there and nowhere else was the center of the town.

It was just as puzzling that the Americans did not live in *vecindades*, like our block on Leandro Valle. Even in the alleys, where people knew one another better, the houses were fenced apart, without central courts to wash clothes, talk, and play with the other children. Like the city, the Sacramento *barrio* did not have a place which was the middle of things for everyone.

In more personal ways we had to get used to the Americans. They did not listen if you did not speak loudly, as they always did. In the

Mexican style, people would know that you were enjoying their jokes tremendously if you merely smiled and shook a little, as if you were trying to swallow your mirth. In the American style there was little difference between a laugh and a roar, and until you got used to them you could hardly tell whether the boisterous Americans were roaring mad or roaring happy.

It was Doña Henriqueta more than Gustavo or José who talked of these oddities and classified them as agreeable or deplorable. It was she also who pointed out the pleasant surprises of the American way. When a box of rolled oats with a picture of red carnations on the side was emptied, there was a plate or a bowl or a cup with blue designs. We ate the strange stuff regularly for breakfast and we soon had a set of the beautiful dishes. Rice and beans we bought in cotton bags of colored prints. The bags were unsewed, washed, ironed, and made into gaily designed towels, napkins, and handkerchiefs. The American stores also gave small green stamps which were pasted in a book to exchange for prizes. We didn't have to run to the corner with the garbage; a collector came for it.

With remarkable fairness and never-ending wonder we kept adding to our list the pleasant and the repulsive in the ways of the Americans. It was my second acculturation.

The older people of the *barrio*, except in those things which they had to do like the Americans because they had no choice, remained Mexican. Their language at home was Spanish. They were continuously taking up collections to pay somebody's funeral expenses or to help someone who had had a serious accident. Cards were sent to you to attend a burial where you would throw a handful of dirt on top of the coffin and listen to tearful speeches at the graveside. At every baptism a new *compadre* and a new *comadre* joined the family circle. New Year greeting cards were exchanged, showing angels and cherubs in bright colors sprinkled with grains of mica so that they glistened like gold dust. At the family parties the huge pot of steaming tamales was still the center of attention, the *atole* served on the side with chunks of brown

346

sugar for sucking and crunching. If the party lasted long enough, someone produced a guitar, the men took over and the singing or *corridos* began.

In the *barrio* there were no individuals who had official titles or who were otherwise recognized by everybody as important people. The reason must have been that there was no place in the public business of the city of Sacramento for the Mexican immigrants. We only rented a corner of the city and as long as we paid the rent on time everything else was decided at City Hall or the County Court House, where Mexicans went only when they were in trouble. Nobody from the *barrio* ever ran for mayor or city councilman. For us the most important public officials were the policemen who walked their beats, stopped fights, and hauled drunks to jail in a patrol wagon we called *La Julia*.

The one institution we had that gave the *colonia* some kind of image was the *Comisión Honorífica*, a committee picked by the Mexican Consul in San Francisco to organize the celebration of the *Cinco de Mayo* and the Sixteenth of September, the anniversaries of the battle of Puebla and the beginning of our War of Independence. These were the two events which stirred everyone in the *barrio*, for what we were celebrating was not only the heroes of Mexico but also the feeling that we were still Mexicans ourselves. On these occasions there was a dance preceded by speeches and a concert. For both the *cinco* and the sixteenth queens were elected to preside over the ceremonies.

Between celebrations neither the politicians uptown nor the *Comisión Honorífica* attended to the daily needs of the *barrio*. This was done by volunteers—the ones who knew enough English to interpret in court, on a visit to the doctor, a call at the county hospital, and who could help make out a postal money order. By the time I had finished the third grade at the Lincoln School I was one of these volunteers. My services were not professional but they were free, except for the IOU's I accumulated from families who always thanked me with "God will pay you for it."

My clients were not *pochos*, Mexicans who had grown up in

California, probably had even been born in the United States. They had learned to speak English of sorts and could still speak Spanish, also of sorts. They knew much more about the Americans than we did, and much less about us. The *chicanos* and the *pochos* had certain feelings about one another. Concerning the *pochos*, the *chicanos* suspected that they considered themselves too good for the *barrio* but were not, for some reason, good enough for the Americans. Toward the *chicanos*, the *pochos* acted superior, amused at our confusions but not especially interested in explaining them to us. In our family when I forgot my manners, my mother would ask me if I was turning *pochito*.

Turning *pocho* was a half-step toward turning American. And America was all around us, in and out of the *barrio*. Abruptly we had to forget the ways of shopping in a *mercado* and learn those of shopping in a corner grocery or in a department store. The Americans paid no

348

attention to the Sixteenth of September, but they made a great commotion about the Fourth of July. In Mazatlán Don Salvador had told us, saluting and marching as he talked to our class, that the *Cinco de Mayo* was the most glorious date in human history. The Americans had not even heard about it.

In Tucson, when I had asked my mother again if the Americans were having a revolution, the answer was: "No, but they have good schools, and you are going to one of them." We were by now settled at 418 L Street and the time had come for me to exchange a revolution for an American education.

The two of us walked south on Fifth Street one morning to the corner of Q Street and turned right. Half of the block was occupied by the Lincoln School. It was a three-story wooden building, with two wings that gave it the shape of a double-T connected by a central hall. It

349

was a new building, painted yellow, with a shingled roof that was not like the red tile of the school in Mazatlán. I noticed other differences, none of them very reassuring.

We walked up the wide staircase hand in hand and through the door, which closed by itself. A mechanical contraption screwed to the top shut it behind us quietly.

Up to this point the adventure of enrolling me in the school had been carefully rehearsed. Mrs. Dodson had told us how to find it and we had circled it several times in our walks. Friends in the *barrio* explained that the director was called a principal, and that it was a lady and not a man. They assured us that there was always a person at the school who could speak Spanish.

Exactly as we had been told, there was a sign on the door in both Spanish and English: "Principal." We crossed the hall and entered the office of Miss Nettie Hopley.

Miss Hopley was at a roll-top desk to one side, sitting in a swivel chair that moved on wheels. There was a sofa against the opposite wall, flanked by two windows and a door that opened on a small balcony. Chairs were set around a table and on the walls hung framed pictures of a man with long white hair and another with a sad face and a black beard.

What Miss Hopley said to us we did not know but we saw in her eyes a warm welcome and when she took off her glasses and straightened up she smiled wholeheartedly, like Mrs. Dodson. We were, of course, saying nothing, only catching the friendliness of her voice and the sparkle in her eyes while she said words we did not understand. She signaled us to the table. Almost tiptoeing across the office, I maneuvered myself to keep my mother between me and the lady. In a matter of seconds I had to decide whether she was a possible friend or a menace. We sat down.

Then Miss Hopley did a formidable thing. She stood up. Had she been standing when we entered she would have seemed tall. But rising from her chair she soared. And what she carried up and up with her was

350

a buxom superstructure, firm shoulders, a straight sharp nose, full cheeks slightly molded by a curved line along the nostrils, thin lips that moved like steel springs, and a high forehead topped by hair gathered in a bun. Miss Hopley was not a giant in body but when she mobilized it to a standing position she seemed a match for giants. I decided I liked her.

She strode to a door in the far corner of the office, opened it, and called a name. A boy of about ten years appeared in the doorway./He sat down at one end of the table. He was brown like us, a plump kid with shiny black hair combed straight back, neat, cool, and faintly obnoxious.

Miss Hopley joined us with a large book and some papers in her hand. She, too, sat down and the questions and answers began by way of our interpreter. My name was Ernesto. My mother's name was Henriqueta. My birth certificate was in San Blas. Here was my last report card of the Escuela Municipal Numero 3 para Varones of Mazatlán, and so forth. Miss Hopley put things down in the book and my mother signed a card.

As long as the questions continued, Doña Henriqueta could stay and I was secure. Now that they were over, Miss Hopley saw her to the door, dismissed our interpreter, and without further ado took me by the hand and strode down the hall to Miss Ryan's first grade.

Miss Ryan took me to a seat at the front of the room, into which I shrank—the better to survey her. She was, to skinny, somewhat runty me, of a withering height when she patrolled the class. And when I least expected it, there she was, crouching by my desk, her blond radiant face level with mine, her voice patiently maneuvering me over the awful idiocies of the English language.

During the next few weeks Miss Ryan overcame my fears of tall, energetic teachers as she bent over my desk to help me with a word in the pre-primer. Step by step, she loosened me and my classmates from the safe anchorage of the desks for recitations at the blackboard and consultations at her desk. Frequently she burst into happy announce- 351

ments to the whole class. "Ito can read a sentence," and small Japanese Ito, squint-eyed and shy, slowly read aloud while the class listened in wonder: "Come, Skipper, come. Come and run." The Korean, Portuguese, Italian, and Polish first graders had similar moments of glory, no less shining than mine the day I conquered "butterfly," which I had been persistently pronouncing in standard Spanish as boo-ter-flee. "Children," Miss Ryan called for attention. "Ernesto has learned how to pronounce *butterfly*." And I proved it with a perfect imitation of Miss Ryan. From that celebrated success, I was soon able to match Ito's progress as a sentence reader with "Come, butterfly, come fly with me."

Like Ito and several other first graders who did not know English, I received private lessons from Miss Ryan in the closet, a narrow hall off the classroom with a door at each end. Next to one of these doors Miss Ryan placed a large chair for herself and a small one for me. Keeping an eye on the class through the open door she read with me about sheep in

the meadow and a frightened chicken going to see the king, coaching me out of my phonetic ruts in words like *pasture*, *bow-wow-wow*, *hay*, and *pretty*, which to my Mexican ear and eye had so many unnecessary sounds and letters. She made me watch her lips and then close my eyes as she repeated words I found hard to read. When we came to know each other better, I tried interrupting to tell Miss Ryan how we said it in Spanish. It didn't work. She only said "oh" and went on with *pasture*, *bow-wow-wow*, and *pretty*. It was as if in that closet we were both discovering together the secrets of the English language and grieving together over the tragedies of Bo-Peep. The main reason I was graduated with honors from the first grade was that I had fallen in love with Miss Ryan. Her radiant, no-nonsense character made us either afraid not to love her or love her so we would not be afraid, I am not sure which. It was not only that we sensed she was with it, but also that she was with us.

Like the first grade, the rest of the Lincoln School was a sampling of the lower part of town where many races made their home. My pals in the second grade were Kazushi, whose parents spoke only Japanese; Matti, a skinny Italian boy; and Manuel, a fat Portuguese who would never get into a fight but wrestled you to the ground and just sat on you. Our assortment of nationalities included Koreans, Yugoslavs, Poles, Irish, and home-grown Americans.

Miss Hopley and her teachers never let us forget why we were at

Lincoln: for those who were alien, to become good Americans; for those who were so born, to accept the rest of us. Off the school grounds we traded the same insults we heard from our elders. The school was not so much a melting pot as a griddle where Miss Hopley and her helpers warmed knowledge into us and roasted racial hatreds out of us.

At Lincoln, making us into Americans did not mean scrubbing away what made us originally foreign. The teachers called us as our parents did, or as close as they could pronounce our names in Spanish or Japanese. No one was ever scolded or punished for speaking his native tongue on the playground. Matti told the class about his mother's down quilt, which she had made in Italy with the fine feathers of a thousand geese. Encarnación acted out how boys learned to fish in the Philippines. I astounded the third grade with the story of my travels on a stagecoach, which nobody else in the class had seen except in the museum at Sutter's Fort. After a visit to the Crocker Art Gallery and its collection of heroic paintings of the golden age of California, someone showed a silk scroll with a Chinese painting. Miss Hopley herself had a way of expressing wonder over these matters before a class, her eyes wide open until they popped slightly. It was easy for me to feel that becoming a proud American, as she said we should, did not mean feeling ashamed of being a Mexican.

The Americanization of Mexican me was no smooth matter. I had to fight one lout who made fun of my travels on the *diligencia*, and my barbaric translation of the word into "diligence." He doubled up with laughter over the word until I straightened him out with a kick. In class I made points explaining that in Mexico roosters said "qui-qui-ri-qui" and not "cock-a-doodle-doo," but after school I had to put up with the taunts of a big Yugoslav who said Mexican roosters were crazy.

But it was Homer who gave me the most lasting lesson for a future American.

Homer was a chunky Irishman who dressed as if every day was 354 Sunday. He slicked his hair between a crew cut and a pompadour. And

Homer was smart, as he clearly showed when he and I ran for president of the third grade.

Everyone understood that this was to be a demonstration of how the American people vote for president. In an election, the teacher explained, the candidates could be generous and vote for each other. We cast our ballots in a shoe box and Homer won by two votes. I polled my supporters and came to the conclusion that I had voted for Homer and so had he. After class he didn't deny it, reminding me of what the teacher had said—we could vote for each other but didn't have to.

The lower part of town was a collage of nationalities in the middle of which Miss Nettie Hopley kept school with discipline and compassion. She called assemblies in the upper hall to introduce celebrities like the police sergeant or the fire chief, to lay down the law of the school, to present awards to our athletic champions, and to make important anouncements. One of these was that I had been proposed by my school and accepted as a member of the newly formed Sacramento Boys Band. "Now, isn't that a wonderful thing?" Miss Hopley asked the assembled school, all eyes on me. And everyone answered in a chorus, including myself, "Yes, Miss Hopley."

It was not only the parents who were summoned to her office and boys and girls who served sentences there who knew that Nettie Hopley meant business. The entire school witnessed her sizzling Americanism in its awful majesty one morning at flag salute.

All of the grades, as usual, were lined up in the courtyard between the wings of the building, ready to march to classes after the opening bell. Miss Shand was on the balcony of the second floor off Miss Hopley's office, conducting us in our lusty singing of "My Country tiz-a-thee." Our principal, as always, stood there like us, at attention, her right hand over her heart, joining in the song.

Halfway through the second stanza she stepped forward, held up her arm in a sign of command, and called loud and clear "Stop the singing." Miss Shand looked flabbergasted. We were frozen with shock.

355

Miss Hopley was now standing at the rail of the balcony, her eyes sparking, her voice low and resonant, the words coming down to us distinctly and loaded with indignation.

"There are two gentlemen walking on the school grounds with their hats on while we are singing," she said, sweeping our ranks with her eyes. "We will remain silent until the gentlemen come to attention and remove their hats." A minute of awful silence ended when Miss Hopley, her gaze fixed on something behind us, signaled Miss Shand and we began once more the familiar hymn. That afternoon, when school was out, the word spread. The two gentlemen were the Superintendent of Schools and an important guest on an inspection.

ERNESTO GALARZA

What's It All About?

1. How was life in Mazatlán, Mexico, different from life in the *barrio* of Sacramento?
2. What goals does Miss Hopley want all her students to reach? What do you think of these goals? Why?

---

1. Who takes care of the daily needs of the barrio? What do these people do?
2. Why does Ernesto like Miss Hopley at their first meeting?
3. How do the students feel about Miss Ryan? Why do they feel this way?
4. Why does Miss Hopley stop the singing at the school assembly? What does this show about her?

PUTTING IDEAS TO WORK

If you were a photographer assigned to do a feature story on life in the Sacramento *barrio*, what scenes would you photograph for the story? Describe five photographs. For each one write a one-sentence caption.

A brass disk was used by the Confederate Army to code messages.

A Code Machine in American History

The brass disk below uses a substitution method to form codes. The inner circle of letters can be turned so that each of its letters can stand for letters in the outer circle. Each code letter on the inner circle can stand for 25 different codes.

Once you know the "setting" of the inner circle, you can easily decode any message. Look at the message below. Find each code letter in the inner circle and write the outer-circle letter it stands for. Do you get the message?

R Z I Z Z Y A J J Y V I Y R V O Z M

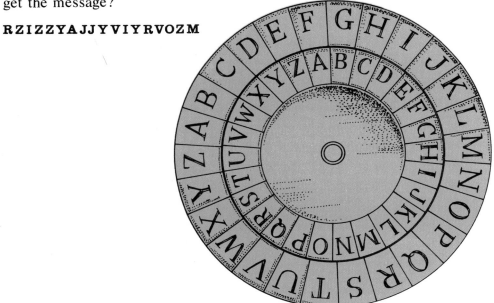

1. Write three messages using the same setting.
2. Put the following messages in code using the disk setting above.

   See you later.   Call me tonight.
   How much is it?   Who said that?

3. Draw your own copy of the disk, but set the inner circle differently from the one above. Make up other messages.

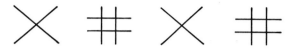

And Now a Brief Message from Middle Earth

Does the writing above look strange and ancient? Maybe so, but it's just another simple substitution code. Sometimes it is known as the "Zig Zag" and sometimes as the "Pig Pen." Here's why.

1) Draw these figures:

2) Now add the letters of the alphabet in some system—known only to you and the receiver of your messages. Here is one way:

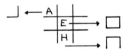

3) Can you see that **A** = ⌐, **E** = □, and **H** = ⊓ ?

4) But we've got a problem. **A** = ⌐, but so does **N**! And **E** = □ , but so does **R**. Well, a few dots will take care of that.

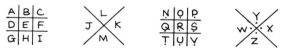

   Now try making up a few messages of your own. Perhaps you would like to change the system of letters to make your codes different. This can be done easily by adding decoration to the present one.

Or maybe you would like to invent a simple substitution code of your own. Here is a clue for you.

Not all codes are used by spies and secret agents to send and receive secret messages. Some codes are used by people who have special needs.

Special Codes

Oral language as we use it is unknown to people who are deaf. In order to receive messages and express themselves, they use a special language, or code. It is called *sign language,* and it consists of the manual alphabet below. Study and practice the alphabet. Can you read the message below?

Manual Alphabet

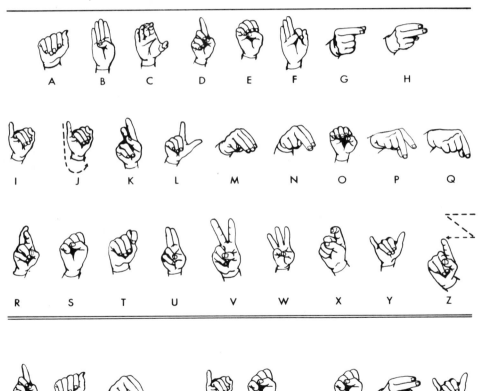

Now practice sending and receiving messages from your classmates.

*Another alphabet—again generally used by a special group, the
blind—uses a series of raised dots to spell out messages.*

The Braille Alphabet

The black dots in each of the blocks below show which dots are
raised for each letter.

    Messages can be written by sticking a pin through the back of a
page to raise each dot. The raised dots can be touched with the fin-
gertips and "read." This is not an easy way to send a message, but it
does give you an idea of how the blind read Braille.

    Study the Braille alphabet. Then try to decode the messages
drawn below. Make up some messages of your own.

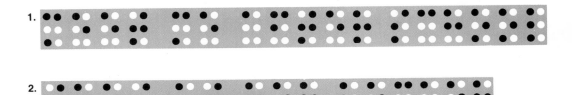

Now write your own messages in Braille using the method
above. Try transferring your message, or the alphabet, to a piece of
sturdy paper by making holes with a thumb tack. Practice "reading"
your messages by touch.

Monaghan's grandfather didn't believe in the Statue of Liberty. What he wanted was a sign that said, "Welcome all!"

GRANDPA and the STATUE

Characters

Characters in the present time of the play:

ANNOUNCER

AUGUST

MONAGHAN (Young Monaghan, a
   soldier)

Characters from the past, heard in the flashback scenes which Young Monaghan remembers:

SHEEAN

MONAGHAN (Grandfather of
   Young Monaghan)

CHILD MONAGHAN (Young
   Monaghan himself, as a child)

GEORGE
CHARLEY ⎫ (neighborhood
JACK   ⎬ children, Child
MIKE   ⎭ Monaghan's friends)
JOE

ALF   ⎫ (passengers on the
GIRL   ⎬ Statue of Liberty
YOUNG MAN ⎭ boat)

MEGAPHONE VOICE

VETERAN (visitor to the Statue)

(*Music: Theme*)

ANNOUNCER: The scene is the
   fourth floor of a giant army
   hospital overlooking New York   363

Harbor. A young man sitting in a wheel chair is looking out a window—just looking. After a while another young man in another wheel chair rolls over to him and they both look. (*Music out*)

AUGUST: You want to play some checkers with me, Monaghan?

MONAGHAN: Not right now.

AUGUST: Okay. (*Slight pause*) You don't want to go feeling blue, Monaghan.

MONAGHAN: I'm not blue.

AUGUST: All you do most days is sit here looking out this window.

MONAGHAN: What do you want me to do, jump rope?

AUGUST: No, but what do you get out of it?

MONAGHAN: It's a beautiful view. Some companies make millions of dollars just printing that view on postcards.

AUGUST: Yeh, but nobody keeps looking at a postcard six, seven hours a day.

MONAGHAN: I come from around here, it reminds me of things. My young days.

AUGUST: That's right, you're Brooklyn, aren't you?

MONAGHAN: My house is only about a mile away.

AUGUST: That so. Tell me, are you looking at just the water all the time? I'm curious. I don't get a kick out of this view.

MONAGHAN: There's the Statue of Liberty out there. Don't you see it?

AUGUST: Oh, that's it. Yeh, that's nice to look at.

MONAGHAN: I like it. Reminds me of a lot of laughs.

AUGUST: Laughs? The Statue of Liberty?

MONAGHAN: Yeh, my grandfather. He got all twisted up with the Statue of Liberty.

AUGUST (*laughs a little*): That so? What happened?

MONAGHAN: Well. My grandfather was the stingiest man in Brooklyn. ''Mercyless'' Monaghan, they used to call him. He even used to save umbrella handles.

AUGUST: What for?

MONAGHAN: Just couldn't stand seeing anything go to waste. After a big windstorm there'd be a lot of broken umbrellas lying around in the streets.

AUGUST: Yeh?

MONAGHAN: He'd go around picking them up. In our house the closets were always full of umbrella handles. My grandma used to say that he would go across the Brooklyn Bridge on the trolley just because he could come back on the same nickel. See, if you stayed on the trolley they'd let you come back for the same nickel.

AUGUST: What'd he do, just go over and come back?

MONAGHAN: Yeh, it made him feel good. Savin' money. Two and a half cents.

AUGUST: So how'd he get twisted up with the Statue of Liberty?

MONAGHAN: Well, way back in 1887 around there they were living on Butler Street. Butler Street, Brooklyn, practically runs right down to the river. One day he's sitting on the front porch, reading a paper he borrowed from the neighbors, when along comes this man Jack Sheean who lived up the block.
(*Music: Sneak into above speech, then bridge, then out*)

SHEEAN (*slight brogue*): A good afternoon to you, Monaghan.

MONAGHAN (*grandfather*): How're you, Sheean, how're ya?

SHEEAN: Fair, fair. And how's Mrs. Monaghan these days?

MONAGHAN: Warm. Same as everybody else in summer.

SHEEAN: I've come to talk to you about the fund, Monaghan.

MONAGHAN: What fund is that?

SHEEAN: The Statue of Liberty fund.

MONAGHAN: Oh, that.

SHEEAN: It's time we come to grips with the subject, Monaghan.

MONAGHAN: I'm not interested, Sheean.

SHEEAN: Now hold up on that a minute. Let me tell you the facts. This here Frenchman has gone and built a fine Statue of Liberty. It costs the Lord knows how many millions to

build. All they're askin' us to do is contribute enough to put up a base for the statue to stand on.

MONAGHAN: I'm not . . . !

SHEEAN: Before you answer me. People all over the whole United States are puttin' in for it. Butler Street is doin' the same. We'd like to hang up a flag on the corner saying— "Butler Street, Brooklyn, is one hundred per cent behind the Statue of Liberty." And Butler Street *is* a hundred per cent subscribed except for you. Now will you give us a dime, Monaghan? One dime and we can put up the flag. Now what do you say to that?

MONAGHAN: I'm not throwin' me good money away for somethin' I don't even know exists.

SHEEAN: Now what do you mean by that?

MONAGHAN: Have you seen this statue?

SHEEAN: No, but it's in a warehouse. And as soon as we get the money to build the pedestal they'll take it and put it up on that island in the river, and all the boats comin' in from the old country will see it there and it'll raise the hearts of the poor immigrants to see such a fine sight on their first look at this country.

MONAGHAN: And how do I know it's in this here warehouse at all?

SHEEAN: You read your paper, don't you? It's been in all the papers for the past year.

MONAGHAN: Ha, the papers! Last year I read in the paper that they were about to pave Butler Street and take out all the holes. Turn around and look at Butler Street, Mr. Sheean.

SHEEAN: All right. I'll do this: I'll take you to the warehouse and show you the statue. Will you give me a dime then?

MONAGHAN: Well . . . I'm not sayin' I would, and I'm not sayin' I wouldn't. But I'd be more *likely* if I saw the thing large as life, I would.

SHEEAN (*peeved*): All right, then. Come along.

(*Music up and down and out*)
(*Footsteps, in a warehouse . . . echo . . . they come to a halt*)
Now then. Do you see the Statue of Liberty or don't you see it?

MONAGHAN: I see it all right, but it's all broke!

SHEEAN: *Broke*! They brought it from France on a boat. They had to take it apart, didn't they?

MONAGHAN: You got a second-hand statue, that's what you got, and I'm not payin' for

366

new when they've shipped us something that's all smashed to pieces.

SHEEAN: Now just a minute, just a minute. Visualize what I'm about to tell you, Monaghan, get the picture of it. When this statue is put together it's going to stand ten stories high. Could they get a thing ten stories high into a four-story building such as this is? Use your good sense, now Monaghan.

MONAGHAN: What's that over there?

SHEEAN: Where?

MONAGHAN: That tablet there in her hand. What's it say? July Eye Vee (IV) MDCCLXXVI . . . what . . . what's all that?

SHEEAN: That means July 4, 1776. It's in Roman numbers. Very high class.

MONAGHAN: What's the good of it? If they're going to put a sign on her they ought to put it: Welcome All. That's it. Welcome All.

SHEEAN: They decided July 4, 1776, and July 4, 1776, it's going to be!

MONAGHAN: All right, then let them get their dime from somebody else!

SHEEAN: Monaghan!

MONAGHAN: No, sir! I'll tell you something. I didn't think there was a statue but there is. She's all broke, it's true, but she's here and maybe they can get her together. But even if they do, will you tell me what sort of a welcome to immigrants it'll be, to have a gigantic thing like that in the middle of the river and in her hand is July Eye Vee MCDVC . . . whatever it is?

SHEEAN: That's the date the country was made!

MONAGHAN: The divil with the date! A man comin' in from the sea wants a place to stay, not a date. When I come from the old country I git off at the dock and there's a feller says to me, "Would you care for a room for the night?" "I would that," I sez, and he sez, "All right then, follow me." He takes me to a rooming house. I no sooner sign me name on the register—which I was able to do even at that time—when I look around and the feller is gone clear away and took my valise in the bargain. A statue anyway can't move off so fast, but if she's going to welcome let her say welcome, not this MCDC. . . .

SHEEAN: All right, then, Monaghan. But all I can say is, you've laid a disgrace on the name of Butler Street. I'll put the dime in for ya.

367

MONAGHAN: Don't connect me with it! It's a swindle, is all it is. In the first place, it's broke; in the second place, if they do put it up it'll come down with the first high wind that strikes it.

SHEEAN: The engineers say it'll last forever!

MONAGHAN: And I say it'll topple into the river in a high wind! Look at the inside of her. She's all hollow!

SHEEAN: I've heard everything now, Monaghan. Just about everything. Good-bye.

MONAGHAN: What do you mean, good-bye? How am I to get back to Butler Street from here?

SHEEAN: You've got legs to walk.

MONAGHAN: I'll remind you that I come on the trolley.

SHEEAN: And I'll remind you that I paid your fare and I'm not repeating the kindness.

MONAGHAN: Sheean? You've stranded me!

(*Music up and down*)

YOUNG MONAGHAN: That was grandpa. That's why I have to laugh every time I look at the statue now.

AUGUST: Did he ever put the dime in?

YOUNG MONAGHAN: Well—in a way. What happened was this: His daughters got married and finally my mom . . . put *me* out on Butler Street. I got to be pretty attached to grandpa. He'd even give me an umbrella handle and make a sword out of it for me. Naturally, I wasn't very old before he began working on me about the statue.

(*High wind*)

CHILD MONAGHAN (*softly, as though grandpa is in bed*): Grampa?

MONAGHAN (*awakened*): Heh? What are you doin' up?

CHILD MONAGHAN: Ssssh! Listen! (*Wind rising up and fading. Rising higher and fading*)

MONAGHAN (*gleefully*): Aaaaaaaah! Yes, yes. This'll do it, boy. This'll do it! First thing in the morning we'll go down to the docks and I'll bet you me life that Mr. Sheean's statue is smashed down and lyin' on the bottom of the bay. Go to sleep now, we'll have a look first thing.

(*Music up and down*)

(*Footsteps*)

CHILD MONAGHAN: If it fell down, all the people will get their dimes back, won't they, grampa? Slow down, I can't walk so fast.

MONAGHAN: Not only will they get their dimes back, but Mr. Sheean and the whole crew that engineered the collection are going to rot in jail. Now

mark my words. Here, now, we'll take a short cut around this shed. . . .

(*Footsteps continue a moment, then gradually . . . disappointedly they come to a halt*)

CHILD MONAGHAN: She's . . . she's still standing, grampa.

MONAGHAN: She is that. (*Uncomprehending*) I don't understand it. That was a terrible wind last night. Terrible.

CHILD MONAGHAN: Maybe she's weaker though. Heh?

MONAGHAN: Why . . . sure, that must be it. I'll wager she's hangin' by a thread. (*Realizing*) Of course! That's why they put her out there in the water so when she falls down she won't be flattening out a lot of poor innocent people. Hey—feel that?

CHILD MONAGHAN: The wind! It's starting to blow again!

MONAGHAN: Sure, and look at the sky blackening over! (*Wind rising*) Feel it comin' up! Take your last look at the statue, boy. If I don't mistake me eyes she's takin' a small list to Jersey already!

(*Music up and down*)

YOUNG MONAGHAN: It was getting embarrassing for me on the block. I kept promising the other kids that when the next

369

wind came the statue would come down. We even had a game. Four or five kids would stand in a semicircle around one kid who was the statue. The statue kid had to stand on his heels and look right in our eyes. Then we'd all take a deep breath and blow in his face. He'd fall down like a stick of wood. They all believed me and grampa . . . until one day. We were standing around and throwing rocks at an old milk can. . . .

(*Banging of rocks against milk can*)

GEORGE (*kid*): What're you doin?

CHILD MONAGHAN: What do we look like we're doin'?

GEORGE: I'm going someplace

370   tomorrow.

CHARLEY (*kid*): I know, church. Watch out, I'm throwin'.
(*Can being hit*)

GEORGE: I mean after church.

JACK: Where?

GEORGE: My old man's going to take me out on the Statue of Liberty boat.
(*Banging against can abruptly stops*)

CHILD MONAGHAN: You're not going out on the statue, though, are you?

GEORGE: Sure, that's where we're going.

CHILD MONAGHAN: But you're liable to get killed. Supposing there's a high wind tomorrow?

GEORGE: My old man says that statue couldn't fall down if all the wind in the world and John L. Sullivan hit it at the same time.

CHILD MONAGHAN: Is that so?

GEORGE: Yeh, that's so. My old man says that the only reason your grandfather's saying that it's going to fall down is that he's ashamed he didn't put a dime in for the pedestal.

CHILD MONAGHAN: Is that so?

GEORGE: Yeh, that's so.

CHILD MONAGHAN: Well, you tell your old man that if he gets killed tomorrow not to come around to my grandfather and say he didn't warn him!

JACK: Hey, George, would your

father take me along?

GEORGE: I'll ask him, maybe he—

CHILD MONAGHAN: What, are you crazy, Jack?

MIKE: Ask him if he'd take me too, will ya, George?

CHILD MONAGHAN: Mike, what's the matter with you?

JOE: Me too, George, I'll ask my mother for money.

CHILD MONAGHAN: Joe! Didn't you hear what my grampa said?

JOE: Well . . . I don't really believe that any more.

CHILD MONAGHAN: You don't be . . .

MIKE: Me neither.

JACK: I don't really think your grampa knows what he's talkin' about.

CHILD MONAGHAN: He don't, heh? (*Ready to weep*) Okay. . . . Okay. (*Bursting out*) I just hope that wind blows tomorrow, boy! I just hope that wind blows!
(*Music up and down*)
(*Creaking of a rocking chair*)
Grampa . . . ?

MONAGHAN: Huh?

CHILD MONAGHAN: Can you stop rocking for a minute?
(*Rocking stops*)
Can you put down your paper?
(*Rustle of paper*)
I—I read the weather report for tomorrow.

MONAGHAN: The weather report . . .

CHILD MONAGHAN: Yeh. It says fair and cool.

MONAGHAN: What of it?

CHILD MONAGHAN: I was wondering. Supposing you and me we went on a boat tomorrow. You know, I see the water every day when I go down to the docks to play, but I never sat on it. I mean in a boat.

MONAGHAN: Oh. Well, we might take the ferry on the Jersey side. We might do that.

CHILD MONAGHAN: Yeh, but there's nothing to see in Jersey.

MONAGHAN: You can't go to Europe tomorrow.

CHILD MONAGHAN: No, but

couldn't we go toward the ocean? Just . . . *toward* it?

MONAGHAN: Toward it. What—what is it on your mind, boy? What is it now?

CHILD MONAGHAN: Well, I . . .

MONAGHAN: Oh, you want to take the Staten Island ferry. Sure, that's in the direction of the sea.

CHILD MONAGHAN: No, grampa, not the Staten Island ferry.

MONAGHAN: You don't mean—(*Breaks off*) Boy!

CHILD MONAGHAN: All the kids are going tomorrow with Georgie's old man.

MONAGHAN: You don't believe me any more.

CHILD MONAGHAN: I do, grampa, but . . .

MONAGHAN: You don't. If you did you'd stay clear of the Statue of Liberty for love of your life!

CHILD MONAGHAN: But, grampa, when is it going to fall down? All I do is wait and wait.

MONAGHAN (*with some uncertainty*): You've got to have faith.

CHILD MONAGHAN: But every kid in my class went to see it and now the ones that didn't are going tomorrow. And they all keep talking about it and all I do . . . Well, I can't keep telling them it's a swindle. I—I

wish we could see it, grampa. It don't cost so much to go.

MONAGHAN: As long as you put it that way I'll have to admit I'm a bit curious meself as to how it's managed to stand upright so long. Tell you what I'll do. Barrin' wind, we'll chance it tomorrow!

CHILD MONAGHAN: Oh, gramp!

MONAGHAN: But! if anyone should ask you where we went you'll say—Staten Island. Are y' on?

CHILD MONAGHAN: Okay, sure. Staten Island.

MONAGHAN (*secretively*): We'll take the early boat, then. Mum's the word, now. For if old man Sheean hears that I went out there I'll have no peace from the thief the rest of m' life.

(*Music up and down*)
(*Boat whistles*)

CHILD MONAGHAN: Gee, it's nice ridin' on a boat, ain't it, grampa?

MONAGHAN: Never said there was anything wrong with the boat. Boat's all right. You're sure now that Georgie's father is takin' the kids in the afternoon.

CHILD MONAGHAN: Yeh, that's when they're going. Gee, look at those two sea gulls. Wee!—look at them swoop! They caught a fish!

MONAGHAN: What I can't understand is what all these people see in that statue that they'll keep a boat like this full makin' the trip, year in and year out. To hear the newspapers talk, if the statue was gone we'd be at war with the nation that stole her the followin' mornin' early. All it is is a big high pile of French copper.

CHILD MONAGHAN: The teacher says it shows us that we got liberty.

MONAGHAN: Bah! If you've got liberty you don't need a statue to tell you you got it; and if you haven't got liberty no statue's going to do you any good tellin' you you got it. It was a criminal waste of the people's money. (*Quietly*) And just to prove it to you I'll ask this feller sitting right over there what he sees in it. You'll see what a madness the whole thing was. Say, mister?

ALF: Hey?

MONAGHAN: I beg your pardon. I'm a little strange here, and curious. Could you tell me why you're going to the Statue of Liberty?

ALF: Me? Well, I tell ya. I always wanted to take an ocean voyage. This is a pretty big boat—bigger than the ferries—

so on Sundays, sometimes, I take the trip. It's better than nothing.

MONAGHAN: Thank you. (*To the boy*) So much for the great meaning of that statue, me boy. We'll talk to this lady standing at the rail. I just want you to understand why I didn't give Sheean me dime. Madam, would you be good enough to . . . Oh pardon me. (*To boy*) Better pass her by, she don't look so good. We'll ask that girl there. Young lady, if you'll pardon the curiosity of an old man . . . could you tell me in a few good words what it is about that statue that brings you out here?

GIRL: What statue?

MONAGHAN: Why, the Statue of Liberty up 'head. We're coming up to it.

GIRL: Statue of Liberty! Is this the Statue of Liberty boat?

MONAGHAN: Well, what'd you think it was?

GIRL: Oh, my! I'm supposed to be on the Staten Island ferry! Where's the ticket man? (*Going away*) Ticket man! Where's the ticket man?

CHILD MONAGHAN: Gee whiz, nobody seems to want to see the statue.

MONAGHAN: Just to prove it, let's see this fellow sitting on this

373

bench here. Young man, say
. . .

YOUNG MAN: I can tell you in one word. For four days I haven't had a minute's peace. My kids are screaming, my wife is yelling, upstairs they play the piano all day long. The only place I can find that's quiet is a statue. That statue is my sweetheart. Every Sunday I beat it out to the island and sit next to her, and she don't talk.

CHILD MONAGHAN: I guess you were right, grampa. Nobody seems to think it means anything.

MONAGHAN: Not only doesn't mean anything, but if they'd used the money to build an honest roomin' house on that island, the immigrants would

have a place to spend the night, their valises wouldn't get robbed, and they—

MEGAPHONE VOICE: *Please keep your seats while the boat is docking. Statue of Liberty—all out in five minutes!*

CHILD MONAGHAN: Look down there, gramp! There's a peanut stand! Could I have some?

MONAGHAN: I feel the wind comin' up. I don't think we dare take the time.
(*Music up and down*)

CHILD MONAGHAN:
Ssssssseuuuuuww! Look how far you can see! Look at that ship way out in the ocean!

MONAGHAN: It is, it's quite a view. Don't let go of me hand now.

CHILD MONAGHAN: I betcha we

could almost see California.

MONAGHAN: It's probably that grove of trees way out over there. They do say it's beyond Jersey.

CHILD MONAGHAN: Feels funny. We're standing right inside her head. Is that what you meant . . . July IV, MCD . . . ?

MONAGHAN: That's it. That tablet in her hand. Now shouldn't they have put Welcome All on it instead of that foreign language? Say! Do you feel her rockin'?

CHILD MONAGHAN: Yeah, she's moving a little bit. Listen, the wind!

(*Whistling of wind*)

MONAGHAN: We better get down, come on! This way!

CHILD MONAGHAN: No, the stairs are this way! Come on!

(*Running in echo. Then quick stop*)

MONAGHAN: No, I told you they're the other way! Come!

VETERAN (*calm, quiet voice*): Don't get excited, pop. She'll stand.

MONAGHAN: She's swayin' awful.

VETERAN: That's all right. I been up here thirty, forty times. She gives with the wind, flexible. Enjoy the view, go on.

MONAGHAN: Did you say you've been up here forty times?

VETERAN: About that many.

MONAGHAN: What do you find here that's so interesting?

VETERAN: It calms my nerves.

MONAGHAN: Ah. It seems to me it would make you more nervous than you were.

VETERAN: No, not me. It kinda means something to me.

MONAGHAN: Might I ask what?

VETERAN: Well . . . I was in the Philippine War . . . back in '98. Left my brother back there.

MONAGHAN: Oh, yes. Sorry I am to hear it. Young man, I suppose, eh?

VETERAN: Yeh. We were both young. This is his birthday today.

MONAGHAN: Oh, I understand.

VETERAN: Yeh, this statue is about the only stone he's got. In my mind I feel it is anyway. This statue kinda looks like what we believe. You know what I mean?

MONAGHAN: Looks like what we believe. . . . I . . . I never thought of it that way. I . . . I see what you mean. It does look that way. (*Angrily*) See now, boy? If Sheean had put it that way I'd a give him me dime. (*Hurt*) Now, why do you suppose he didn't tell me that! Come down now. I'm sorry, sir, we've got to get out of here.

375

(*Music up and down*)
(*Footsteps under*)
Hurry, now, I want to get out of here. I feel terrible. I do, boy. That Sheean, that fool. Why didn't he tell me that? You'd think . . .

CHILD MONAGHAN: What does this say?

(*Footsteps halt*)

MONAGHAN: Why, it's just a tablet, I suppose. I'll try it with me spectacles, just a minute. Why, it's a poem, I believe . . . . "Give me your tired, your poor, your huddled masses yearning to breathe free, the wretched refuse of your teeming shore. Send these, the homeless, tempest-tost to me, I lift . . . my lamp beside . . . the golden door!" Oh, dear. (*Ready to weep*) It had Welcome All on it all the time. Why didn't Sheean tell me? I'd a given him a quarter! Boy . . . go over there and here's a nickel and buy yourself a bag of them peanuts.

CHILD MONAGHAN (*astonished*): Gramp!

MONAGHAN: Go on now, I want to study this a minute. And be sure the man gives you full count.

CHILD MONAGHAN: I'll be right back.

376   (*Footsteps running away*)

MONAGHAN (*to himself*): "Give me your tired, your poor, your huddled masses. . . ."
(*Music swells from a sneak to full, then under to background*)

YOUNG MONAGHAN (*soldier*): I ran over and got my peanuts and stood there cracking them open, looking around. And I happened to glance over to grampa. He had his nose right up to that bronze tablet, reading it. And then he reached into his pocket and kinda spied around over his eyeglasses to see if anybody was looking, and then he took out a coin and stuck it in a crack of cement over the tablet.
(*Coin falling onto concrete*)
It fell out and before he could pick it up I got a look at it. It was half a buck. He picked it up and pressed it into the crack so it stuck. And then he came over to me and we went home.
(*Music: Change to stronger, more forceful theme*)
That's why, when I look at her now through this window, I remember that time and that poem, and she really seems to say, Whoever you are, wherever you come from, Welcome All. Welcome Home.
(*Music: Flare up to finish*)
                                        ARTHUR MILLER

Her friends were raising money for the base of the wonderful new Statue of Liberty. What could the young writer, Emma Lazarus, give?

The Voice of Liberty

Yes, the young girl he once knew had grown into a beautiful woman! So her old friend, William Evarts, remarked to himself when he came to call on her one afternoon. He knew her well enough not to make such a remark aloud. Emma would have dismissed it as sugar-coated flattery. She thought of her features as too angular, not delicate enough. Yet she was beautiful; her face, he mused, like a forest dense with thoughts. He was pleased at the phrase he had chosen. Why, he

smiled to himself, she is turning me into a poet, too!

They chatted for a while, and then he came to the point of his visit. Emma was familiar, was she not, with the noble gift the people of France were planning to donate to this country? It was to be a giant statue, representing the figure of Liberty.

Oh, yes, Emma nodded. There had been much talk about it. Just yesterday she had noticed a display of sketches for the figure in a shop window nearby. And Richard Watson Gilder was planning to publish an article about the man who was modeling the statue.

"Auguste Bartholdi," Evarts said. "Yes, Bartholdi is one of France's finest sculptors. He has executed his design on a truly grand scale. In fact, a bit too grand."

Emma was curious. How could anything be too grand?

"It will require a massive pedestal to support all that weight. The French people have been generous enough to donate the statue. We cannot very well ask them to contribute a base as well."

Evarts went on to explain the problem. "It would be tragic if—for lack of a foundation—the statue could not be put up at all!" Yet it appeared that the American government was not going to supply the money to have a base constructed. It was a costly operation. So now he, Evarts, together with some other private citizens, was forming a committee to raise the necessary funds. He felt that it was a most important and patriotic venture. Bartholdi had labored years at his design, and the finished statue would be a symbol of the continuing friendship between the people of France and the United States.

Emma kept nodding as he spoke. She was in thorough agreement— the French Revolution and the American Revolution had noble ideals in common. The statue, symbolic of that association, ought to be seen by as many people as possible. "Where," she inquired, "were they thinking of setting it up?"

Evarts was enthusiastic. "On Bedloe's Island, out in New York harbor, where it will serve as a beacon light of welcome to all who arrive at these shores."

Emma became caught up in her friend's enthusiasm. Bedloe's Island was a perfect site.

"Now," Evarts continued, "if only we can raise the thousands of dollars that the base will cost. Joseph Pulitzer is conducting a campaign in his newspaper. Even school children are contributing their pennies! But we need something spectacular to wind up with. So we are planning a literary auction of famous manuscripts. We already have one by Longfellow, another from Mark Twain, and Walt Whitman and Bret Harte. And," he bowed, "I am here at this moment to request one from Miss Emma Lazarus."

"I would like very much to help—it is a most worthy cause. But," she paused and frowned, "I really cannot think of anything I have written that would be appropriate."

"Then perhaps you will write something especially for the occasion?"

"Oh, no!" She was aghast at the idea. "I could not possibly write verses to order."

"I suppose not," Evarts agreed politely. Besides, the auction was planned for this coming week. That would not give her enough time, even if she did wish to compose something new. "Well, I hope you will attend the auction, at any rate."

After he left, Emma gazed thoughtfully out the window. She liked the name that had been chosen for the statue: "Liberty Enlightening the World." She also liked Bartholdi's personification of Liberty—as the figure of a woman, with a torch upheld to the sky. The torch of freedom, she mused. Like a light in the darkness, the darkness of intolerance and prejudice.

And light, she thought, as the sacred lamp of learning—enlightenment dispelling the shadows of ignorance. The light of man's knowledge, of his mastery over nature. Yes, liberty and learning went hand in hand. Ignorance was what created prejudice.

Perhaps it was true that she could not write poems "to order." Yet suddenly here was her conscience ordering her to create!

Images sprang to her mind; she had to write rapidly to set one down before the next arose. The statue was gigantic, a veritable colossus. Yet not, to her mind, like the ancient Greek Colossus that had been set up at the city gates of Rhodes. That statue had been war-like.

This figure was a new colossus.

Not like the brazen giant of Greek fame,
With conquering limbs astride from land to land . . .

No. Ours was a democratic harbor.

Here at our sea-washed, sunset gates shall stand
A mighty woman with a torch, whose flame
Is the imprisoned lightning, and her name—

What should be her name, this womanly figure? She was like a mother, calling home the exiled and the deserted. Yes, Liberty as a mother, accepting all, rejecting none. As a mother has no favorite child, but loves equally the fair and the dark, the gifted and the plain. So Liberty, here at our shores, welcoming the refugees.

380

Mother of Exiles. From her beacon hand
Glows world-wide welcome; her mild eyes command
The air-bridged harbor that twin cities frame.
"Keep, ancient lands, your storied pomp," cries she
With silent lips. "Give me your tired, your poor,
Your huddled masses yearning to breathe free,
The wretched refuse of your teeming shore.
Send these, the homeless, tempest-tost to me.
I lift my lamp beside the golden door!"

Emma completed her sonnet within a few swift hours. The lines were to endure forever after as the Voice of Liberty itself.

EVE MERRIAM

381

What's It All About?

1. What does Grandpa think of the Statue of Liberty before he visits it? What does he think at the end of the play?
2. Grandpa and Emma both end up doing something they had refused to do. What does each one do? Why do you think they changed their minds?

---

1. Why does Grandpa refuse to give a dime to the statue fund?
2. What does Grandpa predict will happen to the Statue of Liberty?
3. Why does young Monaghan want to visit the statue? How does he convince Grandfather to take him?
4. What reasons do Alf, the girl, the young man, and the veteran give for visiting the Statue of Liberty?
5. Why does Evarts visit Emma Lazarus?
6. What things does Emma Lazarus especially like about the Statue of Liberty?

PUTTING IDEAS TO WORK

Important ideas can be expressed in both poetry and prose. Write a prose summary, in your own words, of the last six lines of Emma Lazarus's poem. What is she saying about the ''ancient lands'' and this ''new land''?

MEDLEY

A
collection of
poetry
and
prose quotations

U.S.A.

So we march into the present
And it's always rather pleasant
To speculate on what the years ahead of us will see,
For our words and thoughts and attitudes,
All our novelties and platitudes,
Will be Rather Ancient History in 2033.

Will they find us wise—or silly?
Looking backwards, willy-nilly,
At our queer old-fashioned costumes and our quaint
 old-fashioned ways?
When our doings face the ages,
Printed down on textbook pages,
Will they cry, "This Savage Era"? Will they sigh,
 "Those were the days!"?

I don't know—you may be wiser.
Time's a curious capsizer
Of a lot of reputations that seemed certain to endure,
While he'll sometimes make his heroes
Out of people, once thought zeroes,
For the most well-grounded reasons,
 by the solemnly cocksure.

So, instead of prophesying
(Which is fun, but rather trying)
Who they'll pick to be our great ones when the books
 are on the shelves,
Here's the marching panorama
Of our past and present drama
—And we shan't know all the answers till we're history,
 ourselves.

384   ROSEMARY *and* STEPHEN VINCENT BENÉT

Freedom is a hard-bought thing—
A gift no man can give,
For some, a way of dying,
For most, a way to live.

JESSAMYN WEST

By the rude bridge that arched the flood,
    Their flag to April's breeze unfurled,
Here once the embattled farmers stood
    And fired the shot heard round the world.

386   RALPH WALDO EMERSON

An *from* Inaugural Address

We dare not forget today that we are the heirs of that first revolution. Let the word go forth from this time and place, to friend and foe alike, that the torch has been passed to a new generation of Americans—born in this century, tempered by war, disciplined by a hard and bitter peace, proud of our ancient heritage—and unwilling to witness or permit the slow undoing of those human rights to which this Nation has always been committed, and to which we are committed today at home and around the world. . . .

In your hands, my fellow citizens, more than in mine, will rest the final success or failure of our course. Since this country was founded, each generation of Americans has been summoned to give testimony to its national loyalty. The graves of young Americans who answered the call to service surround the globe.

Now the trumpet summons us again—not as a call to bear arms, though arms we need; not as a call to battle, though embattled we are; but a call to bear the burden of a long twilight struggle, year in, and year out, "rejoicing in hope, patient in tribulation"—a struggle against the common enemies of man: tyranny, poverty, disease, and war itself. . . .

And so, my fellow Americans, ask not what your country can do for you: Ask what you can do for your country.

My fellow citizens of the world: Ask not what America will do for you, but what together we can do for the freedom of man.

JOHN F. KENNEDY

Nothing great was ever achieved without enthusiasm.

RALPH WALDO EMERSON

The doors are twisted on broken hinges.
Sheets of rain swish through on the wind
    where the golden girls ran and the panels read:
    We are the greatest city,
    the greatest nation,
    nothing like us ever was.

CARL SANDBURG

388

the greatest city

What do you think endures?
Do you think a great city endures?
Or a teeming manufacturing state? or a prepared
    constitution? or the best built steamships?
Or hotels of granite and iron? or any chef-d'oeuvres of
    engineering, forts, armaments?

Away! These are not to be cherished for themselves,
They fill their hour, the dancers dance, the musicians
    play for them,
The show passes, all does well enough of course,
All does very well till one flash of defiance.

A great city is that which has the greatest
    men and women,
If it be a few ragged huts, it is still the greatest
    city in the whole world.

WALT WHITMAN

the time

There is a time for some things,
And a time for all things;
A time for great things
And a time for small things.

CERVANTES

I frequently tramped eight or ten miles
through the deepest snow to
keep an appointment with a beech tree,
or a yellow birch, or an old
acquaintance among the pines.

HENRY DAVID THOREAU

My horse's hooves
Tramp through the yellow leaves.
As the sun rises
Not a human being is visible
Only the sound of a stream
Through the misty trees.

SUN YÜN-FÊNG

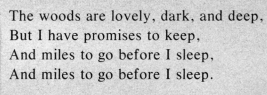

The woods are lovely, dark, and deep,
But I have promises to keep,
And miles to go before I sleep,
And miles to go before I sleep.

ROBERT FROST

391

The world is mine: blue hill, still silver lake,
Broad field, bright flower, and the long white road
A gateless garden, and an open path:
My feet to follow, and my heart to hold.

Edna St. Vincent Millay

The whole world is coming,
A nation is coming, a nation is coming,
The Eagle has brought the message to the tribe.
The father says so, the father says so.
Over the whole earth they are coming.
The buffalo are coming, the buffalo are coming,
The Crow has brought the message to the tribe,
The father says so, the father says so.

Sioux

the EAGLE

He clasps the crag with crooked hands;
Close to the sun in lonely lands,
Ringed with the azure world, he stands.

The wrinkled sea beneath him crawls;
He watches from his mountain walls,
And like a thunderbolt he falls.

ALFRED, LORD TENNYSON

Grandmother's Eagles

Grandmother and I walked the hills when I was a little boy. She loved to watch the eagles fly overhead. One day, high on a ridge, she showed me the eaglets' bed, and she told me how the mother eagle pushed her young ones off. They'd fall, but they would spread their wings and fly high above.

She said, "Son, they'll teach you." I wondered how they could teach me. But I watched, and it was true. They would fly high, so high they'd become like a sand pebble. Then they would plummet down—I guessed because they heard their mother call. But while they were up there, I imagined they'd see far across the land, and it seemed that they were happy.

And Grandmother told me to watch their wings when they flew. They'd spread way out, and they'd gather in the wind so they might fly to places where nobody had been. She said the eagles flew high because they had grown into a world where they had to reach for life.

One day Grandmother felt sick, I did all that I could to make her feel better, but I didn't do much good. She said that everyone had a time when they must go beyond the horizon but that life didn't end; it goes on and on and on. She told me not to wander along the frozen tracks of yesterday but to "go and reach for happiness. Fly, my son; spread your wings and gather in the wind of knowledge. Be strong. We'll meet again, and like the eagles we'll fly." And Grandmother went away.

Today I don't see the eagles. But what Grandmother told me I try to do.

RAY BALDWIN LOUIS

BARTER

Life has loveliness to sell,
    All beautiful and splendid things,
Blue waves whitened on a cliff,
    Soaring fire that sways and sings,
And children's faces looking up
Holding wonder like a cup.

Life has loveliness to sell,
    Music like a curve of gold,
Scent of pine trees in the rain,
    Eyes that love you, arms that hold,
And for your spirit's still delight,
Holy thoughts that star the night.

Spend all you have for loveliness,
    Buy it and never count the cost;
For one white singing hour of peace
    Count many a year of strife well lost,
And for a breath of ecstasy
Give all you have been, or could be.

SARA TEASDALE

YOUTH

We have tomorrow
Bright before us
Like a flame.

Yesterday
A night-gone thing,
A sun-down name.

And dawn-today
Broad arch above the road we came.

We march!

LANGSTON HUGHES

I dwell in Possibility—
A fairer House than Prose—
More numerous of Windows—
Superior—for Doors—

396   EMILY DICKINSON

. . . heads of future things appear,
like mountain-tops whose mists have rolled away.

WILLIAM WORDSWORTH

Glossary

*Pronunciation Key**

a	hat, cap	j	jam, enjoy	u	cup, butter
ā	age, face	k	kind, seek	ù	full, put
ä	father, far	l	land, coal	ü	rule, move
		m	me, am		
b	bad, rob	n	no, in	v	very, save
ch	child, much	ng	long, bring	w	will, woman
d	did, red			y	young, yet
		o	hot, rock	z	zero, breeze
e	let, best	ō	open, go	zh	measure, seizure
ē	equal, be	ô	order, all		
ėr	term, learn	oi	oil, voice	ə	represents:
		ou	house, out		a in about
f	fat, if				e in taken
g	go, bag	p	paper, cup		i in pencil
h	he, how	r	run, try		o in lemon
		s	say, yes		u in circus
i	it, pin	sh	she, rush		
ī	ice, five	t	tell, it		
		th	thin, both		
		ᴛH	then, smooth		

A

a·bate (ə bāt′) *verb.* 1. To reduce in degree; to lessen in intensity: The hurricane raged for hours before it *abated.* 2. To subtract from an amount; to deduct. **abated, abating.** —**abatement** *noun.*

ab·duct (ab dukt′) *verb.* To kidnap; to carry off by force. **abducted, abducting.**

a·byss (ə bis′) *noun.* 1. A bottomless pit; a deep crack in the earth: Only a rope around her waist prevented her from falling into the *abyss* below her. 2. Any depth or void too great to be measured: The loss of his dog sent the boy into an *abyss* of despair.

ad·mit (ad mit′) *verb.* 1. To acknowledge; to confess: He *admitted* his error. 2. To permit to enter: The director *admitted* the tourists to the museum. 3. To grant as being true or valid: The judge *admitted* the new evidence. **admitted, admitting.**

af·ter·ef·fect (af′ tər i fekt′) *noun.* The result of something; that which follows later: The *after-effect* of the hurricane was a great deal of flooding.

aide (ād) *noun.* A helper; an assistant: The military *aide* served breakfast to the general.

al·ien (ā′lyən) *noun.* A non-citizen; a foreigner. *adjective.* 1. Of or relating to another country: an *alien* culture. 2. Strange; abnormal: Anger is *alien* to her personality.

am·pli·fy (am′ plə fī) *verb.* 1. To make stronger; to intensify: They added electrical equipment to *amplify* the sound. 2. To make complete: The diagrams *amplified* the written explanations. 3. To explain at length or in great detail. **amplified, amplifying.**

an·a·gram (an′ ə gram) *noun.* A puzzle in which a word or phrase is formed by reordering the letters of another word or phrase.

an·guished (ang′ gwisht) *adjective.* Painful; filled with suffering: The *anguished* cries of the drowning cat brought rescuers to the icy stream.

an·thol·o·gy (an thol′ ə jē) *noun.* A collection of literary pieces, such as poems, plays, and short stories. —**anthological** *adjective.* —**anthologist** *noun.*

an·tic·i·pa·tion (an tis′ ə pā′ shən) *noun.* The act of foreseeing; the state of expecting: She was filled with *anticipation* about the announcement that would soon be made.

ap·pall (ə pôl′) *verb.* To fill with fear; terrify: The prospect of another hurricane *appalled* us. **appalled, appalling.**

ap·pa·ra·tus (ap′ ə rā′ təs *or* ap′ ə rat′ əs) *noun.* 1. A machine or group of machines designed to perform specific tasks. 2. A political organization. 3. Set of standards for measuring or testing. —**apparatus** or **apparatuses** *plural.*

ap·pre·hen·sion (ap′ ri hen′ shən) *noun.* 1. Fear; dread: The look on the police officer's face confirmed Hank's worst *apprehensions.* 2. Arrest: The *apprehension* of the criminal was made possible by the description given by the victim. 3. Understanding; grasping by the mind: I do not have a clear *apprehension* of the poem's meaning.

ap·pro·pri·ate (ə prō′ prē it) *adjective.* Fitting for the occasion. —*verb* (ə prō′ prē āt) 1. To set aside for a special purpose: The committee *appropriated* the money for the new sidewalks. 2. To take or use without permission. **appropriated, appropriating.** —**appropriately** *adverb.* —**appropriateness** *noun.*

as·cent (ə sent′) *noun.* 1. The act of going up. 2. An upward slope or incline. 3. An advancement in social or economic position.

at·tend (ə tend′) *verb.* 1. To pay attention; to care for. 2. To be present at: to *attend* the meeting. 3. To wait upon, as a servant. 4. To remain ready; to wait. —**attended, attending.**

at·ten·tion (ə ten′ shən) *noun.* 1. Consideration; courtesy: Her hosts gave the visitor a great deal of *attention.* 2. The act of paying attention: The driver paid *attention* to the guide's instructions. 3. Power of attending: The museum guide called our *attention* to the gold leaf decoration. 4. (Plural) Acts of politeness or devotion: The king received many *attentions* from his nobles. 5. A military attitude or posture: The soldier came to *attention* as the general entered the room.

at·ten·tive (ə ten′ tiv) *adjective.* 1. Courteous; considerate: The *attentive* host made certain that his guests were introduced to one another. 2. Showing attention; listening; observant: The *attentive* student watched each step of the laboratory procedure. —**attentively** *adverb.* —**attentiveness** *noun.*

B

bea·con (bē′ kən) *noun.* 1. A signal or marker used to guide or warn. 2. A high tower for a signal. 3. A marker or signal light or radio signal that guides planes and ships through stormy weather.

ben·e·fac·tor (ben′ ə fak′ tər) *noun.* One who gives financial or other assistance.

blind (blīnd) *noun.* 1. A shelter for duck hunters. 2. Any decoy. 3. Something that blocks vision or shuts out light: He closed the venetian *blinds.*

blurt (blėrt) *verb.* To say suddenly on impulse; to speak without thinking. **blurted, blurting.**

bois·ter·ous (boi′ stər əs) *adjective.* 1. Loud; noisy; rowdy: The *boisterous* cheerleaders cheered the team wildly. 2. Stormy; violent. —**boisterously** *adverb.* —**boisterousness** *noun.*

bond (bond) *noun.* 1. Anything that binds, ties, or fastens together. 2. (Plural) Captivity; confinement. 3. The duty, promise, or oath by which one is bound. 4. (Legal) A sum of money paid as bail or surety. 5. (Finance) A certificate of debt promising future payment with interest on a specified date. —*verb.* 1. To place a guarantee on. 2. To furnish money as bail or surety. 3. To join securely with glue or cement. **bonded, bonding.**

bound[1] (bound) *verb.* 1. To leap; to jump forward or upward. 2. To move forward by bounds. **bounded, bounding.** —*noun.* A leap; a jump.

bound[2] (bound) *verb.* 1. To set a limit to. 2. To join or border upon another country or place. 3. To be tied up. 4. To be certain: We are *bound* to be late. 5. To be headed in a particular direction. **bounded, bounding.**

brogue (brōg) *noun.* A strongly marked accent peculiar to a dialect: She speaks English with an Irish *brogue.*

buck·board (buk′ bôrd′) *noun.* An open four-wheeled carriage with the seat fastened to a platform with long, flexible boards extending from the front to the rear axle.

butte (byüt) *noun.* A lone, steep hill found in the western part of the United States. —**buttes.**

C

ca·ble (kā′ bəl) *noun.* 1. A message sent by telegraph. 2. A strong, thick steel or fiber rope. 3. A heavy rope or chain used for mooring a boat. 4. A unit of nautical length equal to 720 feet (216 m) in the United States and 608 feet (182.4 m) in England. —*verb.* To send a message by telegraph. She *cabled* her friends the date of her arrival. **cabled, cabling.**

cache (kash) *verb.* 1. To store in a hiding place for future use. 2. To put together. **cached, caching.** —*noun.* 1. A hole, cave, or similar hiding place used by pioneers for storing supplies. 2. A place for hiding valuables. 3. A store of hidden supplies or valuables.

cal·cu·la·tion (kal′ kyə lā′ shən) *noun.* 1. An estimate. 2. The act or result of calculating. 3. Foresight. —**calculative** *adjective.*

cam·ou·flage (kam′ ə fläzh) *noun.* Any attempt at concealment achieved by making people or things appear to be part of the environment or surroundings.

cas·cade (ka skād′) *verb.* To fall from one level to another continuously: The river *cascaded* down the gorge and rushed on to the sea. **cascaded, cascading.** —*noun.* A waterfall or series of waterfalls over steep hills or mountains.

cause (kôz) *noun.* 1. An idea or movement in which many people are interested and to which they give their assistance. 2. A person, thing, or act which makes something happen. 3. The reason for an event: The birth of their child was the *cause* for a party. —*verb.* To bring about; to make happen: The hurricane *caused* much flooding. **caused, causing.**

cha·os (kā′ os) *noun.* A great confusion; complete disorder: The hurricane left the village in *chaos.*

chute (shüt) *noun.* 1. An inclined or sloped tunnel or passage down which things may pass. 2. A waterfall. 3. (Informal) A parachute.

claim (klām) *verb.* 1. To demand as a right: She produced the bill of sale and *claimed* the car. 2. To state strongly: The snake-oil salesperson *claimed* the medicine would cure all ills. 3. To require; to deserve: My homework *claims* my attention. **claimed, claiming.** —*noun.* 1. A demand: His *claim* to the chair was challenged by the family dog. 2. A declaration of something as a fact: The court decided that the state's *claim* to the land was justified. 3. A title to a tract of land. 4. A statement of one's right to something valuable, such as money or an inheritance.

claim·ant (klā′ mənt) *noun.* One who makes a claim.

clam·ber (klam′ bər) *verb.* To climb awkardly with both the hands and feet. **clambered, clambering.**

clar·i·ty (klar′ ə tē) *noun.* Clearness: The bright sunlight outlined the small boat with remarkable *clarity.*

cli·ent (klī′ ənt) *noun.* 1. A person to whom professional services are provided. 2. A customer or patron. 3. One who is dependent on the services of another.

co·los·sus (kə los′ əs) *noun.* 1. A huge statue. 2. Any gigantic monument; person or institution. —**collosi** or **colluses** *plural.*

Com·mon·wealth (kom' ən welth') *noun.*
1. An association of nations with a common bond. 2. The people who make up a state or nation.

com·pete (kəm pēt') *verb.* 1. To participate in a contest: He is *competing* in the high hurdles. 2. To try hard to win something wanted by others: She *competed* with other students for the science medal. **competed, competing.** —**competitor** *noun.*

com·pet·i·tive (kəm pet' ə tiv) *adjective.* Decided by means of a competition: She took a *competitive* exam to gain admittance to medical school. —**competitively** *adverb.*

con·fi·dent (kon' fə dənt) *adjective.* Having a feeling of confidence; a sense of certainty. —**confidently** *adverb.*

con·glom·er·a·tion (kən glom' ə rā' shən) *noun.* 1. A collection of many different items; a cluster. 2. The process of conglomerating, or collecting in a mass; the state of being conglomerated, or collected in a mass.

con·scious·ness (kon' shəs nis) *noun.* 1. Awareness; condition of being conscious: The injured poodle did not regain *consciousness* for many hours. 2. All the thoughts and feelings of a person.

con·sec·u·tive (kən sek' yə tiv) *adjective.* Following in regular succession. —**consecutively** *adverb.* —**consecutiveness** *noun.*

con·spic·u·ous (kən spik' yü əs) *adjective.* 1. Noticeable; obvious. 2. Gaining attention by being unusual or remarkable. —**conspicuously** *adverb.* —**conspicuousness** *noun.*

con·stant (kon' stənt) *adjective.* 1. Tending to continue without stopping: Two days of *constant* snow made the highways impassable. Continually repeating: The *constant* dripping of the faucet was annoying. 3. Unchanging: Her affection for her mischievous dog was *constant*. 4. Faithful; loyal: His teacher was his *constant* friend. —*noun.* A thing, value, or quantity that is unchanging: The number of days in a week is an important *constant* of our calendar. —**constantly** *adverb.*

con·vey (kən vā') *verb.* 1. To make known; to communicate: His sagging shoulders *conveyed* the message that he had not passed his exams. 2. To take or carry from one place to another: The pipes were *conveyed* by plane to the oilfieds. 3. To conduct; to transmit: The ship's radio *conveyed* the captain's plea for help. **conveyed, conveying.** —**conveyable** *adjective.*

cor·dial (kôr jəl) *adjective.* In a warm and friendly manner: The principal welcomed the parents in a *cordial* manner. —*noun.* 1. Food, drink, or medicine that has a strengthening or stimulating effect. 2. A liqueur. —**cordially** *adverb.*

cor·di·al·i·ty (kôr' jē al' ə tē) *noun.* A warm feeling or quality; heartiness: The ambassador's *cordiality* made him popular with his guests. —**cordialities.**

cor·re·spon·dence (kôr' ə spon' dəns) *noun.* 1. Letters: She hired a secretary to take care of her *correspondence*. 2. The exchange of letters: The boy received a great deal of *correspondence* from his uncle in India. 3. A being in agreement. 4. Similarity: There is a *correspondence* of ideas between the poem and the play.

cove (kōv) *noun.* 1. A small, protected bay or inlet. 2. A protected place in the hills or woods.

crev·ice (krev′ is) *noun.* A narrow opening; a cleft: The mountaineer reached the *crevice* and helped pull his companion to safety.

cul·de·sac (kŭl′ di-sak *or* kool′ di-sak) *noun.* An impasse; a dead-end street: The street was a *cul-de-sac* and was safe for children to play in.

cur·rent (kėr′ ənt) *noun.* 1. The flow or movement of water, air, or any liquid or gas: The swift-moving *current* carried the raft down the stream. 2. The flow of electricity through wires. 3. The amount of electricity measured as it flows past a given point. 4. The general tendency of events or opinions. —*adjective.* 1. Related to the time now passing: Have you read the *current* issue of this magazine? 2. Commonly used or accepted: Several hundred years ago it was a *current* belief that the earth was the center of the universe. 3. Going from person to person, as money. —**currently** *adverb.*

D

de·bark (di bärk′) *verb.* 1. To get off, as from a ship. 2. To unload from a ship. **debarked, debarking.** —**debarkation** *noun.*

de·coy (dē′ koi *or* di koi′) *noun.* 1. A living or artificial animal used to lure animals into a trap or within shooting range. 2. A place used as a trap into which animals are lured. 3. One who leads another into a trap. —*verb.* 1. To lead into danger or a trap. 2. To be lead into a trap. **decoyed, decoying.**

de·ject·ed (di jek′ tid) *adjective.* Depressed; sad: The *dejected* team left the field after losing the championship game. —**dejectedly** *adverb.* —**dejectedness** *noun.*

de·plor·a·ble (di plôr′ ə bəl) *adjective.* 1. Very bad; terrible. 2. Lamentable; grievous. 3. Deserving of severe criticism or discipline. —**deplorably** *adverb.* —**deplorableness** *noun.*

de·scend (di send′) *verb.* 1. To come down from a line of ancestors: He is *descended* from the Pilgrims. 2. To move from a higher to a lower place. 3. To slope or extend downward. 4. To lower oneself in behavior. 5. To arrive in a showy manner: My famous uncle *descended* upon my family like a hurricane. **descended, descending.**

de·scen·dant (di sen′ dənt) *noun.* A person or animal descended from another or others. —**descendent** *adjective.*

de·scent (di sent′) *noun.* 1. The act of coming down. 2. The way down. 3. A sudden attack. 4. (Legal) The transfer of property by inheritance.

de·spite (di spīt′) *proposition.* In spite of, not withstanding: *Despite* the experience of their opponents, the freshman team won the game.

des·ti·ny (des′ tə nē) *noun.* 1. The fate of a person or thing; what becomes of a person: It was her *destiny* to become famous. 2. What is decided for a person and is beyond the person's control or influence: He believed that it was *destiny* that caused him to become shipwrecked. —**destinies.**

dev·as·tate (dev′ ə stāt) *verb.* 1. To destroy; to lay waste: The flood waters *devasted* the farmlands. 2. (Informal) To defeat: Our basketball team *devasted* their rivals in the game. **devastated, devastating.** —**devastatingly** *adverb.* —**devastation** *noun.*

di·lem·ma (də lem′ ə) *noun.* A situation in which a difficult choice must be made. **dilemmas.**

dis·dain (dis dān') *noun.* A show of scorn: The duke treated the peasant farmers with *disdain.* —*verb.* To despise; to treat with contempt. **disdained, disdaining.** —**disdainful** *adjective.*

dis·mal (diz' məl) *adjective.* 1. Gloomy; dreary: The rain made the day a *dismal* one. 2. Dreadful; disastrous: The burned village was a *dismal* sight. —**dismally** *adverb.*

dis·tort (dis tôrt') *verb* 1. To mislead: The newspaper article *distorted* the facts. 2. To twist out of shape. 3. To cause to work in twisted or wrongful manner. **distorted, distorting.**

do·mes·tic (də mes' tik) *adjective.* 1. Relating to one's own country; not foreign: Some magazines publish both a *domestic* and a foreign edition. 2. Relating to the home and family life. 3. Fond of home and family life. 4. Tame; adjusted to civilization; not wild: Dogs and cats are considered *domestic* animals. —*noun.* A household servant: A cook is a *domestic* servant. —**domestically** *adverb.*

drake (drāk) *noun.* A male duck.

drought (drout) *noun.* 1. A long period without rain. 2. A scarcity of anything. —**droughty** *adjective.*

E

ebb (eb) *noun.* 1. A decline: After the stock market crash his fortune was at an *ebb.* 2. The fall of the tide: He liked to walk the shore when the tide was at an *ebb.* —*verb.* 1. To decline. 2. To flow out; to fall away. **ebbed, ebbing.**

e·go·tism (ē' gə tiz' əm) *noun.* 1. A tendency to talk or write about oneself in a boastful manner; conceit. 2. The quality of being overly concerned with oneself; selfishness.

el·i·gi·ble (el' ə jə bəl) *adjective.* Qualified; fit to be chosen: Students had to be sixteen years old in order to be *eligible* for the drivers education course.

em·bark (em bärk') *verb.* 1. To board a ship. 2. To set out on a journey or adventure. 3. To invest in a business venture. **embarked, embarking.** —**embarkation, embarkment** *noun.*

en·dure (en dür' *or* en dyür') *verb.* 1. To last; to remain: Steel *endures* for a long time. 2. To bear; to withstand: The Pilgrims *endured* a perilous voyage to come to America. **endured, enduring.**

en·dur·ing (en door' ing *or* en dyoor' ing *or* in door' ing) *adjective.* 1. Patient. 2. Lasting: The library is an *enduring* monument to its' founder. 3. Chronic; undecided: an *enduring* problem. —**enduringly** *adverb.* —**enduringness** *noun.*

en·light·en (en līt' n) *verb.* To give truth and knowledge; to inform: The director *enlightened* her staff. **enlightened, enlightening.**

en·light·en·ment (en līt' n mənt) *noun.* Information; instruction: The news reporter provided some *enlightenment* on the judge's decision.

ep·i·dem·ic (ep' ə dem' ik) *noun.* 1. Any contagious disease that spreads quickly. 2. A brief, widespread popularity of a fad or fashion: Playing with hula hoops was a fad that once reached *epidemic* proportions among young people.

ex·ile (eg' zīl *or* ek' sīl) *verb.* To force a person from his native land; to banish. **exiled, exiling.** —*noun.* 1. One who is exiled. 2. The state of being exiled.

ex·ploit (ek' sploit) *noun.* Bold, daring deeds: She liked to read about Robin Hood's *exploits.* —*verb.* (ek sploit') 1. To make use of: That mine is *exploited* for its coal. 2. To take unfair advantage of: Some countries used to *exploit* their colonies. **exploited, exploiting.**

404

F

fol·ly (fol′ ē) *noun.* 1. Foolish; without good sense or foresight. 2. Any silly act. 3. An act which has a tragic or expensive result: Jack named the boat he couldn't afford to keep, "Jack's *Folly.*" — **follies.**

for·mi·da·ble (fôr′ mə də bəl) *adjective.* 1. Admirable; awesome. 2. Causing fear or alarm. 3. Difficult to defeat or overcome. —**formidably** *adverb.* —**formidableness** *noun.*

for·ti·fi·ca·tion (fôr′ tə fə kā′ shən) *noun.* 1. A fort; something that protects or defends. 2. The act of fortifying.

frus·tra·tion (frus trā′ shən) *noun.* 1. Discouragement; disappointment. 2. One that causes discouragement.

G

gal·lows (gal′ ōz) *noun.* (Plural) 1. A structure consisting of two upright beams supporting a crossbeam from which a noose is hung and used for execution by hanging. 2. Any similar structure used for this purpose.

game (gām) *adjective.* Spirited; brave: She was *game* for a white water canoe ride.

ghast·ly (gast′ lē) *adjective.* 1. Horrible; dreadful: The rescued miner told the *ghastly* tale of the mine explosion. 2. With a sick or deathlike appearance: The sleepwalker had a *ghastly* look on his face. —*adverb.* 1. Horribly; terrible. 2. Ghostly. —**ghastliness** *noun.*

grand (grand) *adjective.* 1. Great; impressive: The monument was built on a *grand* scale. 2. Large and of fine appearance. 3. Noble quality. 4. High rank: She was the *Grand* Duchess of Austria. 5. Complete: the *grand* total. (Informal) Very satisfactory: We had a *grand* time at the picnic. (Slang) A thousand dollars. —**grandly** *adverb.* —**grandnness** *noun.*

grave (grāv) *adjective.* 1. Dignified in behavior; serious. 2. Critical: She is recovering from a *grave* illness. 3. Important; weighty: The president tried to find a solution to the *grave* crisis. — **gravely** *adverb.* —**graveness** *noun.*

grim (grim) *adjective.* 1. Without mercy; harsh: The rain made it a *grim* day. 2. Without yielding: The losing army fought on with *grim* determination. 3. Horrible; frightening: The car accident was a *grim* sight. —**grimly** *adverb.* — **grimness** *noun.*

grin·go (gring′ gō) *noun.* In Latin America, a foreigner; especially, a person from North America or England. Used contemptuously. (Spanish: *gringo*, originally meant an unknown tongue, gibberish.) —**gringos.**

grudge (gruj) *verb.* To have a feeling of resentment caused by some slight or insult. **grudged, grudging.**

grudg·ing·ly (gruj′ ing lē) *adverb.* In a reluctant manner; unwillingly: She *grudgingly* praised the performance of her competitor.

gru·el·ing (grü′ ə ling) *adjective.* (Informal) Exhausting; draining; tiring: The ten mile race was *grueling.*

gulch (gulch) *noun.* A small, shallow canyon with steep, smooth sides; a small ravine.

H

ha·bit·u·al (hə bich′ ü əl) *adjective.* 1. Done often unconsciously and regularly: His habitual nail-chewing kept his fingernails ragged. 2. Done deliberately and regularly: A *habitual* chess player is one who plays the game regularly. 3. Usual; customary: Her *habitual* breakfast is bacon and eggs. —**habitually** *adverb.* —**habitualness** *noun.*

hap·haz·ard (hap haz′ ərd) *adjective.* Casual; unplanned; random: He had a *haphazard* system for keeping his papers. —*adverb.* By chance; casually: The flowers were strewn on the table in a *haphazard* way. —**haphazardly** *adverb.* —**haphazardness** *noun.*

haunt (hônt) *verb.* 1. To visit often: He *haunted* his old neighborhood looking for familiar friends. 2. To be often with: Memories of her youth *haunted* the woman. **haunted, haunting.** —*noun.* A place frequently visited: The old swimming hole was the favorite *haunt* of the children on a hot day. —**hauntingly** *adverb.*

heir·loom (er′ lüm′ *or* ar′ lüm′) *noun.* A possession handed down from generation to generation: My great grandfather's watch is a family *heirloom.*

hem·lock (hem′ lok) *noun.* An evergreen tree found in North America and eastern Asia. The *hemlock* tree has short, flat needles and small cones.

her·it·age (her′ ə tij) *noun.* Something which is handed down from one generation to another: The love of singing is a strong part of the cultural *heritage* of the Welsh people.

I

id·i·o·cy (id′ ē ə sē) *noun.* 1. Foolish. 2. Great stupidity. 3. A foolish action or statement. —**idiocies.**

im·age (im′ ij) *noun.* 1. The public concept or impression created by someone or something: That politician has an informal *image* with the voters. 2. A reproduction of the appearance of a person or object. 3. A counterpart; a double; a representation of something. 4. A mental picture of something not real or present. 5. A mental picture created by words. —*verb.* 1. To copy; to portray. 2. To mirror or reflect. 3. To symbolize. 4. To describe or recall. **imaged, imaging.**

in·ad·e·qua·cy (in ad′ ə kwə sē) *noun.* 1. Inability; failure. 2. A defect; a lack. —**inadequacies.**

in·cred·u·lous (in krej′ ə ləs) *adjective.* 1. Disbelieving; doubtful; uncertain. 2. Expressing disbelief: He had an *incredulous* look on his face when he heard the shocking news. —**incredulously** *adverb.*

in·dif·fer·ent (in dif′ ər ənt) *adjective.* 1. Having no concern for. 2. Not partial; having no bias. 3. Insignificant; unimportant. 4. Being neither too much or too little; moderate. —**indifferently** *adverb.*

in·dig·nant (in dig′ nənt) *adjective.* Angry at some insult or injury: The waiter's rudeness made her *indignant.* —**indignantly** *adverb.*

in·dig·na·tion (in′ dig nā′ shən) *noun.* Anger at something unworthy, unjust or mean: The proposed taxation stirred his *indignation.*

i·ni·ti·ate (i nish′ ē āt) *verb.* 1. To admit a person with special ceremonies into a group. 2. To start; to begin: The President *initiated* the baseball season by throwing out the first ball. 3. To introduce someone to a new subject, art, or craft: The girl's father *initiated* her into the fine art of tying a lure. **initiated, initiating.** —(i nish′ ē it *or* i nish′ ē āt)

in·scribe (in skrīb′) *verb.* 1. To mark or write words or names on stone, metal, or paper: His name was *inscribed* on the bracelet. To dedicate or address a book or picture: The author *inscribed* the book to her teacher. 3. To impress deeply: Her parting words were *inscribed* in his memory. 4. To list. **inscribed, inscribing.**

in·tense (in tens′) *adjective.* 1. Extreme in degree. 2. Showing strain. 3. Depth of feeling. —**intensely** *adverb.* —**intenseness** *noun.*

in·ten·si·ty (in ten′ sə tē) *noun.* Unusually high concentration, power, or force. —**intensities.**

in·ter·na·tion·al (in′ tər nash′ ə nəl) *adjective.* 1. Having to do with relations among nations: The countries signed *international* agreements about the use of the oceans. 2. Between or among nations. —**internationally** *adverb.*

in·tol·er·ance (in tol′ ər əns) *noun.* 1. Unwillingness to let others do and think as they choose. 2. Inability to endure.

irk (ėrk) *verb.* To irritate; to annoy: Her political beliefs *irked* her friends. **irked, irking.**

ir·res·o·lute (i rez′ ə lüt) *adjective.* Indecisive; wavering; unable to make up one's mind: *Irresolute* people are of little help in a crisis. —**irresolutely** *adverb.*

J

jaun·ty (jôn′ tē) *adjective.* 1. Brisk; carefree: She strode down the lane with a *jaunty* air. 2. Stylish in appearance: The flower in his lapel gave him a *jaunty* appearance. —**jauntily** *adverb.* —**jauntiness** *noun.*

jin·rik·i·sha (jin rik′ shə *or* jin rik′ shô) *noun.* A small, two-wheeled, oriental carriage drawn by one or two people.

L

la·ser (lā′ zər) *noun.* A light beam which repeats itself in a predictable, orderly pattern.

lav·a·liere (lav′ ə-lûr′ *or* la va lyâr′) *noun.* A pendant; a brooch often worn on a chain around the neck.

leg·a·cy (leg′ ə sē) *noun.* 1. Something that has been handed down from one generation to another or from the past: The boy decided that the memory of his father's wit was the best *legacy* he could have. 2. Money or property left to a person by a will. —**legacies.**

life·line (līf′ līn′) *noun.* 1. A signaling line used by divers. 2. A secured line thrown as a support to someone falling or drowning. 3. The methods of transport or the route by which necessary supplies are sent.

list (list) *noun.* A leaning to one side; tilt. —*verb.* To lean or tilt to one side. **listed,** listing.

long (lông) *verb.* To wish earnestly; to hope for; to yearn: He looked at the ocean and *longed* to take a swim. **longed, longing.**

loom (lüm) *verb.* To appear dimly as a large threatening shape: Suddenly the last peak of the mountain *loomed* through the clouds and we knew the expedition was not over. **loomed, looming.** —*noun.* A frame for weaving cloth.

lurk (lėrk) *verb.* 1. To exist unobserved or unexpected; to be hidden. 2. To sneak; to slink: We could hear a wild animal *lurking* in the bushes. 3. To lie in wait, as in ambush. **lurked, lurking.**

M

mal·lard (mal′ ərd) *noun.* A wild duck of which the male has a green head and neck.

mar·ket (mär′ kit) *noun.* 1. The demand for something: There is always a *market* for used cars. 2. A trade center: Europe is a *market* for sugar. 3. A store for the sale of food: a fruit and vegetable *market.* 4. A place where people meet to buy and sell goods, cattle, or stocks and bonds. 5. The people at such a market: The arrival of the crossbred sheep stirred the *market.* —*verb.* 1. To buy or sell in the market. 2. To sell: Farmer's are unable to *market* their wheat due to low prices. **marketed, marketing. — marketer** *noun.*

men·ace (men′ is) *noun.* 1. A threatening or troublesome person. 2. A threat. 3. The act of threatening. —*verb.* To threaten: The enemy submarines *menaced* the cargo ships. **menaced, menacing. —menacingly** *adverb.*

merge (murj) *verb.* To blend together so as to lose identity: The two companies *merged* and became a new business firm. **merged, merging. —merger** *noun.*

mod·er·ate (mod′ ər it) *adjective.* 1. Not excessive; fair in quantity, quality, or extent: He charged a *moderate* fee for repairing the car. 2. Not violent; calm: The islands have *moderate* weather during the winter. —*noun.* A person who has temperate opinions in politics or religion. —*verb.* (mod′ ə rāt) 1. To make less severe or extreme. 2. To govern or occupy the place of authority: She was chosen to *moderate* the discussion. **moderated, moderating. —moderately** *adverb.*

mol·ten (mōlt′ n) *adjective.* 1. Brightly glowing: The piece of quartz had a *molten* beauty. 2. Melted and fused together by intense heat or pressure.

mor·ti·fy (môr′ tə fū) *verb.* 1. To feel humble; to humiliate; to make ashamed: He was *mortified* to discover that his shirt was inside out. 2. To overcome by pain or denial: The hermit *mortified* his desire for rich food by living on plants and berries. 3. To die; decay. **mortified, mortifying.**

moti·va·tion (mō′ tə vā′ shən) *noun.* Something that encourages an action; encouragement: The prospect of getting a bicycle was *motivation* to save her money.

mount (mount) *verb.* 1. To get up on: He *mounted* his horse and rode off. 2. To climb. 3. To provide with a horse: The stable *mounted* the new rider with a gentle mare. 4. To provide with scenery, as in a theatrical production. 5. To put in readiness and begin an action: With the guns in place the soldiers *mounted* the attack. 6. To increase in intensity or number: The suspense *mounted* as the villain crept toward the unsuspecting victim. **mounted, mounting. —noun.** 1. A horse, animal, or vehicle on which to ride. 2. An object which serves as a base or pedestal for another object.

mov·ing (mü′ ving) *adjective.* 1. Touching; pathetic: That was a *moving* poem. 2. That moves: Watch out for *moving* cars! 3. Causing action: He was the *moving* spirit in planning for the banquet. **—movingly** *adverb.*

mum (mum) *adjective.* Silent, saying nothing: *Mum's* the word. (Informal) Be silent: say nothing.

N

non·cha·lant (non′ shə lənt *or* non′ shə länt′) *adjective.* Casual; unconcerned. **—nonchalantly** *adverb.*

O

odds (odz) *noun* (Plural) 1. The likelihood of one result occurring over another. 2. (In games) An advantage given to the weaker of two opponents.

oc·cu·py (ok′ yə pū) *verb.* 1. To take possession of and keep control over an area by military conquest: The Roman Empire sent troops to *occupy* the provinces. 2. To live in; to dwell: He *occupies* an apartment in that building. 3. To hold or fill (an office or position): She *occupied* the office of vice-president for ten years. 4. To fill up: The guided tour of the museum *occupied* most of the day. 5. To employ; to busy oneself: He *occupied* himself with a magazine while he waited for the plane. **occupied, occupying.**

op·pres·sive (ə pres′ iv) *adjective.* 1. Causing physical or mental distress: The heat wave lasted several days and had been *oppressive*. 2. Harsh; tyrannical: The farmers thought the land tax was *oppressive* and refused to pay it.

or·der·ly (ôr′ dər lē) *adjective.* 1. In order; with a regular method or arrangement: The boy kept his books in an *orderly* row on the shelf. 2. Keeping order; well behaved: The kindergartners were an *orderly* class. —*noun.* 1. A soldier who attends a superior officer. 2. A hospital attendant who keeps things clean and in order. —**orderlies.**

o·ver·ride (ō′ vər rūd′) *verb.* 1. To prevail over; to overcome. 2. To ride across. 3. To trample upon. 4. To set aside. **overrode, overridden.**

P

pa·cif·ic (pə sif′ ik) *adjective.* 1. Peaceful; calm: He wandered down the *pacific* country lane and listened to the birds twitter in the trees. 2. Tending to calm; appeasing. —**pacifically** *adverb.*

pa·tron (pā′ trən) *noun.* 1. A sponsor: The banker was a *patron* of the museum. 2. A person who regularly uses a particular establishment's goods and services: He was a frequent *patron* of the restaurant. 3. A protector; a guardian. —*adjective.* Protecting or guarding: a *patron* saint.

ped·e·stal (ped′ i stəl) *noun.* 1. Base for a statue. 2. Any base or support. 3. The base of a large vase or lamp.

per·sua·sive (pər swā′ siv) *adjective.* Having the ability to win over or convince someone by urging or arguing: The *persuasive* salesperson convinced them that they needed the gadget. —**persuasively** *adverb.* —**persuasiveness** *noun.*

pe·ti·tion (pə tish′ ən) *noun.* 1. A formal request to an authority asking for a right or benefit: The people signed a *petition* requesting additional parking spaces be made available in the town square. 2. A prayer; an entreaty. —*verb.* To request a right or benefit from a person or group in authority. **petitioned, petitioning.**

pierce (pirs) *verb.* 1. To penetrate. 2. To make a hole or opening. 3. To make a path through: The explorer *pierced* her way through the dense jungle. 4. To make a sharp sound: The siren *pierced* the stillness of the night. 5. To succeed in understanding: Einstein *pierced* the mystery of the atom. 6. To move deeply: The sad news *pierced* his heart with pain. **pierced, piercing.** —**piercingly** *adverb.*

pitch (pich) *noun.* 1. (Slang) A speech designed to persuade. 2. The act of pitching. 3. (Baseball) A ball thrown by the pitcher. 4. Any slant or angle. 5. (Music) A standard used in the tuning of instruments. —*verb.* 1. To throw; to toss. 2. To put up: The scouts *pitched* their tents for the night. 3. To slope downward. 4. To plunge or fall forward. 5. To set the course: The politician *pitched* his speed to the moods of his audience. —**pitched, pitching.**

pla·cate (plā′ kāt *or* plak′ āt) *verb.* To pacify; to appease; to yield: The king tried to *placate* his enemies by giving them jewels. **placated, placating.** —**placative** *adjective.* —**placatory** *noun.*

plod·der (plod′ ər) *noun.* A person who works or moves in a slow, labored manner.

prac·tice (prak′ tis) *noun.* 1. The work of a professional person: Although she was young, the hardworking lawyer soon had a busy *practice.* 2. An action done repeatedly to perfect a skill: Daily *practice* at the piano is the best way to become a good pianist. 3. A customary way of doing things: It was his *practice* to read the newspaper at the breakfast table. 4. The following of a profession: He is engaged in the *practice* of medicine. —*verb.* 1. To do or perform customarily; to make a habit of. 2. To do or perform in order to gain a skill: She *practiced* basketball daily. 3. To work at a profession: He studied hard so that he might *practice* law one day. 4. To follow a rule or ritual: He *practiced* his religion faithfully. **practiced, practicing.**

pre·car·i·ous (pri ker′ ē əs *or* pri kar′ ē əs) *adjective.* 1. Dangerous; perilous: Their descent down the mountain was made more *precarious* by frequent rock slides. 2. Unstable; insecure: Because it is unpopular with the people, the government is in a *precarious* position. — **precariously** *adverb.*

prej·u·dice (prej′ ə dis) *noun.* 1. Unfair opinion not based on facts. 2. Harm or injury. —*verb.* 1. To cause a prejudice. 2. To harm or injure. **prejudiced, prejudicing.**

prime (prīm) *noun.* 1. The best part; the best time: He is in the *prime* of his life. 2. The beginning; the first part. 3. Springtime.

prop·er·ly (prop′ ər lē) *adverb.* Correctly; exactly; thoroughly. —**proper** *adjective.* —**properness** *noun.*

prow (prou) *noun.* The front part of a ship; the bow: The captain stood near the *prow* of the boat and watched the upcoming shore.

R

ra·di·ate (rā′ dē āt) *verb.* 1. To spread out, as the spokes in a wheel: The flower beds *radiate* from the center of the garden. 2. To issue or send out rays: The microwave antenna collected the energy *radiated* from the distant station. **radiated, radiating.** —**radiative** *adjective.*

raf·ter (raf′ tər) *noun.* A sloping beam that supports a pitched roof.

ram·shack·le (ram′ skak′ əl) *adjective.* Likely to fall apart; loose and rickety: The farmer made few repairs on the *ramshackle* barn.

range (rānj) *noun.* 1. The distance to a target. 2. The extent of knowledge, experience, or ability: The *range* of her research in Greek history makes her an expert. 3. The maximum distance a vehicle can travel before exhausting its fuel supplies. 4. (Music) The series of tones within the capacity of a voice or instrument: The wide *range* of her voice made her a valuable member of the chorus. 5. A group or series: a mountain *range.* 6. (Aerospace) A testing area for rockets and missiles. —*verb.* 1. To travel over an area; to explore. 2. To vary within limits: His emotions *ranged* from laughter to tears. 3. To extend in one direction: The river *ranged* from the foothills to the sea. **ranged, ranging.**

rapt (rapt) *adjective.* 1. Overcome by strong, noble emotion. 2. Deeply engrossed. 3. Expressing rapture: The children watched the circus with *rapt* looks on their faces.

re·al·i·ty (rē al′ ə tē) *noun.* 1. A real thing or fact. 2. Actual state of affairs: Leprechauns have no place in *reality.*

re·bel·lious (ri bel′ yəs) *adjective.* 1. The quality of being a rebel. 2. Participating in a rebellion. 3. Unruly; undisciplined; out of control. —**rebelliously** *adverb.* —**rebelliousness** *noun.*

re·cep·tion (ri sep′ shən) *noun.* 1. Manner of receiving or welcoming: The fans gave their favorite player a warm *reception* as he strode to the mound. 2. A being received: He was happy about his *reception* into the club. 3. A gathering to meet and welcome people: The school alumni association had a *reception* for its members. 4. The quality of sound reproduced by a radio or of the sound and picture in a television.

rec·og·nize (rek′ əg nīz) *verb.* 1. To consider; to acknowledge: Smoking is a *recognized* health hazard. 2. To be aware of something from past experience; to identify: She *recognized* the valuable painting by the signature in the left-hand corner. 3. To acknowledge as a speaker: The young woman waited for the moderator to *recognize* her. 4. To greet: Walking along the old familiar street she *recognized* many a neighbor. 5. To accept or acknowledge the national status of a new government. **recognized, recognizing.** —**recognizable** *adjective.* —**recognizer** *noun.*

rec·ol·lec·tion (rek′ ə lek′ shən) *noun.* 1. Memory. 2. The act of recollecting.

ref·use (ref′ yüs) *noun.* Useless stuff; trash; waste.

re·luc·tant (ri luk′ tənt) *adjective.* Unwilling; opposing: The child was *reluctant* to share the blocks with his new playmate. —**reluctantly** *adverb.*

re·prove (ri prüv′) *verb.* Scold; admonish; show disapproval: She *reproved* the student for his sloppy work. **reproved, reproving.**

re·pug·nance (ri pug′ nəns) *noun.* The state of feeling extreme dislike or disgust.

re·pul·sive (ri pul′ siv) *adjective.* 1. Disgusting: A *repulsive* odor came from the old garbage can. 2. Tending to repel. —**repulsively** *adverb.* —**repulsiveness** *noun.*

rep·u·ta·tion (rep′ yə tā′ shən) *noun.* 1. The general opinion held of a person or thing: She has the *reputation* of being a reliable electrician. 2. The state of being well thought of: His *reputation* as a conscientious worker is well known. 3. Fame: a well-publicized *reputation*.

re·sent (ri zent′) *verb.* To feel angry at; to feel indignation: The baby *resents* anyone else gaining her mother's attention. **resented, resenting.**

re·sist (ri zist′) *verb.* 1. To remain firm; to withstand: The rebel forces *resisted* the king's army. 2. To abstain; to keep from giving in to: He *resisted* the tempting dessert and stayed on his diet. **resisted, resisting.**

res·pite (res′ pit) *noun.* 1. Relief of a temporary nature: Sitting on a bench gave her a brief *respite* from a day of shopping. 2. A reprieve from punishment. —*verb.* 1. To give temporary relief. 2. To grant a stay in punishment. **respited, respiting.**

re·strain (ri strān′) *verb.* 1. To control; to check: She *restrained* her desire to walk out of class. 2. To deprive of freedom or liberty. 3. To limit or restrict: He *restrained* his dog when the cat passed. **restrained, restraining.** —**restrainable** *adjective.* —**restrainedly** *adverb.*

rev·er·ie (rev′ ər ē) *noun.* 1. Daydreaming. 2. A daydream: The ringing telephone woke her from her *reveries* of girlhood days.

re·vive (ri vīv′) *verb.* 1. To improve the spirits or emotions: The touchdown *revived* the spirits of the team. 2. To restore to life or consciousness: The lifeguard applied artificial resuscitation until the swimmer was *revived*. 3. To restore to health, use, notice, activity or effectiveness. **revived, reviving.**

rheu·ma·tism (rü′ mə tiz′ əm) *noun.* A disease which affects the muscles, tendons, joints, bones, and nerves. It causes great pain and disability.

411

right (rīt) *noun.* 1. (Plural) The privileges accorded citizens by law, such as the right to vote. 2. That which is morally or legally proper. 3. The right-hand side or direction. 4. That which is due by law, tradition, or nature. 5. A conservative opinion, idea, or political viewpoint. — *verb.* 1. To restore to an upright position: She *righted* her overturned boat and continued the race. 2. To put in order; to correct. 3. To make amends; right a wrong. **righted, righting.** —*adjective.* 1. In a proper, legal, or moral manner. 2. Correct: That is the *right* answer. 3. On the right side: Please turn *right* at this corner. —*adverb.* 1. In a straight line: Can you look me *right* in the eye and say that? 2. Conveniently; correctly: That shirt doesn't fit *right*. 2. At once: He will be *right* here.

rite (rīt) *noun.* 1. The customary form for conducting a ceremony. 2. Any formal practice, custom, or procedure. 3. A religious ceremony.

ri·val (rī′ vəl) *noun.* 1. A competitor: They were *rivals* in sports. 2. An equal; something that can be matched to another. —*verb.* 1. To compete: The gas stations *rivaled* each other in service to customers. 2. To equal; to match. **rivaled, rivaling.** —*adjective:* The *rival* team had a band play during intermission.

S

sa·ga (sä′ gə) *noun.* 1. Any long, historical account. 2. An Icelandic prose narrative of the 12th and 13th centuries telling historical and legendary events and deeds.

schol·ar·ship (skol′ ər ship) *noun.* 1. Money or other help given to a student to pay for some or all of the tuition. 2. Possession of knowledge in a particular field of study.

sem·i·con·scious (sem′ i kon′ shəs) *adjective.* Not fully conscious. —**semiconsciousness** *noun.*

se·ren·i·ty (sə ren′ ə tē) *noun.* 1. Calmness; peacefulness; dignity: The face of the old woman had a *serenity* more beautiful than youthfulness. 2. Clearness; brightness; brillance. —**serenities.**

shun (shun) *verb.* 1. To avoid deliberately: She *shunned* her old neighborhood with its unhappy memories. 2. To avoid through fear: They *shunned* the most direct route, as it had been flooded by heavy rain. **shunned, shunning.**

sig·nif·i·cant (sig nif′ ə kənt) *adjective.* 1. Having meaning: The old letter contained a *significant* reference to a historical figure. 2. Important, valuable. —**significantly** *adverb.*

silt (silt) *noun.* 1. Fine particles of earth and sand carried by ocean or river water and left as sediment: The army engineers dug tons of *silt* from the harbor.

si·mul·ta·ne·ous·ly (sī′ məl tā′ nē əs lē) *adverb.* At the same time; at once.

skin·ny (skin′ ē) *adjective* 1. Very thin; scrawny; lanky: Abraham Lincoln was described as being tall and *skinny*. **skinnier, skinniest.** —**skinniness** *noun.*

smoke (smōk) *verb.* 1. To preserve meat or fish by exposing it to the smoke of burning hardwood, usually after pickling it in salt water. 2. To draw in and exhale the smoke of a cigarette, pipe, or cigar. 3. To change the color of glass by exposing it to smoke. 4. To force out of a place of hiding by or as if by the use of smoke. 5. To reveal to the public. **smoking, smoked.** —*noun.* 1. The vapor resulting from a fire. 2. Any cloud of fine particles. 3. (Informal) A cigarette.

snub (snub) *verb.* 1. To stop a rope suddenly by turning it about a post. 2. To make an animal secure in this manner. 3. To treat coldly or with contempt: He *snubbed* his classmates after he won the scholastic award. **snubbed, snubbing.** —*noun.* 1. A sudden stop. 2. Scornful treatment. —*adjective.* Blunt, stunted, or short at the tip: A *snub* nose.

sol·emn (sol′ əm) *adjective.* 1. Serious; impressive: Graduation was a *solemn* occasion. 2. Gloomy; somber. 3. Ceremonious; established: The marchers began their *solemn* parade. 4. Invoking the force of religion; sacred. —**solemnly** *adverb.*

spec·u·late (spek′ yə lāt) *verb.* 1. To guess: We *speculated* about possible endings to the story. 2. To consider; to think carefully: The mathematician *speculated* about the next step in the problem. 3. To buy or sell when there is a large risk in the hope of making a profit: She *speculated* in South American oil wells. **speculated, speculating.**

spec·u·la·tor (spek′ yə lā′ tər) *noun.* A person engaged in the buying or selling of a product with a certain amount of risk on the chance of great profit.

spent (spent) *adjective.* 1. Used up; exhausted; consumed: His energy was *spent* so he dropped out of the race. 2. Passed; come to an end; over with.

squeam·ish (skwē′ mish) *adjective.* 1. Easily made ill or nauseated. 2. Easily hurt; oversensitive. —**squeamishly** *adverb.* —**squeamishness** *noun.*

stal·wart (stâl′ wərt) *adjective.* 1. Robust strength. 2. Unwilling to come to a mutual agreement; not subject to change. —*noun.* 1. One who is physically strong. 2. One who is morally strong; a loyal supporter of a cause or group.

stanch (stänch) *adjective.* A variant spelling of staunch (See *staunch*).

staunch (stônch) *adjective.* 1. Loyal; true: They had been *staunch* friends for many years. 2. Having a strong makeup. **stauncher, staunchest.** —**staunchly** *adverb.* —**staunchness** *noun.*

sti·fle (stī′ fəl) *verb.* 1. To hold back; to repress: He *stifled* a scream at the sight of the corpse. 2. To kill by cutting off air; to suffocate. 3. To interrupt the voice or breath. **stifled, stifling.** —**stifler** *noun.* —**stiflingly** *adverb.*

stock (stok) *noun.* 1. The wooden or metal handle of a gun, pistol, or rifle to which the barrel and mechanism are attached. 2. The long, mooring beam of a field gun carriage that rests on the ground.

stoop (stüp) *noun.* Front door steps; a small porch or staircase leading to the front of a building.

stu·pe·fy (stü′ pə fi *or* styü′ pə fī) *verb.* 1. To amaze or shock: The sight of the strange creature *stupefied* him. 2. To overwhelm the senses of; to put into a stupor. **stupefied, stupefying.**

sub·merge (səb mėrj′) *verb.* 1. To plunge under water: The submarine *submerged* beneath the sea. 2. To cover with water: She *submerged* the carrots in the pan of boiling water. 3. To cover; to hide from view: The antique clock was *submerged* under a pile of old clothes. **submerged, submerging.**

suf·fra·gist (suf′ rə jist) *noun.* A person who supports the cause of giving voting right to women.

sul·len (sul′ ən) *adjective.* 1. Sulky; gloomy: The *sullen* child complained when he was refused a second dessert. 2. Sluggish; slow: The band played a *sullen* tune. —**sullenly** *adverb.* —**sullenness** *noun.*

413

sus·tain (sə stān′) *verb.* 1. To support; to keep from falling. 2. To keep alive; to maintain: The liquid diet contained vitamins and *sustained* the critically-ill patient. 3. To bear up under; to endure: Despite the hardships they *sustained,* the American troops did not surrender at Valley Forge. 4. To support the spirits; to encourage: The knowledge that his family loved him *sustained* him during his time of trouble. **sustained, sustaining.**

swag·ger (swag′ ər) *noun.* A bold manner of walking, acting, or talking. —*verb.* To walk or talk boldly, boastfully: The player *swaggered* onto the tennis court confident of victory. **swaggered, swaggering.**

T

tap·es·try (tap′ i strē) *noun.* 1. A textile fabric with a multi-colored design woven across the warp and used for wall hangings and furniture. 2. A textile fabric imitating this. —*verb.* 1. To decorate with tapestry. 2. To make or weave in a tapestry. **tapestried, tapestrying.**

tar·nish (tä′ nish) *verb.* 1. To become spoiled or tainted; to spoil or taint. 2. To become dull; to lose luster: The brass plate became *tarnished* over the years. **tarnished, tarnishing.** —*noun.* 1. The state of being tarnished. 2. The state of being spoiled. —**tarnishable** *adjective.*

taunt (tônt) *verb.* 1. To ridicule; to jeer: The children *taunted* their new classmate because of his unusual name. 2. To aggravate into action: The girl *taunted* her friend into climbing the high wall. **taunted, taunting.** —*noun.* Jeers; insults: Their *taunts* made the boy cry.

taut (tôt) *adjective.* 1. Pulled tight; not loose or slack. 2. Tense; stiff; strained: The rower's muscles remained *taut* as he rowed toward the finish line. 3. Kept tidy; in order: The captain insisted that the crew keep a *taut* ship. **tauter, tautest.** —**tautly** *adverb.* —**tautness** *noun.*

teem (tēm) *verb.* To be full to overflowing; to swarm: The pond *teemed* with frogs, turtles, and other animals. **teemed, teeming.**

ten·der[1] (ten′ dər) *noun.* 1. A crew member responsible for taking care of a deep-sea diver and equipment. 2. A small boat used to ferry passengers and supplies to a ship or to shore. 3. A railroad car located behind the locomotive and used to carry fuel and water. 4. A person who tends a machine or equipment.

ten·der[2] (ten′ dər) *adjective.* 1. Soft; delicate: A flower is too *tender* to be handled roughly. 2. Easily hurt; sensitive: The baby's skin is *tender.* 3. Expressing gentle feelings: The sight of the little kitten made them feel *tender* and protective. **tenderer, tenderest.** —**tenderly** *adverb.*

ten·e·ment (ten′ ə mənt) *noun.* 1. A city building divided into many apartments, usually located in a poor neighborhood. 2. A dwelling or part of a dwelling occupied by a tenant.

thor·ough·fare (thėr′ ō fer′ *or* thėr′ ō far′) *noun.* 1. A main street or road; a public highway. 2. Any place of passage from one location to another. 3. A heavily traveled passage.

thrive (thrīv) *verb.* To grow strong; to be rich; to prosper: Those flowers *thrive* on frequent waterings. **thrived, thriving.**

414

ti·dal flats (tī′ dl flats) *noun.* Low coastal land; shoals.

tol·e·rate (tol′ ə rāt′) *verb.* 1. To put up with; to endure. 2. To allow; to permit: The principal *tolerated* the wearing of blue jeans to school. 3. To recognize; to respect: We should *tolerate* the customs of various cultures. **tolerated, tolerating.**

trea·son·a·ble (trē′ zn ə bəl) *adjective.* Relating to acts of betrayal to one's country; having to do with a betrayal of trust.

trem·u·lous (trem′ yə ləs) *adjective.* Shaking; quivering, as with fear.

trib·ute (trib′ yüt) *noun.* 1. An acknowledgement of respect or gratitude: The school held a banquet in *tribute* to its athletic coach. 2. Money paid for peace, protection, or because of an agreement: All nations paid *tribute* to Rome when it held power two thousand years ago.

triv·i·al (triv′ ē əl) *adjective.* 1. Ordinary. 2. Of little importance; insignificant. 3. Concerned with petty things.

tyr·an·ny (tir′ ə nē) *noun.* 1. A government in which a single ruler has complete power. 2. Absolute power exercised unjustly and cruelly. **—tyrannies.**

U

un·can·ny (un kan′ ē) *adjective.* 1. Strange; causing fear and wonder. 2. Unusually keen; sensitive: His analysis of the problem was *uncanny.* **—uncannily** *adverb.* **—uncanniness** *noun.*

un·for·tu·nate (un fôr′ chə nit) *adjective.* Unlucky; regrettable: It was *unfortunate* for the speaker to be introduced incorrectly. **—unfortunately** *adverb.*

u·ni·ty (yoo′ nə tē) *noun.* 1. A union of parts into a whole; solidarity. 2. A state of being one; singleness. 3. A singleness of purpose or action. 4. An arrangement of parts that results in harmony. 5. A uniformity of character.

V

va·lise (və lēs′) *noun.* A bag used to carry clothes while traveling.

val·ued (val′ yüd) *verb.* 1. To prize; to hold in high regard: The nurse was a *valued* member of the hospital staff. 2. To determine the worth of something; to evaluate: The antique dealer *valued* the old coins at three hundred dollars. **valued, valuing.** **—noun.** 1. The worth or merit of a person or thing. 2. The fair price or return for goods or services. 3. A standard or ideal considered worthwhile. 4. (Music) The duration of a sound or rest. 5. (Mathematics) A determined or calculated numerical quantity. 6. Precise meaning of a word.

ven·ture (ven′ chər) *noun.* A brave or daring adventure or project. **—verb.** 1. To expose to risk or danger. 2. To dare to say or do. **ventured, venturing.**

vice (vīs) *noun.* 1. Any clamping device which holds an object in position. 2. A clamping tool opened and closed by a screw or lever and used in carpentry or metal working. **—variant spelling of** vise.

W

wa·ver (wā′ vər) *verb.* 1. To move back and forth; to flutter: The image *wavered* on the television screen. 2. To vary in strength; to flicker: The lights seemed to *waver* in the fog. 3. To hesitate: He *wavered* between keeping his old jacket and buying a new one. 4. To begin to give way: Her decision to work late began to *waver* as she got sleepy. **wavered, wavering.** **—noun.** The act of wavering. **—waveringly** *adverb.* **— waverer** *noun.*

415

whet (hwet) *verb.* To make eager; to stimulate: Just the sight of the ocean *whetted* her desire to take a swim. 2. To sharpen a took, such as a knife. **whetted, shetting.**

wince (wins) *verb.* 1. To withdraw suddenly: He *winced* when he hit his thumb instead of the nail with the hammer. **winced, wincing.** —*noun.* The act of wincing: Seeing the *wince,* his friend handed him a bandage.

wreathe (rēth) *verb.* 1. To curl; to twist around in a wreath–like shape. 2. To coil or curl: The vine *wreathed* itself around the pine tree. 3. To crown or decorate with a wreath. **wreathed, wreathing.**

wretch·ed (rech′ id) *adjective.* 1. Miserable; unhappy: He was a *wretched* criminal. 2. Very bad: They lived in a *wretched* hut. —**wretchedly** *adverb.* — **wretchedness** *noun.*

BCDEFGHIJ 080798
Printed in the United States of America